For
reference

SCHOOL LAW

DEBATING ISSUES
in American Education

EDITORIAL BOARD

SCHOOL LAW

VOLUME EDITOR

CHARLES J. RUSSO

UNIVERSITY OF DAYTON

8

VOLUME

DEBATING ISSUES
in American Education

SERIES
EDITORS

CHARLES J. RUSSO
ALLAN G. OSBORNE, JR.

⑤SAGE reference

Los Angeles | London | New Delhi
Singapore | Washington DC

Los Angeles | London | New Delhi
Singapore | Washington DC

FOR INFORMATION:

SAGE Publications, Inc.
2455 Teller Road
Thousand Oaks, California 91320
E-mail: order@sagepub.com

SAGE Publications Ltd.
1 Oliver's Yard
55 City Road
London EC1Y 1SP
United Kingdom

SAGE Publications India Pvt. Ltd.
B 1/I 1 Mohan Cooperative Industrial Area
Mathura Road, New Delhi 110 044
India

SAGE Publications Asia-Pacific Pte. Ltd.
3 Church Street
#10-04 Samsung Hub
Singapore 049483

Publisher: Holt A. Janke
Acquisitions Editor: Jim Brace-Thompson
Assistant to the Publisher: Michele Thompson
Developmental Editors: Diana E. Axelsen, Carole Maurer
Production Editor: Tracy Buyan
Reference Systems Manager: Leticia Gutierrez
Reference Systems Coordinator: Laura Notton
Copy Editor: Robin Gold
Typesetter: C&M Digitals (P) Ltd.
Proofreader: Jennifer Thompson
Indexer: Mary Mortensen
Cover Designer: Janet Kiesel
Marketing Manager: Carmel Schrire

Copyright © 2012 by SAGE Publications, Inc.

Printed in the United States of America.

Library of Congress Cataloging-in-Publication Data

School law / editors-in-chief, Charles J. Russo, Allan G. Osborne, Jr. ; volume editor, Charles J. Russo.

p. cm. – (Debating issues in American education ; v. 8)

Includes bibliographical references and index.

ISBN 978-1-4129-8758-5 (cloth : alk. paper)

1. Educational law and legislation—United States. I. Russo, Charles J. II. Osborne, Allan G., Jr.

KF4119.S35 2012
344.73'07–dc23   2011040902

12 13 14 15 16 10 9 8 7 6 5 4 3 2 1

CONTENTS

ABOUT THE EDITORS-IN-CHIEF

Charles J. Russo, JD, EdD, is the Joseph Panzer Chair in Education in the School of Education and Allied Professions and adjunct professor in the School of Law at the University of Dayton. He was the 1998–1999 president of the Education Law Association and 2002 recipient of its McGhehey (Achievement) Award. He has authored or coauthored more than 200 articles in peer-reviewed journals; has authored, coauthored, edited, or coedited 40 books; and has in excess of 800 publications. Russo also speaks extensively on issues in education law in the United States and abroad.

Along with having spoken in 33 states and 25 nations on 6 continents, Russo has taught summer courses in England, Spain, and Thailand; he also has served as a visiting professor at Queensland University of Technology in Brisbane and the University of Newcastle, Australia; the University of Sarajevo, Bosnia and Herzegovina; South East European University, Macedonia; the Potchefstroom Campus of North-West University in Potchefstroom, South Africa; the University of Malaya in Kuala Lumpur, Malaysia; and the University of São Paulo, Brazil. He regularly serves as a visiting professor at the Potchefstroom Campus of North-West University.

Before joining the faculty at the University of Dayton as professor and chair of the Department of Educational Administration in July 1996, Russo taught at the University of Kentucky in Lexington from August 1992 to July 1996 and at Fordham University in his native New York City from September 1989 to July 1992. He taught high school for 8½ years before and after graduation from law school. He received a BA (classical civilization) in 1972, a JD in 1983, and an EdD (educational administration and supervision) in 1989 from St. John's University in New York City. He also received a master of divinity degree from the Seminary of the Immaculate Conception in Huntington, New York, in 1978, as well as a PhD Honoris Causa from the Potchefstroom Campus of North-West University, South Africa, in May 2004 for his contributions to the field of education law.

Russo and his wife, a preschool teacher who provides invaluable assistance proofreading and editing, travel regularly both nationally and internationally to Russo's many speaking and teaching engagements.

Allan G. Osborne, Jr. is the retired principal of the Snug Harbor Community School in Quincy, Massachusetts, a nationally recognized Blue Ribbon School of Excellence. During his 34 years in public education, he served as a special education teacher, a director of special education, an assistant principal, and a principal. He also served as an adjunct professor of special education and education law at several colleges, including Bridgewater State University and American International University.

Osborne earned an EdD in educational leadership from Boston College and an MEd in special education from Fitchburg State College (now Fitchburg State University) in Massachusetts. He received a BA in psychology from the University of Massachusetts.

Osborne has authored or coauthored numerous peer-reviewed journal articles, book chapters, monographs, and textbooks on legal issues in education, along with textbooks on other aspects of education. Although he writes and presents in several areas of educational law, he specializes in legal and policy issues in special education. He is the coauthor, with Charles J. Russo, of five texts published by Corwin, a SAGE company.

A past president of the Education Law Association (ELA), Osborne has been an attendee and presenter at most ELA conferences since 1991. He has also written a chapter now titled "Students With Disabilities" for the *Yearbook of Education Law*, published by ELA, since 1990. He is on the editorial advisory committee of *West's Education Law Reporter* and is coeditor of the "Education Law Into Practice" section of that journal, which is sponsored by ELA. He is also on the editorial boards of several other education journals.

In recognition of his contributions to the field of education law, Osborne was presented with the McGhehey Award by ELA in 2008, the highest award given by the organization. He is also the recipient of the City of Quincy Human Rights Award, the Financial Executives Institute of Massachusetts Principals Award, the Junior Achievement of Massachusetts Principals Award, and several community service awards.

Osborne spends his time in retirement writing, editing, and working on his hobbies: genealogy and photography. He and his wife Debbie, a retired elementary school teacher, enjoy gardening, traveling, attending theater and musical performances, and volunteering at the Dana Farber Cancer Institute in Boston.

ABOUT THE
VOLUME EDITOR

Charles J. Russo, JD, EdD, is the Joseph Panzer Chair in Education in the School of Education and Allied Professions and adjunct professor in the School of Law at the University of Dayton. He has authored or coauthored more than 200 articles in peer-reviewed journals; authored, coauthored, edited, or coedited 40 books; and has more than 800 publications.

Before joining the faculty at the University of Dayton as professor and chair of the Department of Educational Administration in July 1996, Russo taught at the University of Kentucky in Lexington and at Fordham University in New York City. He earned a BA degree in classical civilization in 1972, a JD degree in 1983, and an EdD degree in educational administration and supervision in 1989, all from St. John's University in New York City. He also earned a master of divinity degree from the Seminary of the Immaculate Conception in Huntington, New York, in 1978.

ABOUT THE CONTRIBUTORS

Robert C. Cloud is a professor of educational administration and higher education at Baylor University. Cloud holds four academic degrees and has 43 years of experience in higher education at all administrative and instructional levels. His current research interests include education law and policy, administration, leadership, governance, and current issues in education.

Amanda Harmon Cooley is an assistant professor of law at South Texas College of Law. She earned her JD and BA from the University of North Carolina at Chapel Hill.

Bruce S. Cooper is a professor of school policy and leadership at Fordham University's Graduate School of Education. He is a noted scholar on private and religious education and is editor of the *Private School Monitor*. His interests include Catholic and Jewish schools, which he has analyzed now for 40 years. One of his latest books is the coedited *Handbook on Education Politics and Policy*.

Luke M. Cornelius is an associate professor of educational leadership at the University of North Florida. He teaches and researches in the areas of education law, school finance, educational policy and politics, and sports law.

Margie W. Crowe spent 30 years teaching general and special education in public and private schools before joining the special education faculty at the University of Southern Mississippi. Her interests include assistive technology, differentiating instruction, and curriculum design.

Todd A. DeMitchell is a professor in and chair of the Department of Education, and the Lamberton Professor in the Justice Studies Program at the University of New Hampshire. Most recently, he was named Distinguished Professor. His research focuses on the legal mechanisms that affect schools and colleges. He has authored or coauthored 5 books and more than 145 publications.

Marilyn Denison is the executive director of elementary education for Spring Independent School District, Houston, Texas. She has more than 17 years' experience in public education. She earned her bachelor's degree from the University of New Mexico, two master's degrees from East Central University, and a doctorate from Sam Houston State University.

Stacey L. Edmonson is a professor in and the chair of the Department of Educational Leadership and Counseling at Sam Houston State University in Huntsville, Texas. She has previously served Texas public schools as a central office administrator, principal, and teacher. Her research interests include educator burnout, legal issues in education, and ethics.

Allison S. Fetter-Harrott is an assistant professor of political science at Franklin College in Franklin, Indiana. Her research interests include public school anti-harassment measures, free speech, and the interplay between public schools and the First Amendment's religion clauses.

Richard Fossey is a professor and Mike Moses Endowed Chair in Educational Leadership at the University of North Texas. He received his JD from the University of Texas School of Law and his EdD from Harvard University. He is editor of the *Journal of Cases in Educational Leadership* and *Catholic Southwest.*

Michelle Gough McKeown is the assistant director of legal affairs at the Indiana Department of Education. She is currently at the dissertation stage of her graduate coursework in education policy and leadership at Indiana University School of Education. She earned her JD from Indiana University–Bloomington Maurer School of Law in 2006 and her BA in English literature from DePauw University in 2003. She has practiced education law at the law firm of Deatherage, Myers & Lackey in Hopkinsville, Kentucky.

Michael J. Jernigan is a mathematics and physics teacher, Miami Valley Career Technology Center, Clayton, Ohio. He received his PhD in educational leadership from the University of Dayton. His research interests included collective bargaining; school law; teacher preparation; and science, technology, engineering, and math (STEM).

Mark Littleton is a professor of educational leadership and policy studies at Tarleton State University. He serves as coordinator of the educational leadership doctoral program and routinely writes on the topic of sexual harassment in schools.

James L. Mawdsley received his BA from Yale University, an MA in English from Kent State University, and a JD from Cleveland-Marshall School of Law. He currently is an English instructor at Stark State College of Technology. A member of the Education Law Association and the Australia New Zealand Education Law Association, he has authored or coauthored numerous publications, including the "Employees" chapter of the *Yearbook of Education Law.*

Ralph D. Mawdsley holds a JD from the University of Illinois and a PhD from the University of Minnesota. He has authored more than 500 publications on the subject of education law. Mawdsley was president of the Education Law Association in 2001 and was awarded that organization's Marion A. McGhehey Award in 2004. He has received two Fulbright Awards, one to South Africa and one to Australia.

Timothy E. Morse is an associate professor at the University of Southern Mississippi Gulf Coast, where he directs the Mississippi Department of Education's Autism Project. In addition to having taught undergraduate and graduate special education courses at the university, he has worked as a public school special education administrator and teacher.

Emily Richardson is a PhD candidate in education policy at Indiana University–Bloomington School of Education. She received her JD from Indiana University Maurer School of Law.

Robert J. Safransky is an adjunct professor of school law and American government, Nova Southeastern University. He received a BA from St. Francis College, an MA from Stetson University, and a PhD from Florida State University. He has worked as a high school teacher, junior high school and adult vocational school principal, and a central office administrator.

Ralph Sharp is the director of School Administration Programs at East Central University in Ada, Oklahoma, where he has taught educational administration courses for nearly 30 years. He has authored several dozen articles and chapters, generally dealing with academic freedom and employment discrimination, in books and peer-reviewed journals.

Clayton H. Slaughter is chief financial officer for Greencastle Community Schools in Greencastle, Indiana, and an attorney-at-law.

Jeffrey C. Sun is an associate professor of educational leadership and affiliate professor of law at the University of North Dakota. He holds a JD from the Moritz College of Law at the Ohio State University and a PhD from Columbia University. Sun teaches and writes about education law.

INTRODUCTION

As reflected by the wide array of debates on the controversial legal topics addressed in this book, as well as by related entries sprinkled throughout this series of volumes, school law, often referred to as education law, is a dynamic discipline that brings to mind the observation of the Greek philosopher Heracleitus, "One cannot step into the same river twice." Heracleitus's comment highlights that school law, like the ever-flowing waters of the river, is constantly evolving to meet the needs of today's schools.

Evidence of the evolving nature of school law can be seen in the debates contained in this book, which range from whether there should be limits on the free speech expressive rights of students and teachers, particularly given the emergence of social media on the Internet, to whether students and teachers should be subjected to drug testing. Essays also debate such emerging issues as the limits of how copyrighted materials are used in schools, the educational rights of students who are homeless, and whether parents should be able to sue for educational malpractice if their children do not receive an education.

As readers examine issues in school law, perhaps for the first time, it is worth keeping in mind that the debates in this volume typically rely on systematic inquiry in the form of historical-legal research. This approach differs from the qualitative and quantitative research methodologies that are typically used in the social sciences, including education. School law involves the interpretation and explanation of legislative, executive, and judicial actions and an examination of the impact of legal issues on educators, students, and others in K–12 school settings.

In perusing these chapters, readers who are unfamiliar with the way in which the law and legal research operate may be surprised that in debates on topics such as student drug testing and the free speech rights of teachers, among others, researchers often rely on the same cases but interpret them differently and thus reach different conclusions. Given that cases, statutes, and other sources of law are subject to divergent interpretations, readers need to keep in mind that school law is an applied, rather than purely theoretical, discipline that addresses real-life concerns in ways that tend to be reactive rather than proactive. In other words, school law, as part of the U.S. legal system, usually develops rules only after real cases or controversies have been litigated or legislative or executive bodies have responded to needs that had yet to be addressed or resolved. In fact, *Brown v. Board of Education* (1954) is a typical example of how the law can be seen as reactive, insofar as *Brown* would not have been litigated when it was if public school officials in Topeka had met the needs of their African American students.

As readers grapple with the issues in this volume, the goal of these debates is to assist readers in thinking creatively about controversial issues in education and in developing proactive responses that can offer solutions before difficulties arise. Adopting a proactive approach is consistent with the notion of preventative law wherein knowledgeable educators can identify potential problems in advance by examining differing perspectives on issues as educators work to ensure these issues do not develop into crises.

In reading these debates, students should keep in mind that legal disputes may begin with a single issue but can have far-reaching implications in ways that the original parties never anticipated, exemplifying the principle of unintended consequences in action. In *Brown,* for example, the most important education case in the history of the United States, the Supreme Court invalidated racial segregation in U.S. public schools. Yet, it is highly debatable whether the parties to *Brown* could have anticipated, or foreseen, how it would lead to an era that ushered equal educational opportunities in the United States while transforming U.S. society in unimaginable ways, from schooling to housing to the job market. At the same time, although it is a topic that is admittedly beyond the scope of this volume, it is worth noting that *Brown* has served as a beacon of hope for equal educational opportunities that can lead to better lives for millions throughout the world (Russo, Beckmann, & Jansen, 2005). The chapters in this volume, like the others in the series, begin with head note essays before turning to point–counterpoint debates. Like the other volumes in this series, this book uses a debate format that presents point and counterpoint essays on each topic, in the hope of spurring readers to develop creative solutions for new and evolving issues in the world of education.

APPLIED SCHOOL LAW

Among the most significant legal advances that *Brown* spawned in helping ensure equal educational opportunities was the enactment of two federal statutes, both of which are subjects of debates in this volume. These two laws, Title IX of the Educational Amendments of 1972 and the Individuals with Disabilities Education Act (IDEA), initially codified as the Education for All Handicapped Children Act in 1975, have profoundly affected the lives of millions of Americans, providing them with opportunities that most could not have imagined a mere 40 years ago.

Title IX was designed to create gender equity in intercollegiate sports but later served as a tool in efforts to eliminate sexual discrimination and harassment generally, the subject of one of the debates in this volume. In the debate in Chapter 9, the authors reach divergent perspectives even though they rely on essentially the same cases from the Supreme Court in addressing whether the tests that the Justices created are adequate to the serious task of eliminating sexual harassment in schools, whether the students were subjected to harassment by teachers (*Franklin v. Gwinnett County Public Schools*, 1992; *Gebser v. Lago Vista Independent School District*, 1998) or by peers (*Davis v. Monroe County Board of Education*, 1999).

The author of the point essay maintains that the tests that the Supreme Court enunciated work effectively because they provide clear guidance that balances the need to protect boards from unnecessary liability and students from harassment by teachers or peers when they are in school settings. The counterpoint essay responds that the tests leave something to be desired, arguing that given the abuses that technology has engendered via social media, for instance, the Court needs to revamp the tests to meet the evolving needs of the current day.

At the same time, the IDEA, arguably the most effective of all federal educational statutes insofar as it has largely achieved the goals that it was designed to accomplish by providing educational placements for students with disabilities, presents unique challenges for school officials. Given the impact that the IDEA has had on school systems, two debates focus on issues related to students with disabilities.

The first of the two debates involving the IDEA focuses on one of the thornier issues confronting educators—whether its disciplinary standards are fair to all students. The point essay in Chapter 6 asserts that rather than creating different disciplinary standards for students with disabilities, the law affords students with disabilities additional procedural rights before they can be subjected to serious disciplinary sanctions that are related to their disabilities. The essay explains that these protections, which are needed because of the history of discriminatory treatment toward children with disabilities, strike a fair balance between the need for school officials to maintain safe schools and the rights of these students to a free appropriate public education (FAPE). The counterpoint essay argues that insofar as the IDEA does not allow school officials to discipline students with disabilities in the same way as their peers who are in regular classes, this teaches students to disrespect authority. This essay concludes that students with special educational needs should be treated in the same way as their peers and that they should be responsible for their own behavior so that they can benefit from their rights to FAPEs as delineated in the IDEA.

The second debate goes to the heart of the IDEA in its goal of providing a FAPE in the least restrictive environment (LRE) for students with disabilities, which has transformed the way U.S. public schools operate. The point essay in Chapter 7 acknowledges that school officials need to use the IDEA continuum of placements, reiterating that the appropriate use of pullout programs is supported by both the IDEA and case law. This essay makes the case that school officials often meet the IDEA's requirement of providing a FAPE in the LRE even when students are placed in pullout programs. The counterpoint essay responds that educators should do all that they can to serve students with disabilities in inclusive settings. Even though the author concedes that there may be reasons for occasionally removing students with disabilities from inclusive placements, she contends that they should do so only when it is in the children's best interests because pullout settings are usually not the most effective placements for many of these children.

THE NATURE OF SCHOOL LAW

Like the authors of debates in this volume, readers need to look to the past, present, and future in making sense of the evolving nature of school law. By placing legal issues in perspective, adopting this approach can help inform students and educators about the meaning and status of the law and provide them with tools to raise questions for issues that have yet to emerge.

Rooted in the historical nature of the law and its reliance on precedent, school law calls on readers to look to the past for authority to govern the outcome of the debates at issue. The law adopts this approach because the Anglo-American legal system is grounded in the principle of precedent, the notion that an authoritative ruling of the highest court in a given jurisdiction is binding on lower courts within its purview. In other words, a ruling of the U.S. Supreme Court is binding on all courts on the same issue, but a judgment of a state high court is controlling only within the boundaries of its home state.

Given the more or less reactive nature of law, those who use the legal system to address current concerns look to see how past decisions have dealt with the same issue. If cases support their points of view, then they can argue that precedent should be followed. However, if precedent is contrary to their positions, then they can seek to distinguish their situations and reach different outcomes in attempting to demonstrate that precedent cases are sufficiently different and inapplicable to the facts at hand, particularly when developing policies for new and evolving issues such as student free speech on the Internet and the impact of social media in the world of education.

Along with the issues that this introductory essay has already highlighted, the remainder of this volume examines controversial topics relating to a variety of other issues that have arisen in school law. The essays in the rest of this book, then, present an array of controversial topics under the broad headings of student rights, faculty rights, and institutional issues.

STUDENT RIGHTS
Policies on School Uniforms

Amid considerable concern for enhancing student safety and learning outcomes, debate has emerged regarding a practice that has long been used in nonpublic schools but is relatively new to public education, namely requiring students to wear uniforms, even if doing so limits their purported First Amendment right to free expression. The point essay in Chapter 3 posits that officials in public schools should have the authority to require students to wear school uniforms. This essay contends that to the extent that educators carefully craft nondiscriminatory policies to achieve such important interests as school safety and improving learning in a way that does not suppress student expression, then they should be free to operate their schools as they see fit. Conversely, the counterpoint essay responds that educational leaders should not have the power to require public school students to comply with school uniform policies because they are not as effective as their supporters claim. This essay argues that because little data support the arguments of those who support uniforms for students, uniform policies serve as little more than "quick fixes" that fail to offer long-term chances for success in improving schooling.

Student Drug Testing

Insofar as schools have not avoided the scourge of drug use, disputes have arisen regarding the extent to which educational officials can require all students, not just those involved in interscholastic athletics, to submit to drug testing. As reflected in the debate in Chapter 4, the two authors rely on largely the same cases in addressing whether school officials have the authority, under the Fourth Amendment in the U.S. Constitution and comparable language in state constitutions, to subject students to random drug testing.

According to the point essay, because educators have special custodial duties for students, they should be free to use random drug testing to help ensure safe and orderly learning environments. In seeking to protect the majority in schools who may be at risk because of the few who use drugs, this essays stands for the proposition that officials should be free to subject students to random drug testing to help keep schools safe. In arguing that random drug testing is a bad idea, the counterpoint essay questions the point essay's reliance on Supreme Court rulings on the Fourth Amendment. At the same time, the counterpoint essay expresses serious reservations about the costs of testing, both financial and nonfinancial and raises concerns about ways in which officials can use information on students who tested positive for drug use, arguing that educators should not have such potentially invasive power.

Homeless Students

The debates in Chapter 8 ask whether current state and federal legislation, most notably the federal McKinney-Vento Homeless Assistance Act, adequately meets the needs of the approximately 800,000 students in the United States who are homeless. The point essay takes the position that the McKinney Act has been effective because it affords school boards flexibility in deciding how to provide services for children who are homeless. The essay thus raises the concern that insofar as its implementation is already expensive, having to offer additional protections could take funding away from other necessary programs. In response, the counterpoint essay posits that although the McKinney Act provides a good start, it has not done enough to protect the interests of homeless children. This essay argues that given two major challenges with the law—namely, that it has not been implemented as intended and that there are few reliable mechanisms to make sure that schools are following its mandates—too many homeless children are not having their needs met, and further efforts are needed.

Free Speech

As reflected in the debate in Chapter 11, one of the hallmarks of U.S. schools is the extent to which the law protects the free speech rights of students. The essays in this chapter rely essentially on the same Supreme Court cases, starting with the seminal *Tinker v. Des Moines Independent Community School District* (1969), in reaching different results on whether officials in public schools should have the authority to limit the First Amendment free speech rights of students.

The point essay questions the wisdom of cases that have given school officials the authority to regulate student speech only when it occurs in schools and causes, or is likely to cause, material and substantial disruptions. This essay maintains that more recent forms of student speech, as exemplified in emerging electronic communications, reveal that the *Tinker* substantial disruption standard should be expanded to include speech and expression that may have originated outside of schools but that affect activities within schools. The counterpoint essay retorts that the courts have too often permitted educational officials to limit student speech unfairly. This essay asserts that the judiciary needs to be more vigilant in protecting the free speech rights of students because only in doing so can school officials avoid interfering with parental rights and focus on implementing the educational missions of their schools as they inculcate societal values.

TEACHER RIGHTS

Six sets of essays address key legal issues concerning the rights of teachers in K–12 public schools.

Academic Freedom and Free Speech

As reflected in a pair of debates, two related issues that are of great interest to teachers are the interrelated topics of academic freedom and free speech. More specifically, even though the Supreme Court's analysis in *Tinker* pointed out, "It can hardly be argued that either students or teachers shed their constitutional rights to freedom of speech or expression at the school-house gate" (1969, p. 506), educators in public schools certainly do not have unfettered rights to teach, or speak, in their classrooms as freely as they might wish.

Long a staple of higher education, debate has ensued regarding whether K–12 teachers should have academic freedom that would grant them greater control over the content of school curricula. The point essay in Chapter 1 takes the position that insofar as teachers are the most qualified individuals in their districts to design and implement curricula, they should have the freedom to teach as they see fit. Further, the essay rejects the practice of allowing unqualified lay people such as school board members and politicians to make curricular decisions, preferring that they be made by professionally prepared teachers who can act autonomously in designing curricula.

Conversely, the counterpoint essay answers that because states and local boards are responsible for schools, they alone should have the authority to decide what children learn. The author buttresses her position by adding that insofar as local school boards and educational leaders are responsible for raising student achievement while closing the educational gap between children, they, working with state officials, and occasionally the federal government, must preserve their control over schools so that they, rather than teachers, can ensure standardized quality of curricular content for all.

Chapter 12 addresses issues related to the important right of free speech. In a series of cases beginning the year before it rendered its judgment in *Tinker*, the Supreme Court recognized that teachers have the right to speak out on matters of public concern absent compelling state interests to limit what they have to say (*Pickering v. Board of Education of Township High School District 205*, 1968). The essays in this chapter use essentially the same major cases in reaching different outcomes.

The author of the point essay concedes that although teachers should be free to speak out on school-related issues of public concern without fear of dismissal, there are good reasons why their rights in this regard have long been limited. The essay concludes that because some speech can damage working relationships in schools and otherwise create distractions, the courts have wisely balanced the rights of teachers and their boards by limiting their comments to matters of public concern.

The author of the counterpoint essay replies that there should be no limits on the free speech rights of teachers other than those reasonably necessary to advance the educational missions of schools. If anything, although recognizing that the judiciary has acknowledged that schools have unique organizational cultures, the essay posits that the courts have gone too far in restricting the speech rights of teachers and that, as professionals, they should be free to practice their profession as they deem appropriate.

Drug Testing

Just as concerns have arisen over the extent to which students use drugs in schools, so, too, have boards had similar worries about their teaching staffs. In light of more than a quarter of a century of litigation on this important topic, the debates in Chapter 5 address whether teachers should be subject to suspicionless drug testing.

The author of the point essay who favors testing of students also supports the authority of boards to test their teachers. Observing that teachers have a unique role in U.S. society in helping shape the minds of young people in what amounts to a sacred trust, this essay puts forth the opinion that educators will be unable to perform their jobs adequately if there are concerns that they used drugs. The counterpoint author answers that because random drug testing of teachers intrudes on their reasonable expectations of privacy, it is not justified by any special need. Relying on recent litigation, the author of this essay is convinced that insofar as teachers are not in so-called "safety sensitive" positions, in which their actions could place the well-being of students at immediate risk of harm, they should not be subject to potentially intrusive random drug testing.

Charges of Sexual Misconduct

An unfortunate reality in schools is that occasionally teachers must be disciplined or dismissed for misbehavior that limits or eradicates their ability to fulfill their jobs effectively. As reflected in this debate, questions have arisen over whether charges of sexual misconduct involving teachers should be public records and whether current laws and procedures dealing with teacher dismissal provide educators with adequate due process protections.

It goes without saying that teachers who engage in sexual misconduct, especially with students, should be removed from their positions. However, disagreements have arisen over whether the records of teachers who face such charges should be made public immediately, especially in situations where teachers are later vindicated or the charges against them are proven to be false. Against this backdrop, the essays in Chapter 10 address the sensitive topic of whether charges of sexual misconduct involving educators should be treated as public records given the need to balance the privacy rights of teachers with the right of parents and students to know when educators are accused of such misdeeds.

Although conceding that educators can be falsely accused of misconduct, the point essay supports making charges of sexual misconduct against teachers public based on the fact that they have avenues of redress available. Although recommending that investigations into teacher sexual misconduct be handled at the state rather than the local level, the essay argues that if these records are not made public, then confidence in education is likely to erode.

The author of the counterpoint essay opposes making such information public because it risks doing irreparable harm to the reputations of teachers who have been unjustly accused because mere mention of sexual misdeeds can destroy their careers. The counterpoint essay disagrees with the point essay in declaring that there is no evidence that state level investigations would be any more effective than those conducted at the local level and that available remedies do little to restore the reputations of those who have been falsely accused.

Due Process in Teacher Dismissal

Moving away from the narrower confines of actions concerning teacher sexual misconduct, another debate addresses whether teachers who are subject to dismissal receive adequate due process protections. According to the point essay in Chapter 14, poorly written tenure statutes have limited the rights of teachers who are subject to dismissal. The author believes that insofar as the laws were designed to protect teachers with good records, they did little to address the status of teachers who broke the law or are not tenured. The essay concludes that it is not so much that teachers need greater rights as that laws should be more precisely written to protect educators from wrongful nonrenewal or termination of their contracts.

The author of the counterpoint responds that teacher employment statutes combined with collective bargaining agreements adequately protect the rights of teachers faced with dismissal. Rather than make it easier for school boards to dismiss teachers who are ineffective, the extensive due process procedures that have emerged have made it difficult to dismiss even those who are not performing adequately. The essay posits that these protections harm education as a whole because the expense devoted to ridding the system of the relatively few undeserving educators diverts resources and attention from their more deserving colleagues who are actually meeting the needs of students.

Unions and Collective Bargaining

At a time when there is a great deal of controversy nationally over the status and continuing viability of teacher unions, the debate in Chapter 15 examines whether teacher unions and collective bargaining improve the terms and conditions of teacher employment in U.S. public education. The point essay takes the decidedly pro-union position that teacher unions provide economic (by providing members with chances to make decent livings), political (by exercising their rights in ways that affect all levels of government), social (by allowing them to remain in contact with colleagues), and organizational (by affording them opportunities to speak out on issues of concern) benefits for their members and to education as a whole.

The counterpoint essay disagrees, noting that by focusing on salaries and benefits for the members, unions do not necessarily advance teaching and learning or improve the quality of teaching. This essay stands for the proposition that it is incumbent on teachers to recognize their ability to represent themselves in a professional manner when negotiating salary and benefits. Instead, the essay suggests that teachers have no need to rely on unions to act as their bargaining representatives because unions have done little to improve their terms and conditions of employment.

INSTITUTIONAL ISSUES

Two debates in this volume do not fit neatly under either of the earlier headings; they are presented here because the issues that they consider are more likely to affect school systems as a whole rather than individual teachers or students.

Copyright

The evolving nature of technology as it interacts with intellectual property and the growth in online teaching have contributed to a growing controversy regarding the appropriate limits on the use of copyrighted material by educators.

The point essay in Chapter 2 maintains that federal copyright law cannot be interpreted in a way that violates the intellectual property interests of authors. To this end, the author concedes that as important as it is to find a balance between permitting users access to educational materials, it is also important to safeguard the intellectual property rights of creators. Conversely, the counterpoint essay takes the position that as important as it is to make educational materials available, unless adequate protection is in place to protect the rights of those who develop new materials, they might be dissuaded from creating new works that might benefit the educational enterprise.

Educational Malpractice

As reflected in this debate, an issue that has been percolating for years addresses whether school systems should be liable for educational malpractice when students are unable to read or write at grade level. The point essay in Chapter 13 takes the position that if educators are to be treated as the professionals that they wish to be viewed as, then they should be subject to the same malpractice standards as doctors, lawyers, and other professionals. The counterpoint essay responds that creating the tort of educational malpractice would do more harm than good because it might deter qualified individuals from pursuing careers in education for fear of the risk of liability, would likely driving up costs of schooling, and would have little or no appreciable impact on student learning.

CONCLUSION

Given the impact that school law has on the world of K–12 education, one can wonder how the judiciary will ultimately respond to the ongoing and emerging topics that this book has addressed. Perhaps most notably, it will be interesting to observe how the judiciary crafts the rules for student, and teacher, free speech in cyberspace involving the use of social networking sites because the law, like the ever-flowing river that Heraclitus mentioned, cannot seem to keep pace with developments in technology. Given the legal and educational concerns that this, and other issues raise, those interested in school law must share in the job of developing and implementing policies to enhance the school environment for all.

In sum, as noted, perhaps the only constant in school law is that as it evolves to meet the demands of a constantly changing world, it is likely to remain of utmost importance for those interested in teaching and learning. The seemingly endless supply of new statutes, regulations, and cases speaks of the need to be ever vigilant regarding how legal developments affect education. A challenge for educators, then, is to harness their knowledge of this ever-growing field so that they can make the schools better places for all children. Aware of this, the contributors to this book of debates provide different perspectives on school law in the hope that they can assist those who are seeking solutions for ongoing quests for educational equity and to be prepared to address new and evolving issues.

Charles J. Russo
University of Dayton

Further Readings and Resources

Permuth, S., & Mawdsley, R. D. (2006). *Research methods for studying legal issues in education.* Dayton, OH: Education Law Association.

Russo, C. J. (2008). Introduction. In C. J. Russo (Ed.), *The encyclopedia of education law* (pp. xxxi–xxxvii). Thousand Oaks, CA: Sage.

Russo, C. J. (2010). School law: An essential component in your toolbox. *School Business Affairs, 75*(9), 36–38.

Russo, C. J., Beckmann, J., & Jansen, J. (Eds.). (2005). *Equal educational opportunities: Comparative perspectives in education law:* Brown v Board of Education *at 50 and Democratic South Africa at 10.* Johannesburg, South Africa: Van Schaik.

Court Cases and Statutes

Brown v. Board of Education, 347 U.S. 483 (1954).

Davis v. Monroe County Board of Education, 526 U.S. 629 (1999), *on remand*, 206 F.3d 1377 (11th Cir. 2000).

Education for All Handicapped Children Act of 1975, now Individuals with Disabilities Education Act, 20 U.S.C. § 1401 *et seq.*

Franklin v. Gwinnett County Public Schools, 503 U.S. 60 (1992), *on remand*, 969 F.2d 1022 (11th Cir. 1992).

Gebser v. Lago Vista Independent School District, 524 U.S. 274 (1998).

Individuals with Disabilities Education Act, 20 U.S.C. §§ 1400 *et seq.*

McKinney-Vento Homeless Assistance Act, 42 U.S.C. §§ 11302 *et seq.*, 11431 *et seq.*

Pickering v. Board of Education of Township High School District 205, 391 U.S. 563 (1968).

Tinker v. Des Moines Independent Community School District, 393 U.S. 503 (1969).

Title IX of the Educational Amendments of 1972, 20 U.S.C. § 1681.

Academic freedom: Should K–12 teachers have greater control of the content of the curricula they teach?

POINT: Ralph Sharp, *East Central University*

COUNTERPOINT: Marilyn Denison, *Spring Independent School District, Houston, Texas*

OVERVIEW

The concept of academic freedom emerged in Enlightenment Prussia, flowered in late-19th-century German universities, and made its way to the United States in the early 20th century. Today, educators typically assert rights to academic freedom in higher education rather than K–12 educational settings. As described by one court, academic freedom is "the principle that individual instructors are at liberty to teach that which they deem to be appropriate in the exercise of their professional judgment" (*Aguillard v. Edwards*, 1985, p. 1257). Insofar as there is a significant difference between the instructional duties of faculty members in institutions of higher learning and teachers in K–12 schools, the debate in this chapter focuses on academic freedom in elementary and secondary schools.

In *Tinker v. Des Moines Independent Community School District* (1969), the Supreme Court expanded the First Amendment speech and expression rights of students in upholding their right to wear black armbands in protest of U.S. involvement in Vietnam. *Tinker* focused on the rights of students. However, in *Tinker's* immediate wake, in cases that apparently reflected the tenor of the social upheaval of the times, lower courts initially lent something of a sympathetic ear to the claims of K–12 teachers who asserted rights to academic freedom under the broad rubric of protected First Amendment speech. For example, in a controversy admittedly more about threatened cutbacks in educational programming than instructional issues per se, the Supreme Court of California, relying on *Tinker*, ruled that school officials could not limit teacher protests unless their actions demonstrated a "clear and substantial threat to order and efficiency" (*Los Angeles Teachers Union v. Los Angeles City Board of Education*, 1969, p. 836).

More to the point, in two cases from New York that reached the Second Circuit, and in which the Supreme Court refused to hear appeals, the court made passing references to academic freedom. In the first case, the court upheld the right of a teacher to wear a black armband in class as a protest against U.S. involvement in Vietnam (*James v. Board of Education of Central School District No. 1, Addison*, 1972 a, b). Within the year, the same court agreed that a school board in New York could not dismiss a teacher who refused to participate in the flag-salute ceremony but simply stood silently at attention during its recitation (*Russo v. Central School District No. 1, Towns of Rush*, 1972, 1973).

Following the initial flurry of cases granting K–12 teachers some rights to academic freedom in the 1970s, the pendulum swung back as courts now ordinarily recognize that teachers lack any right to deviate from established school board curricula. In this regard, courts have been unresponsive to claims of academic freedom when teachers refused to follow directions regarding such issues as curricular activities (*In re Proposed Termination of James E. Johnson's Teaching Contract with Independent School District No. 709*, 1990); course content and methodologies (*Bradley v. Pittsburgh Board of Education*, 1990); supplemental reading materials (*Kirkland v. Northside Independent School District*, 1989, 1990); and showing violent, sexually suggestive R-rated movies without previewing them and identifying an educational purpose (*Fowler v. Board of Education of Lincoln County, Ky.*, 1987a, b). Courts also rejected academic freedom claims from teachers who employed (*In re Bernstein*, 2001), or allowed students to use (*Lacks v. Ferguson Reorganized School District R-2*, 1998), inappropriate language in class.

Courts continue to demonstrate their continued support for school boards when teachers depart from established school curricula to express their political opinions in class. In one such case, the Seventh Circuit affirmed that in refusing to renew the employment contract of a probationary elementary school teacher who had voiced her opposition to U.S. involvement in Iraq as part of a discussion with students, a board in Indiana did not violate the teacher's rights (*Mayer v. Monroe County Community School Corp.*, 2007a, b). The court noted that the First Amendment does not permit educators in elementary and secondary schools who address captive audiences of students to cover topics or advocate perspectives that deviate from the approved curricula of their boards, rejecting her claim that she was protected by academic freedom. Subsequently, in a variation of this theme, the Sixth Circuit, relying partly on the case from Indiana, affirmed that a teacher in Ohio lacked a First Amendment right to academic freedom that allowed her to select books and methods of instruction for class-room use without interference from public school officials (*Evans-Marshall v. Board of Education of Tipp City Exempted Village School District*, 2010, 2011).

Against this backdrop, the debates in this chapter consider two very different perspectives on whether teachers in K–12 settings should enjoy the right to academic freedom. In the point essay, Ralph Sharp (East Central University) takes the position that insofar as teachers are the most qualified individuals in their school systems to design and implement curricula, they should have the freedom to teach as they see fit. As such, he is critical of allowing unqualified lay people such as school board members and politicians to make curricular decisions, preferring that they be made by professionally prepared educators, including teachers. Sharp concludes that students and communities are "far better served by increasing the autonomy of classroom educators to design and adapt the curricular content in their classrooms."

Marilyn Denison's (Spring Independent School District, Houston, Texas) counterpoint essay responds that teachers should not have greater control of the content of curricula because academic freedom is essentially "nothing more than a fine-sounding, vague guideline with little appreciable value in application in K–12 schools." She asserts that because states and local boards are responsible for schools, they alone should have the authority to decide what children in public schools learn. Denison adds that if educational leaders are to increase achievement among top students while closing gaps between other groups of children, then local school boards, joined in particu-lar by state officials, and occasionally the federal government, must maintain their control to ensure standardized quality of curricular content. She distin-guishes between control of content and instruction and does see a place for freedom in developing the latter.

As you read these debates about academic freedom in K–12 schools, ask yourself two questions. First, should teachers in public elementary and second-ary schools have the right to academic freedom allowing them to teach as they see fit? Second, how far can or should local school boards go in directing what teachers teach and how they teach it, regardless of educator claims of a right to academic freedom?

Charles J. Russo
University of Dayton

POINT: Ralph Sharp
East Central University

A t a time when activists across the spectrum challenge the content of public school curricula, it is worth recalling that the concept of academic freedom, based on First Amendment freedom of speech, encompasses the abstract right to teach freely and without reprisal. In a general sense, as a federal appellate court declared in 1985, "Academic freedom embodies the principle that individual instructors are at liberty to teach that which they deem to be appropriate in the exercise of their professional judgment" (*Aguillard v. Edwards*, 1985, p. 1257).

Typically, conflicts involving claims of academic freedom pit the rights of teachers to teach what and how they deem appropriate against the authority of states or local school boards to determine the nature and content of curricular programs. Often, classroom teachers claim a right to set curricula against external endeavors (by the state government, typically the legislature or state board of education) or internal attempts (by the local school board or district administrators) to regulate what students study. Moreover, teachers' assertions of academic freedom may extend to what they teach (curriculum) and how they teach (instruction).

The concept of academic freedom in U.S. education originated in higher education, not long after the beginning of the 20th century but witnessed a growth when conflicts involved communism and loyalty issues after World War II. The extension of academic freedom from higher education to K–12 schooling developed slowly in the second half of the 20th century. Two impediments to the development of a universally recognized concept of academic freedom in K–12 education have been the tradition of local school board control, including authority over school curricular programs, and the fact that public school students are minors in need of protection. Nonetheless, a small number of courts recognized academic freedom in K–12 as a vigorous, possibly essential right in ruling in favor of teachers in disputes involving curricular challenges. For example, where a teacher's use of a masculinity survey was controversial and sensitive but did not materially or substantially disrupt the operation or discipline of the high school, the court declared that "a teacher has a constitutional right protected by the First Amendment to engage in a teaching method of his or her own choosing, even though the subject matter may be controversial or sensitive" (*Dean v. Timpson Independent School District*, 1979, p. 307). This point essay argues for the proposition that K–12 teachers should have greater control of the content of the curricula they teach.

ARGUMENTS IN FAVOR OF ACADEMIC FREEDOM

Arguments in favor of allowing K–12 teachers greater control of the curricula they teach presume that teachers select suitable curricular content and materials for their classrooms when given the opportunity to do so. Most teachers are effective professionals capable of designing their own curricula in ways that are appropriate and not significantly disruptive. Building-level administrators, with local board support, should dismiss or not renew the contracts of educators who cannot or do not develop and implement effective and suitable classroom curricula. Even so, the way boards handle unsatisfactory teaching performances is not a direct issue in a discussion of academic freedom. Beyond these low or nonperforming educators, classroom teachers should have greater control of the content of the curricula they teach, as three courts from 1969 to 2001 agreed, with others rejecting teachers' specific claims but presenting a defense of the general concept of academic freedom. Arguments in favor of increasing teachers' control of classroom curricula center around protecting freedom of thought and allowing teachers to shape curricula because they are better prepared and skilled than others are to do this.

Arguments Based on Freedom of Ideas

K–12 teachers should have greater control of the curricula they teach primarily because of the significant contribution that academic freedom makes to a democratic society. The Supreme Court has noted that the value of academic freedom extends to all, not merely the affected teachers. By indirectly protecting the rights of students to learn or hear, academic freedom both promotes freedom of thought and the free exchange of ideas.

As a federal trial court in Illinois wrote more than 20 years ago, a key aspect of public education is that "a public school system strives to develop inquisitive minds and independent thought. . . . [this] function cannot be achieved unless the individual teachers are given some measure of academic freedom" (*Krizek v. Board of Education of Cicero-Stickney Township High School, District No. 201, Cook County, Illinois*, 1989, p. 1137). In this regard, protecting teachers' autonomy and control of curricula, with the resulting freedom of thought, combats attempts at censorship and the imposition of the prevailing majority viewpoints.

Related to the protection of freedom of thought is the argument that greater freedom of ideas serves as a shield from political and community involvement and other non-instructional, non-pedagogical influences. In essence, academic freedom insulates curricula from outside pressures based on noneducational grounds. As noted, today's schools are a battleground for competing special interest groups advocating their particular beliefs and attempting to impose their viewpoints on school programs. Most classroom educators teach from academic rather than politically based approaches, or at least far less politically than special interest groups teach. However, at the state level, legislatures and state boards of education often attempt to impose their political and social agendas on the public school curricula. As that 1985 federal appellate court stated so eloquently, "The principle of academic freedom abjures state interference with curriculum or theory as antithetical to the search for truth" (*Aguillard v. Edwards*, 1985, p. 1257).

One need only look to the May 2010 revisions in the Texas social studies curriculum to find an example of politicization of school curricula by including materials that, for example, stressed the role of capitalism while questioning whether the founding fathers were dedicated to an entirely secular government. In the eyes of many, the slant given to social studies curricula, approved by straight party line voting, distorts history instruction. Interestingly, the Texas State Board did not seek input from historians, sociologists, or economists—those theoretically most inclined to provide nonpartisan viewpoints on social studies curricula.

Some local school boards similarly attempt to impose their political, social, and religious viewpoints on their instructional programs with administrators frequently succumbing to the pressures brought by their boards and community groups. Local board members and administrators often lack the courage or inclination to stand up to complaining and meddling patrons, whether they are acting individually or in organized groups. Although some administrators have good intentions and are dedicated to quality school programs, others, not to mention board members, unquestionably are more interested in avoiding or quieting public controversy than in providing the most academically sound curricular program to their students. Only by allowing educators greater control of curricula in their classrooms will public education be able to neutralize this outside, non-pedagogical tampering with what students learn.

By way of illustration, a 2001 case from Kentucky recognized the freedom of teachers to exercise control of the curricula in their classrooms. At issue was the dismissal of an elementary school teacher who invited the actor Woody Harrelson to speak about the benefits and environmental uses of industrial hemp, even though commonwealth law prohibits the use of both industrial hemp and marijuana. At the same time, Harrelson added that he was not arguing for legalization of marijuana. The Sixth Circuit agreed that the teacher's "speech," in the form of her selection of speakers for curricular purposes, was constitutionally protected by the First Amendment (*Cockrel v. Shelby County School District*, 2001).

Related to the argument for greater K–12 teacher control of curricula to preserve and promote freedom of thought is the legal protection of teachers' speech. Led by a series of U.S. Supreme Court cases, lower courts have protected the right of teachers to speak on controversial issues in their classrooms and beyond, provided their speech deals with matters of public concern and does not unduly disrupt the workplace harmony or normal school operations.

An early case from Texas provides a classic example of the need to protect teacher free speech. A federal trial court found that a school board violated the speech rights of a civics teacher when it discharged him for personally refusing to oppose interracial marriage in response to a student's question and for engaging in curricular activities that could have been interpreted as indirectly supporting some anti–Vietnam War activities. The principal, through the social studies department chair, had directed the teacher to refrain from discussing controversial issues and to teach the current events class from the textbook.

The trial court provided a ringing endorsement of a teacher's free speech within the curriculum when it declared,

> The freedom of speech of a teacher and a citizen of the United States must not be so lightly regarded that he stands in jeopardy of dismissal for raising controversial issues in an eager but disciplined classroom. (*Sterzing v. Fort Bend Independent School District*, 1972, p. 661)

This legal protection of teachers who discuss controversial or sensitive topics within their curricula is vital to preserve freedom of thought as well as the free exchange of ideas while educating children by introducing them to conflicting viewpoints on controversial or sensitive topics. To do otherwise is in essence a form of censorship by the prevailing majority viewpoints in local communities and ill prepares students to become active and contributing members in a democratic society nationally.

Arguments Based on Teacher Effectiveness and Expertise

The strongest argument that K–12 teachers should have greater control of the content of curricula is that classroom educators are the most qualified to determine curricula and often the only ones capable of designing the most effective curricula for their students. Through formal college training and teaching experience, classroom teachers are specialists in their subjects and grade levels. Public education should both allow and require teachers to exercise their professional judgment in designing topics and materials for their classrooms.

Further, classroom teachers obviously have direct ownership in the outcome of the decision making, unlike local and state officials whose stake in the success of the curricular decisions is more indirect.

Moreover, the alternative, namely allowing local and state officials to shape curricula, turns curricular decision making over to administrators, board members, and politicians—groups typically clueless as to how to teach a specific subject or grade. Only in public education does society allow untrained laypeople or professional administrators untrained in the specific subject to make policy decisions overriding or ignoring trained professionals. Trained instructional educators are far better suited to make curricular decisions about their specific school programs than either local or state officials. If one carries the theories of "local control" and "site-based management" to their logical conclusions, classroom teachers know best their specific subjects, their classroom environments, and individual students, far better than do board members, meddling administrators not in classrooms for any length of time, or far-removed state officials with political agendas.

Still another educational benefit from giving K–12 teachers greater control of curricular content of what they teach is that such increased autonomy helps work against the modern trend of rigid, stifling uniformity of curricula. Increasing state mandates, the emergence of step-by-step textbook programs such as Saxon Math that emphasize repeated practice rather than development of higher-level thinking skills and limit teacher discretion in shaping classroom instruction, and emphasis on "high stakes" testing have taken school curricula closer to a "canned" approach where teachers mechanically follow outlined procedures and exercise little judgment in their instruction. Greater autonomy in curricular decision making allows classroom teachers to teach to their individual students' needs. At the same time, increased autonomy enables teachers to use their instructional strengths and general creativity and to teach more responsively to their settings and students. To do otherwise forces teachers to teach curricula less suited to their teaching styles and their students' needs.

An Oklahoma teacher's battles with her school board illustrate this point. The Tenth Circuit upheld a school board's action not to reemploy the elementary teacher when she refused to use its adopted "learning modules" for science instruction. In its analysis, the court rejected the teacher's argument that it should have allowed her, a veteran of more than 30 years' experience, to continue using her traditional science methods and materials that she posited were superior to the modular curriculum. In the end, the board achieved its desired uniformity of elementary science curriculum, but at the price of forcing at least one elementary teacher to use a less effective (for her) method of teaching students science or lose her job (*Greenshields v.*

Independent School District I-1016 of Payne County, Oklahoma, 2006). What other profession directs its members exactly how to perform tasks, removes individual judgment, and then holds the professionals accountable for the success (test results) of the tasks?

Giving teachers greater control of curricula also increases their opportunities to adjust and adapt the content of their lessons within their classrooms, a fundamental tenet of instructional techniques. Less state and district control of curricula should provide greater opportunities for teachers to make immediate changes and adjustments to reflect successes and failures in student progress. In addition, such an approach, when compared with state-mandated curricula, enables teachers to shape their instructional programs to reflect community values, traditions, and history—those curricular aspects that hold student attention.

It is commonly accepted that instructional objectives include such elements as selecting activities to meet individual student and group needs while relating subjects and topics to existing student experiences. Greater teacher curricular control will enable classroom educators to teach more effectively and will facilitate their ability to meet such instructional objectives. Conversely, greater board and state control creates roadblocks to such strong instructional approaches and decreases the chances for teachers' success in the classroom.

A final argument for allowing teachers greater control of the K–12 curricular content they teach is that doing so should bolster the quality of the teaching force, albeit indirectly and difficult if not impossible to document quantifiably. Greater teacher control of curricula, allowing classroom educators to exercise daily autonomy in their teaching, will help attract and retain capable people who are passionate about teaching. Allowing teachers to exercise professional judgment in selecting curricular topics and materials should provide stimulating challenges in their careers and bring greater respect in their chosen profession. Ideally, by putting greater curricular responsibility in the hands of classroom instructors, with the assumed resulting additional time commitment, one could anticipate another benefit—the more apathetic, unambitious, and low-performing teachers will voluntarily leave their jobs and the profession.

CRITICISMS AND RESPONSES

Turning to the argument of the counterpoint essay that the legal principle of academic freedom is not as concrete and clearly established as statutory law, it is nonetheless a general concept extended to classroom teachers. As such, it is a weak argument to write academic freedom off simply because it is more abstract than legislative action. One can trace the roots of academic freedom back to German universities in the 19th century, and as early as 1940 when references to this concept began to appear in litigation. Moreover, some contemporary judicial opinions have embraced the concept, and the Supreme Court has acknowledged that it may be an issue in teacher speech cases. Academic freedom is a benefit bestowed on teachers at least in the abstract, and public education would be strengthened by granting K–12 classroom teachers greater control of the curricula they teach.

Although one cannot dispute that the public schools belong to their local communities and states, providing the financial support to maintain schools does not justify exercising considerable control of their actual operation nor ensure that such extensive authority results in the best educational programs. There is considerable distance between state government and local school systems in geography, awareness of conditions, and direct interest in the success and welfare of the schools and communities, and laypeople serving on local boards of education or administrators long removed from the classroom seldom understand what effective teaching entails. Although state and local governments provide financial support for hospitals, roadways, and airports, they seldom attempt to tell those trained professionals how to perform their specific duties.

The argument that appears convincing on the surface but is most superficial is that giving teachers increased autonomy regarding the curricula undermines state and local efforts to align curricula and establish benchmarks to determine effectiveness. The push for curricular alignment, at the expense of individualized student learning, is typical of the emphasis on format and procedure coming from governance at the state and local levels. Though one should not question the value of high expectations, genuine expectations are set by individual teachers who insist that their students achieve at the highest level possible. Student learning and achievement come from effective classroom teaching, not from state or district curricular alignment. Yet, states and communities want standards and accountability in an oversimplified format that the general public thinks it understands, and standards determined by benchmarks rely too heavily on test scores and do not accurately measure actual teaching and learning. As such, alignment of ill-founded standards is a weak defense for restricting teachers' autonomy within their classrooms.

Consistency is not a legitimate argument, either. Emphasis on consistency leads to the primary goal of striving for sameness and uniformity rather than increased learning. Classrooms are unique and their students vary, particularly in learning styles. By adjusting for these many differences, teachers increase learning; consistency for the sake of sameness does not. Variation and individualization are strengths in teaching and generally are effective, because teachers adapt the curriculum to the specific students in the classroom.

In addition, giving K–12 classroom teachers greater control of the curricula they teach is a way to recognize and show respect for the teaching profession. Veteran classroom teachers are trained and experienced professionals who know best what and how to teach the students in their classrooms. Such educators have, or should be required to find, time to adapt their curricula to the students within their classrooms. To oppose giving teachers greater curricular control because of a few incompetent members of the profession is a weak argument.

CONCLUSION

In sum, although states and local school boards must retain some control of K–12 curricula, the authority of teachers regarding curricular content should be increased. Giving local school board members and school administrators, not to mention state officials, greater control of the curricular content than classroom educators have invites unresponsive, standardized curricula that will likely fail to reach most students, poorly prepare them one day for college and work, and result in lower standardized test scores. Students and their communities are far better served by increasing the autonomy of classroom educators to design and adapt the curricular content in their classrooms. Teachers, not others, know best what their students need and what they are capable of teaching most effectively.

COUNTERPOINT: Marilyn Denison
Spring Independent School District, Houston, Texas

A fundamental reason to oppose allowing classroom teachers greater control of the curricula they teach is that such an idea is founded on an unjustified premise. Although educators are quick to shout "academic freedom," it is at most a general, abstract concept in K–12 public education. Although courts often make general reference to the theory, only a few court rulings have recognized a specific, concrete right to academic freedom in public school classrooms. Thus, the concept of academic freedom in the abstract sounds good, but seldom is it viewed as a specific right that classroom educators actually possess in their daily work. In essence, this counterpoint essay maintains that academic freedom is nothing more than a fine-sounding, vague guideline with little appreciable value in K–12 schools; therefore, teachers should not have greater control of the content of the curricula they teach.

LOCAL CONTROL OF SCHOOLS BELONGS TO COMMUNITIES

In general, states and school boards, rather than classroom educators, should exercise primary control of curricula because U.S. public schools belong to their local communities, not the professional educators that they employ. From the founding of the American colonies to the present, our nation has structured its system of education around public schools governed under the concept of local control. Fundamentally, each community, not those professionals employed to work in the schools, "controls" its local schools. Our schools belong to the local communities, not to the teachers who answer to the community through their local school boards. Though some may argue that local boards and their administrators are too political and cave in to the whims of vocal patrons and community interest groups, such reactions are simply responsive to the community that owns the schools and reflect the community's values and standards.

STATE AND LOCAL GOVERNMENTS PAY FOR PUBLIC EDUCATION

A related reason why states and local school boards should not allow K–12 teachers to exercise greater control of the curricula they teach ties back to financial support for public education. Through legislative appropriations and local property tax revenues, state governments and local communities provide the overwhelming financial support for maintaining public education. These levels of support justify the right of legislatures and communities to retain control of curricula to ensure that they are operated in a manner reflecting local values. Why should state governments and local communities "foot the bill" for their public schools and then hand curricular control off to teachers who are merely employees? Such an argument comes close to nothing more than turning the asylum over to the inmates.

MAINTAINING STANDARDS AND ASSESSMENTS

Legislatures create common academic standards as a focus for improving teaching and learning to reassure parents and communities that high school graduates in every part of the nation have the knowledge and skills necessary for college or a competitive job market. Having students meet standards creates opportunities designed to develop better choices in their lives. These standards define the knowledge and skills students should have to succeed in entry-level, credit-bearing, academic college courses and in workforce training programs. With all students prepared for their future, our nation will be positioned to compete in today's global economy. The standards are designed to measure how well students perform based on mastery of the standards. To measure what is taught and mastered, assessments, curricula, and professional development must be aligned with the standards.

Local boards of education and administrators have an interest in maintaining fundamental curricular standards and have a responsibility to ensure such basic standards. Local school boards, through their administrators, monitor student achievement and exercise general supervision over schools. Boards and administrators recognize that student success is the overriding concern. Student achievement is the ultimate measure of educational value, so policies and resources for schools must focus on promoting student achievement. Further, policies of this nature communicate priorities and expectations, sending a clear signal to staff, parents, and communities about board visions and goals.

States hold both school boards and administrators in individual building sites accountable for student achievement. What reflects whether a given school is successful comes down to how well teachers prepare their students for the state assessments covering state standards. To better prepare students for the state assessments, many local boards develop a form of benchmark testing to monitor the teaching and learning process. This informative process identifies struggling students and teachers early enough in the school year to provide correctional support. Without common curricula and these frequent checkpoints, intervention would be near impossible to implement.

Increasing teacher control of their classroom curricula would result in some, perhaps many, teachers "setting the bar" too low for their students. With the range of abilities that students possess, it is likely some teachers may "dumb down" curricula to reach the lowest performers, thus missing material that is designed to meet the range of students' mixed abilities, from low to high achieving, in classrooms. Giving teachers greater control of creating curricula and accountability systems may create significant gaps between aspirations and reality. Teachers may have the best intentions but their curricula may be filled at times with bias, opinion, and low expectations. Teachers' expectations for their students can indeed influence student performance. Not being held to high standards with accountability measures, teachers may lead their students in many directions such that preparing them for higher education or the work force will be a hit-or-miss action.

CURRICULAR ALIGNMENT BY STATES AND LOCAL BOARDS

Another argument in opposition to granting individual classroom educators greater curricular control is that such individualized instructional decision making can work against state and local school board efforts to align curricula to prepare students for standardized testing. As a focus on closing the achievement gaps with the No Child Left Behind Act, educational legislation began to hold schools more accountable through the increase of standardized tests. With the attention on district accountability requirements, the role of curricular alignment gains more attention. State departments of education align state standards with state assessments. In turn, school boards write or adopt curricula aligned with the state documents. Local curricula also build on the skills learned in one grade level for the next as teachers align classroom instruction with district curricula. At the same time, school boards provide professional development that meets curricular and instructional alignment. Improved student performance as measured by state assessments can result when teachers align instruction with district curricula. It would thus be illogical to increase classroom teachers' autonomy to alter and adapt curricula when, or as, they see fit because such changes would negate the efforts to align curricula across and within school systems.

VARIATION AND INCONSISTENCY

On the other side of the coin regarding the argument of curricular alignment, a fundamental flaw in giving classroom teachers greater control is the resulting variation and individualization. A state primarily has a legitimate interest in seeking some level of basic consistency from its school boards as they operate their districts. Moreover, local boards need, and have a right to insist on, some minimum consistency in curricula among classrooms within specific grade levels and from building to building. Although minor adaptations by teachers are effective, school boards unquestionably have the right to insist on curricular uniformity. It is both reasonable and educationally sound to demand that each grade and subject cover assigned objectives and lessons. This approach is essential given both the emphasis on high-stakes testing and the degree to which students move between and among buildings within district school systems in states.

Giving teachers the academic freedom to interpret and develop curricula leaves student achievement as measured by state assessments to chance. Without mandated comprehensive curricula, teachers have the freedom to design instructional programming for their classes. Consequently, curricula could vary from teacher to teacher even at the same grade level and in the same school. Individual teachers would then decide what students should learn, how they would receive instruction, and when instruction would take place during a school year. Even though students may be learning what teachers are teaching, they might be learning different curricula from one classroom to the next.

Without required curricula, there would be no guarantee that prerequisite skills would be taught in previous grades or courses, possibly causing gaps in the learning process. In addition, there will be no protection from redundancy of concepts in consecutive grades allowing students to repeat units of instruction or miss gaining skills altogether. Increased learning gaps either frustrate teachers when they assume grade appropriate material was not covered previously or they have concerns that students have learning problems, which may lead to having students inappropriately being placed in special education settings.

Instead of student achievement gaps closing, allowing teachers greater curricular control could allow the gap to continue to widen. What happens when students move to other schools in districts or across states? Will those children miss out on specific skills that are needed or will they be able to continue with the appropriate educational process? If teachers decide when and what to teach, the students who are affected by mobility may lose their opportunities to learn important grade-level skills because the content of curricula may not be consistent from one teacher to the next. Should this occur, students who miss out on parts of curricula would then be behind, making it difficult for them to ever catch up as they fall farther and farther behind academically. Students who do not master the basic skills would then be required to repeat grade levels or run the risk of being tracked into remedial classes with low expectations.

THE TEACHING PROFESSION: THE WORK ROUTINE

Assuming teachers have the time and the enthusiasm for developing the curricula for the classes they teach, is it fair to assume all educators are adequately prepared to create an innovative, real-world curricula that engages each student in the learning process? Would requiring more work retain teachers or encourage them to find other careers even quicker in an already high rate of career turnover with almost half of teachers leaving the profession after 5 years?

Providing curricula and assessments supports for teachers allows them more time to prepare their classes and instructional strategies. The academic freedom that K–12 teachers should have is to align instructional strategies to meet the needs of the learning styles of the students within mandated curricula. Teachers can then focus on creative and innovative instruction. Teachers can also focus on the "how" to teach instead of the "what" to teach. Moreover, teachers should pay attention to setting up their classrooms with safe environments so that students feel free to take the necessary risks for learning. Teachers should provide the systems of support for each individual student to learn the intended curriculum through models such as differentiation or tutelage. This also allows time for teachers to attend appropriate staff development to acquire knowledge and skills aligned with curricula. As such, the freedom to create curricula and assessments should not be that of teachers. Their time is better served by allowing teachers opportunities for instructional development.

Most teachers are qualified to teach in public schools with only bachelors' degrees in education. More recently, alternative credentialing programs provide fast-track avenues for teacher certification requiring bachelors' degrees in areas of specialization other than education without the study of pedagogical practices. Neither of these modes of certification requires teachers to be experts in the areas within which they are hired to instruct. An upshot is that teachers who are less knowledgeable may stick to facts and rules while missing conceptual, problem solving, and inquiry aspects of their subjects. Teachers must keep in mind that curricular materials are tools providing pedagogical guidance and support that allows them to do their best work with students. Their academic freedom concerns aside, without guaranteed, viable curricula, teachers may not have the resources to meet their duty of providing effective and productive instruction.

LACKING PROFESSIONAL DISCERNMENT

Another justification for opposing increasing control by K–12 teachers to set the curricula in their classrooms is that many fail to exercise sound professional judgment. One need only follow the daily news to witness accounts of teacher behavior that is unsound and indefensible while jeopardizing student learning and sometimes student safety, leaving many to scratch their heads in bewilderment. For example, in the spring of 2010, a teacher in Oklahoma fired a cap gun, which could have been converted to use live ammunition, in his classroom or hallway, and previously sprayed a disinfectant on the students in his class. Further, there are numerous accounts of teachers who duct taped students for their poor behavior and who put children in closets as a form of discipline.

Incidents of bizarre behavior do not represent the conduct of typical teachers, but they are fairly regular and cause the general public to lose confidence in public school teachers generally. Although the "top" of the teaching profession is filled with responsible, capable classroom educators who exercise wise judgment in their work, there are too many teachers whose inconsistent, irrational, and sometimes bizarre actions place their students at risk. These teachers simply do not instill public confidence that more curricular decision making should be turned over to them. Nothing says that most teachers are qualified to exercise, competently, greater control of curricula with the result that students benefit. Moreover, rarely, it seems, do administrators remove these "looney" teachers from their classrooms unless forced to by public reaction to their bizarre behavior.

THE NEED FOR BOUNDARIES

For K–12 teachers to have academic freedom, there first must be boundaries. Without specific boundaries, teachers would be left to decide what material is most important for their students to learn and when it is appropriate for them to learn the material. Having an established curricular and assessment process with timelines for student mastery of material is a determining boundary.

The National Governors Association Center for Best Practices and the Council of Chief State School Officers are the educational drivers for developing the Common Core State Standards. The development of national standards was not left to a hodgepodge of noneducational legislators with personal bias. Instead, these standards define the knowledge and skills that students need from kindergarten to 12th grade to graduate ready for higher education and the workforce. These standards do not cover all of the content that students should learn; therefore, the standards should be complemented by a well-developed, content-rich curriculum provided by the state.

State curricula become a protection and guide for teachers. If teachers are responsible for writing their own curricula, there is no guarantee that students would receive an education preparing them for college or the workforce. If students are not successful beyond high school, parents can then blame the educational system and teachers for not providing guaranteed and viable curricula to prepare their children for the future. Also, by following curricular guidelines, teachers can stay away from covering material that can be inappropriate, libelous, obscene, or likely to lead to lawbreaking or controversial disorder. Mandated curricula leave room for students to learn to debate issues while maintaining workplace harmony and the normal operation of the school.

K–12 teachers may be the most qualified to determine the strategies used to instruct lessons but not to set curricula. If anything, teachers are already being stretched by growing expectations and having to deal with an ongoing and increasing array of social problems. Granting teachers in elementary and secondary schools the right to academic freedom and expecting them to write their own curricula adds pressure that in the end may lead to higher rates of teacher stress and burnout.

In education, the curriculum is known as a unit of study or the content offered at a grade level or course. The curriculum is the "what" in teaching, the path for teaching, learning, and assessments for a given course of study. A lesson is known as a unit of instruction. It is the "how" in teaching. Simply because states and local school boards provide curricula does not mean that instruction will become a "canned" approach. For example, in many states, the third grade curriculum requires students to learn multiplication facts. Teachers have the authority to design creative and innovative lessons to teach this curriculum. Also, the curriculum in science may require students to classify samples of matter as solids, liquids, and gas. The lessons may look different in classrooms as one teacher might have students act out how atoms react in solids, liquids, and gasses, and another teacher may have students working at centers cutting out pictures and sorting examples of solids, liquids, and gasses. In this scenario, both teachers are providing lessons that cover the objective in the curriculum but the lessons look fairly different from one another.

States and local school boards, not teachers, must maintain control of K–12 curricula to ensure a practicable education for all children. Standardization eliminates the creation of curricula lacking focus while inviting a secure path to best prepare students for the future. It reduces potential legal issues by avoiding controversial material. Parents, teachers, and students are familiar with educational expectations and can deliver to them. Therefore, lesson design, not curriculum writing or academic freedom, is best left to teachers to create and deliver instruction for learning.

CONCLUSION

Areas of concern can be addressed when individuals have ways of discovering their weakness. What is going right can be emulated if teachers have ways to expose the truth. From this revelation, strategic plans ensuring consistency among curricula goals, resources, capacity, and assessment can be aligned for the good of all students, teachers, administrators, and school boards.

In today's educational system, the focus is on student achievement. As a measure of value, each country is competing for a top ranking for the best in education. Likewise, each state in the United States is vying for the rank of having exemplary institutions. The rankings of top states in student achievement are based on the outcome of test scores, graduation rates, and how many students earn higher education certifications. To continue increasing student achievement while closing the gaps between student population groups, local and state boards, acting in conjunction with the federal government, must maintain control of what curricula is to be taught and assessed. With this alignment, students' assessments provide a clear picture of what is learned across the nation, among states, and within school districts. Therefore, K–12 teachers should not have academic freedom to assert greater control of the content of the curricula they teach.

Further Readings and Resources

Daly, K. C. (2001). Balancing act: Teachers' classroom speech and the First Amendment. *Journal of Law and Education, 30*, 1–62.

DeMitchell, T. A., & Connelly, V. J. (2007). Academic freedom and the public school teacher: An exploratory study of perceptions, policy, and the law. *Brigham Young University Education and Law Journal, 2007*, 83–117.

Fries, K., Connelly, V. J., & DeMitchell, T. A. (2008). Academic freedom in the public K–12 classroom: Professional responsibility or constitutional right? A conversation with teachers. *Education Law Reporter, 227*, 505–524.

Sharp, R. (2008). Academic freedom. In C. J. Russo (Ed.), *Encyclopedia of education law* (pp. 12–14). Thousand Oaks, CA: Sage.

Sharp, R. (2008). Academic freedom and censorship. In K. E. Lane, M. Gooden, J. Mead, P. Pauken, & S. Eckes (Eds.), *The principal's legal handbook* (4th ed., pp. 383–389). Dayton, OH: Education Law Association.

Wenkart, R. D. (2006). Public school curriculum and the free speech rights of teachers. *Education Law Reporter, 214*, 1–17.

Wright, R. G. (2007). The emergence of First Amendment academic freedom. *Nebraska Law Review, 85*(2007), 793–829.

Court Cases and Statutes

Aguillard v. Edwards, 765 F.2d 1251 (5th Cir. 1985), 482 U.S. 578 (1987).

Bernstein, In re, 726 N.Y.S.2d 474 (N.Y. App. Div. 2001).

Bradley v. Pittsburgh Board of Education, 910 F.2d 1172 (3d Cir. 1990).

Cockrel v. Shelby County School District, 270 F.3d 1036 (6th Cir. 2001).

Dean v. Timpson Independent School District, 486 F. Supp. 302 (E.D. Tex. 1979).

Evans-Marshall v. Board of Education of Tipp City Exempted Village School District, 624 F.3d 332 (6th Cir. 2010), *reh'g and reh'g en banc denied* (2011).

Fowler v. Board of Education of Lincoln County, Ky., 819 F.2d 657 (6th Cir. 1987), *cert. denied*, 484 U.S. 986 (1987).

Greenshields v. Independent School District I-1016 of Payne County, Oklahoma, 174 Fed. Appx. 426 (10th Cir. 2006).

James v. Board of Education of Central School District No. 1, Addison, 461 F.2d 566 (2d Cir.1972), *cert. denied*, 409 U.S. 1042 (1972).

Kirkland v. Northside Independent School District, 890 F.2d 794 (5th Cir.1989), *cert. denied*, 496 U.S. 926 (1990).

Krizek v. Board of Education of Cicero-Stickney Township High School, District No. 201, Cook County, Illinois, 713 F. Supp. 1131 (N.D. Ill. 1989).

Lacks v. Ferguson Reorganized School District R-2, 147 F.3d 718 (8th Cir. 1998).

Los Angeles Teachers Union v. Los Angeles City Board of Education, 455 P.2d 827 (Cal. 1969).

Mayer v. Monroe County Community School, 474 F.3d 477 (7th Cir. 2007a), *reh'g and reh'g en banc denied* (7th Cir. 2007), *cert. denied*, 552 U.S. 823 (2007b).

No Child Left Behind Act of 2001, 20 U.S.C. §§ 6301 *et seq.*

Proposed Termination of James E. Johnson's Teaching Contract with Independent School District No. 709, In re, 451 N.W.2d 343 (Minn. Ct. App. 1990).

Russo v. Central School District No. 1, Towns of Rush, 469 F.2d 623 (2d Cir. 1972), *cert. denied*, 411 U.S. 932 (1973).

Sterzing v. Fort Bend Independent School District, 376 F. Supp. 657 (S.D. Tex. 1972).

Tinker v. Des Moines Independent Community School District, 393 U.S. 503 (1969).

Should the current limits on educational use of copyrighted materials and intellectual property be revised to give schools more latitude and guidance?

POINT: Clayton H. Slaughter, *Greencastle Community Schools*
COUNTERPOINT: Amanda Harmon Cooley,
South Texas College of Law

OVERVIEW

Protection under the Copyright Act of 1976 applies only to "original works of authorship fixed in any tangible medium of expression," subject to the act's "fair use" provision that permits an exemption from copyright infringement "for purposes such as criticism, comment, news reporting, teaching (including multiple copies for classroom use), scholarship, or research . . ." (Copyright, §§ 102(a), 107).

The test for originality for purposes of the Copyright Act is not substantial. This principle is reflected in *West Publishing Co. v. Mead Data Center* (1986) where, in granting injunctive relief to *West*, the Eighth Circuit observed, "To be the original work of an author, a work must be the product of some 'creative intellectual or aesthetic labor.' However, 'a very slight degree of such labor[,] . . . almost any ingenuity in selection, combination or expression, no matter how crude, humble or obvious, will be sufficient' to make the work copyrightable" (p. 1223). Although the four factors discussed later constituting "fair use" are a defense against charges of violating the Copyright Act, their interpretation has never been easy or consistent (Mawdsley, 2009).

The basic aspect of copyright is to prevent others from reproducing or copying original works without permission. It extends only the copyrightable portions of an author's output to the format in which ideas are expressed and to substantial similarity between copies and the originals. Thus, the threshold question under the Copyright Act is always whether that which has been copied was copyrightable. In *Clark v. Crues* (2008), the Federal Circuit held that a teacher who developed a hall pass system did not have a copyrightable interest in that system for purposes of an infringement action against the school's development of a similar program. Instead, the court viewed the teacher's work as only a "business idea" that is excluded from Copyright Act protection.

The classic infringement case is *Marcus v. Rowley* (1983), where a high school teacher (Marcus) who developed a 35-page booklet, "Cake Decorating Made Easy," found herself in the awkward position of being charged with plagiarism by her own students after another teacher (Rowley) copied portions of her booklet without attribution and distributed them to students. Worth noting is that the plaintiff, Marcus, placed the copyright symbol, ©, in each booklet, followed by "1973 Eloise Marcus." In the plaintiff's subsequent copyright act suit against the defendant's plagiarism, the Ninth Circuit ruled that a copyright violation was present and remanded for damages. With respect to the doctrine of fair use, the court pointed out that there were violations because the defendant's use had been "for the same intrinsic purpose for which the copyright owner intended." The court added that it was not conceivable that "the copying of all, or substantially all, of a copyrighted [item] can be held to be a fair use" (*Marcus*, 1175, 1176).

Original ideas can still be excluded from copyright protection for the creator where they constitute "works for hire." Works that are created as part of an employment relationship are considered "works for hire," and under the Copyright Act, "the employer or other person for whom the work was prepared is considered the author . . . unless the parties have expressly agreed otherwise in a written instrument signed by them, owns all of the rights comprised in the copyright" (Copyright Act, § 201(b)).

In *Pavlica v. Behr* (2005), for example, a federal trial court decided that there was a triable question of fact whether a manual that a high school teacher developed to use in a new course involving science research represented a work for hire. The legal theory in *Pavlica* is interesting in that the school board raised the work for hire claim, arguing essentially that, because the manual had been developed to be used in the plaintiff's high school teaching, it was a work for hire that precluded his infringement claim. The teacher eventually prevailed in part and was awarded some damages for copyright infringement. Even so, this case is a reminder that materials that teachers develop and use for their classes can be subject to "work for hire" challenges to copyright protection.

The authors in this chapter debate whether teachers should be given greater latitude and additional guidance regarding their use of copyrighted materials in the classroom. Both authors are in agreement that original works need to be protected but differ in regard to the limits that are placed on teachers for classroom use of copyrighted materials and intellectual property. Clayton H. Slaughter's (Greencastle Community Schools) point essay suggests that, although protection of intellectual property under the Copyright Act is a worthy goal, it should not be imposed in such a way as to frustrate the deliverance of high quality education. The tension, as he indicates, is that failure to adequately protect copyrighted material will have the effect of creating a disincentive to create new works. He suggests that although limits to the use of these materials are necessary, current limits should be reduced so that teachers have more latitude when using such materials for instructional purposes. He further suggests that clearer guidelines are needed.

In the counterpoint essay, Amanda Harmon Cooley (South Texas College of Law) argues that the Copyright Act should not be interpreted so expansively that it violates the intellectual property interests of authors, but nonetheless, should reflect the increased emphasis on electronic learning. She supports the narrow interpretation that courts have given to "fair use," reasoning that judicial language about the use of others' material should be clear enough to those in education. Cooley also finds support in the Technology, Education and Copyright Harmonization (TEACH) Act. She concludes that even in the electronic age, the current restrictions on the use of copyrighted material for instructional purposes are reasonable. She also feels that current guidelines are adequate.

As you read these essays, ask yourself the following three questions. First, are the laws governing the use of copyrighted materials in schools workable, particularly with respect to technology? Second, if not, how can they be improved? Third, how have the rapid changes in technology, coupled with the growth of online instruction and the use of virtual, nonprint media, changed the way copyright laws apply in today's schools?

Ralph D. Mawdsley
Cleveland State University

POINT: Clayton H. Slaughter
Greencastle Community Schools

The pervasiveness of books, workbooks, posters, compact discs, DVDs, computer software, digital photographs, PDFs, and online videos is evident in most K–12 schools today. Computers and the Internet have revolutionized the way education is delivered. The predecessors to the computer printout—the photocopy and mimeograph machine—are still present in schools today. All of these items are tools to meet the goal of providing high quality education. These tools also have another element in common: They are potentially protected by federal copyright law.

The tension between two noble goals, providing high quality education and protecting copyright, is highlighted with exceptional clarity in school settings. Teachers strive to educate students even as most schools work under tighter fiscal restraints than ever before. This combination of increased expectations and scarce resources makes schools ripe for duplicating copyrighted works in the name of educating students.

The goal of protecting copyrights is also noble. It may seem at first blush that educating students should trump the rights of whoever has secured a copyright on a worksheet, photograph, or DVD. However, the very goal of educating students is exactly why school officials should respect copyrights. Violating copyrights will, over time, reduce educators' ability to provide a quality education. This point essay argues that the solution to potential educator copyright infringement is to provide clearer standards for what constitutes acceptable use of copyrighted works under the "fair use" exception and reducing the time a work is protected by copyright to allow educators access to more work sooner.

PURPOSE OF COPYRIGHT

The purpose of a copyright is to provide a limited-term monopoly on the use of a work. During the duration of the limited monopoly, the copyright holder can control who can use the copyrighted material; thus, the holder can choose to allow only those paying for the materials to use them. There are limited exceptions to the monopoly of a copyright and limits to the length of time it applies. This limited monopoly is designed to provide authors and artists with incentive to write and create. The limited monopoly allows the copyright holder a limited time after authorship to recoup the cost of writing or creating.

After the copyright expires, the work becomes part of the public domain for everyone to use without cost or restriction. Copyright holders can also waive their copyright and place their work directly into public domain. All materials created by the U.S. government are automatically in the public domain.

This safeguard for copyright holders also supports educators and subsequently their students. If authors and artists are not protected, then their works can be taken immediately after writing or publishing and used by anyone, anywhere, with no financial remuneration to those who created the work. Under this system, without copyright, there is no financial incentive for writing or creating. If this system persists, then new workbooks, textbooks, and creative works will slow or even stop. Some financially wealthy artists or authors may continue to write, but any author or artist attempting to make a living wage will be forced out of business. The teacher who photocopies mass amounts of workbook pages to save school money has achieved short-term savings for the school board but has damaged education in the long run because these acts are like stealing. The current copyright system breaks down when the length of copyright protection far exceeds the time needed to recover the sunk costs of writing or creating. The current copyright law protects works for 70 years *after* the death of the author. Works created after January 1, 1978, are protected for the life of the author plus 70 years; for corporate authors, it is the shorter of 95 years from the work's first publication or 120 years from when the work was created. If a work was created before 1978, the term is whichever is shorter: the life of the author plus 70 years or December 31, 2047. The purpose of copyright protection is to allow authors to recover sunk costs and potentially make a profit from their work. The goal is not to allow the author's family to receive royalties forever.

Educators could be using several decades' worth of materials for educational purposes that are no longer making a profit for the publishers, except that copyright law protects works for far too long and thus prevents educators from using materials for educational purposes for several decades. The length of copyright protection was extended in 1998 by the Copyright Term Extension Act (CTEA). The act is also known as the Sonny Bono Copyright Term Extension Act of 1998. In extending the copyright protection for a few lucrative works, Congress extended what is effectively a ban on educators' ability to use others' works.

Critics of the current copyright law complain that it constrains educators from making real-time adjustments to their curriculum to reflect current events and incorporate recently available materials. This claim is inaccurate. The current law allows educators more discretion to use copyrighted works than any other group of people have. This exception is incorporated in the law as the "fair use" exception. The problem in the fair use exception is that it is loosely defined and creates a chilling effect on use by educators. An exception that is difficult to use does not provide much of a safe harbor for educators attempting to provide students with a quality education.

FAIR USE BALANCING TEST

Fair use is a term of art in the law and has a specific definition. This definition outlines a subjective balancing test. Like any balancing test, defined elements or variables must be examined. The weight given to each variable and the resultant aggregate is subjective, resulting in a lack of clarity in application. Educators are uncertain when fair use applies and when it does not. Because of this uncertainty, educators either disregard copyright protection, thus opening the school corporation to legal liability, or shy away from using copyrighted works. The tendency not to use works even when they are within the fair use exception and would enrich the learning experience of the student is the "chilling effect" that makes educators less likely to use works they are rightfully entitled to use. Either of these results—blatant disregard or diminished use—is unhealthy for the education community.

Nonprofit Use

The four elements of the fair use balancing test, which are subject to varying interpretations, are nonprofit use, brevity, spontaneity, and cumulative effect. None of these elements is controlling except for nonprofit use. Commercial use of a product abrogates fair use. To claim fair use, educators must be using material in a nonprofit manner. All of the elements must be examined with their aggregate effect determining if the use of a copyrighted work is a permissible exception under the fair use doctrine.

Brevity

Brevity refers to the amount of copyrighted work copied for educational use. The amount of copying allowed depends on the type of work being used. The policy goal is to allow educators to use portions of otherwise protected works for educational purposes, but not to allow them to use substantial portions of the work. Using substantial portions of the material allows the educator to, in effect, create a substitute for the protected material. Clear explanations of how much material can be used are not provided in the law. Attempts have been made to provide guidance on the amount of material that can be borrowed, but these suggestions are just that—suggestions based on past copyright cases and legislative history. These recommendations need to be codified to provide educators with a clear definition or clear indication of how much material they can use.

Examples of recommendations for acceptable copying under the brevity portion of the test include poems shorter than 250 words and articles less than 2,500 words. Guidelines are also in place and available for plays, novels, letters, picture books, charts, graphs, drawings, cartoons, and pictures. The reasoning that teachers are uncertain about what and how much of a work may be copied seems only to be a guise for lack of knowledge about the copyright, until it becomes obvious that these suggestions are not binding in a court of law. How can educators, who are untrained in copyright law, apply and balance such a complex subjective legal test? It has been argued that ignorance of the law is no excuse, but when the law is unclear, it is impossible to know what is legal. This vagueness of the fair use test variables leaves much room for clarification.

Spontaneity

Spontaneity refers to the length of time the copyrighted material has been located before use in the classroom. This element is not an excuse or crutch for the underprepared educator. Rather, it is an exception to copyright law to allow for the use of current material in classrooms. An example of this exception might be the use of a previous day's newscast in a classroom as a writing or discussion prompt. This exception is not intended to allow educators to record a documentary and show it year after year in their classroom.

The issue of concern is the gray area between material that is a day old and that which is a year or several years old. This rule requires educators who intend to reuse materials year after year to seek permission from copyright holders before subsequent uses, an understandable approach. The law should provide a clear cutoff for the spontaneity time frame based on when material is published, not when an educator locates it. This time frame should be extended to a minimum of 1 year. If a teacher is covering a current event, it is burdensome to have some recent stories regarding the event be acceptable for use, but the articles that are a month old be protected. In the time that students are working with an article, it could easily move from permissible use to protected status if the time allowed is too short.

The copying of recent periodicals is frequently allowed under the spontaneity portion of fair use, but educators need to be cognizant of the amount of material used. All portions of the fair use test must be met. Simply because a periodical is recent does not mean that the entire magazine or newspaper can be copied—the brevity portion of the fair use test must also be applied. By applying all of the sections of the fair use test, a more holistic approach can be achieved to balance the competing goals of high quality education and copyright protection. This goal of high quality education is undermined by forcing educators to apply a legal test that is used differently in different jurisdictions. We are asking educators to become copyright fair use experts.

Cumulative Effect

Cumulative effect refers to the overall result from using the copyrighted work. Frequently, courts will look to see if the copy or allegedly infringing work is a "market substitute" for the copyrighted work. For example, a photocopy of a workbook is a market substitute. Rather than buying another workbook, a copy is used in its place. A work that would not be a market substitute would be one where the original is not supplanted by the copy. For example, the use of a few lines of text out of a novel to discuss a literary metaphor would not be a market substitute for the entire novel. What constitutes a market substitute is unclear in many other cases. Does the use of an entire chapter from a book constitute a substitute? What about the use of only the graphics or flowcharts in a book? Educators are not positioned to determine the cumulative effect of using copyrighted works.

Fair use does not allow for copying of consumable items such as workbooks, worksheets, and answer sheets. Materials that would normally be "consumed" or destroyed in the education process cannot be copied under the fair use exception. These copies would serve as a market substitute. This rule should be a model for the other elements of the copyright law. It provides more clarity than the other elements of the fair use test provide.

GUIDELINES FOR QUALITY EDUCATION WITHIN FAIR USE

The bounds of the fair use exception are unclear. Until Congress clarifies the elements of the fair use exception, educators can stay within the safe bounds of copyright law and protect the incentives of authors and artists by following a few basic principles.

Start with the narrow default position that all written and visual works are protected by copyright and thus belong to someone.

Determine if a work is part of the public domain. Has the author allowed for public use? If one cannot prove that a work is in the public domain, then assume that it is copyrighted. If a work bears the copyright symbol, ©, then it is not part of the public domain.

Will the copyrighted work be used for nonprofit purposes? This question is likely to be yes for most all educators, but should not be skipped. Commercial use voids a claim to fair use.

Consider how much of a work one plans to use. Apply your intended use to one of the available allowable fair use tables. If a planned use is in the permissible column, then it is most likely fair use. If a planned use is in the impermissible column, then either adjust the amount of work used, or do not use the work because the planned use is most likely a copyright violation. Remember these tables provide suggestions only. They are not definitive safe harbors for the bounds of permissible use.

If copyrighted works are used to illustrate contemporary issues, do not keep the work for next semester. If works are to be used semester after semester, purchase or secure the rights to use a copyrighted work.

Never photocopy a workbook without written permission from the publisher. This permission will most likely be in the form of a license and will cost money.

Approach copyrighted works as a tool. Look for fundamentally sound ways to adjust curricula and teaching practices to avoid copying works protected by copyright. The educative ingenuity of teachers will most likely result in a better learning environment than will simply copying in mass from a copyrighted work.

Develop one's own materials. This option may take time, even several semesters, but a well-written worksheet, text, or photograph can illustrate a point without any copyright issues.

CONCLUSION

The availability of currently copyrighted materials to educators can be increased through decreasing the length of the copyright protection to a length of time that better reflects the purpose of copyright protection—to help authors recoup sunk costs and incentivize authors to write. The body of work available to educators can also be increased by clarifying the elements of the fair use exception. Additional guidance regarding how much material can be used and for how long will reduce the chilling effect currently in place for educators who want to use copyrighted materials but are afraid of running afoul of the law. When these clarifications are made to the copyright law, effort should be made to maximize the availability of materials to educators without undermining the goals of copyright.

ADDITIONAL CONSIDERATIONS

The current requirements of the Copyright Act severely restrict student exposure to new ideas. Although providing clearer definition to the aspects of fair use and reducing the number of years of copyright protection represent a step in the direction of broadening access to ideas, educators are still left struggling with whether their disclosures of copyrighted material to classes would constitute a copyright violation. Under the current Copyright Act, violators can face substantial penalties. A better course of action might be to permit use of copyrighted material for instructional purposes but then require that educators furnish appropriate attribution for the materials used. The requirement of attribution within the context of plagiarism is much broader than fair use and has the salutary effect of creating a level academic playing field for both students and educators. Arguably, attribution is a concept much easier for educators to understand and avoids having to furnish definition to such amorphous copyright concepts as fair use.

COUNTERPOINT: Amanda Harmon Cooley
South Texas College of Law

I t is inarguable that in the current competitive global environment, school systems and officials should do all that they can to provide their students with access to as many educational resources as possible. However, this assertion becomes problematic when educators begin to use materials in a way that infringes on the rights of the creators of those resources. Clearly, it is important to find a balance between educational access to materials and intellectual property rights. If this balance is to be an equitable one for all parties, then it must involve certain limits on how school staff can use copyrighted materials and intellectual property in schools. For the use of copyrighted materials inside traditional classrooms, this balance should be struck based on the established and expansive doctrine of "fair use" as outlined by statute and court decisions.

Yet, in an era of emerging technologies and instructional methodologies, schools can no longer be defined solely in terms of traditional classrooms. More and more education is being conducted online. This relatively new medium for teaching and learning has resulted in a series of questions about how school officials may use copyrighted materials in virtual classrooms. Although the fair use doctrine is still relevant to online education, Congress has added other important protections that apply specifically to this form of teaching. Consequently, for the use of copyrighted materials via distance learning platforms, the balance between educational access and intellectual property rights should be struck based on the requirements of the Technology, Education and Copyright Harmonization (TEACH) Act.

In sum, this counterpoint essay maintains that there should be limits to how school staff can use copyrighted materials in schools. The same limits that are applied to the general public's use of intellectual property, with the expansions that are built into the fair use doctrine and the TEACH Act, should govern school usage of intellectual property. Specifically, for copyrighted materials, the limiting question should be whether such use complies with the fair use doctrine and the TEACH Act. If the answer to this question is in the affirmative, then the school should continue to use those resources. If the answer to this question is in the negative, school staff should refrain from such use.

As a matter of law and equity, educational institutions should be treated similarly to the general public in their use of copyrighted materials. Just as all other individuals and entities must abide by the copyright law as established by Congress and courts, schools, colleges, and universities should also ensure that their use of copyrighted material without the permission of owners complies with the rightful requirements of the fair use doctrine and the TEACH Act. To argue the contrary would be unfair to copyright owners and would dilute the meaning of intellectual property rights.

COPYRIGHT PROTECTIONS AND THE FAIR USE DOCTRINE

Protection of intellectual property, in the form of copyrights and patents, is an integral part of the U.S. government. Article I, Section 8, Clause 8 of the U.S. Constitution specifically gives Congress the power "To promote the progress of science and useful arts, by securing for limited times to authors and inventors the exclusive right to their respective writings and discoveries." The inclusion of this congressional power in the Constitution, after unanimous approval, demonstrates the importance that the founders of the United States placed on safeguarding the rights of authors.

Pursuant to this constitutional grant, Congress enacted a series of copyright laws to ensure that authors had (1) the exclusive right to produce, reproduce, distribute, perform, and display their original works of authorship and (2) the exclusive right to authorize others to do so. These laws include the Copyright Act of 1976, which codified the fair use doctrine. Before the passage of this federal statute, the fair use doctrine, which grants a limited privilege of lawful use of copyrighted material by someone other than its owner without the owner's permission, had been developed as a defense to copyright infringement claims through a number of judicial opinions. The purpose of the fair use doctrine is to provide a defense against claims by copyright owners that one has violated their intellectual property rights. Under a broad approach, one could argue that, in an educational context, the objective of the fair use doctrine is to ensure the advancement of knowledge, learning, and scholarship.

Consequently, the Copyright Act of 1976, as amended, governs the use (and the fair use) of copyrighted material by individuals and entities other than the owner of the copyright. Importantly, Section 107 of the act states, "The fair use of a copyrighted work . . . for purposes such as criticism, comment, news reporting, teaching (including multiple copies for classroom use), scholarship, or research, is not an infringement of copyright." Under this statute, four factors are used to determine whether the use of a copyrighted work is fair use. These factors are as follows:

1. The purpose and character of the use, including whether such use is of a commercial nature or is for nonprofit educational purposes;

2. The nature of the copyrighted work;

3. The amount and substantiality of the portion used in relation to the copyrighted work as a whole; and

4. The effect of the use upon the potential market for or value of the copyrighted work. (Copyright Act, 107)

An examination of the 1976 Copyright Act clearly shows that Congress wanted (and continues to want) to ensure broad educational use of copyrighted work, so long as such use does not infringe on the intellectual property rights of the author of the work. Given the expanded legal scope that school officials have regarding their use of copyrighted materials for educational purposes under the fair use doctrine, it would be inequitable to the creators of those materials to advocate for the limitless use of copyrighted materials and intellectual property in schools. To call for such use would be contrary to a key foundational right that has been examined and upheld throughout U.S. history.

Opponents of the proposition that there should be limits on how school staff can use copyrighted materials in schools might argue that the fair use doctrine is too restrictive, that it does not clearly define the differences between copyright infringement and lawful fair use, or that it does not adequately address the issues that are raised in the relatively new medium of distance teaching and learning. In response to the first claim, the fair use doctrine is an expansive (rather than a restrictive) doctrine in the context of legal rights in schools. In response to the second claim, the fair use doctrine and its interpreting guidelines provide appropriate guidance for schools' lawful usage of copyrighted materials. Finally, in response to the third claim, the TEACH Act supplements the fair use doctrine by providing additional guidance on the use of copyrighted materials in the new technologies that are present in online education. Consequently, the contention that there should be no limits on how school staff can use copyrighted materials and intellectual property in schools is a misguided argument that should be rejected.

FAIR USE: AN EXPANSIVE (RATHER THAN RESTRICTIVE) DOCTRINE IN THE CONTEXT OF LEGAL RIGHTS IN SCHOOLS

In a multitude of opinions, the Supreme Court has reaffirmed that neither teachers nor students lose their legal rights when they enter the schoolhouse door. Despite this language, there have been a fair number of recent cases in federal and state courts where the judges, in looking at the constitutional rights or other legal rights of teachers or students, have construed these rights narrowly. Examples of the limitations that are being placed on students and teachers include situations involving First and Fourth Amendment rights under the U.S. Constitution. The restriction of legal rights of teachers and students has become a cause for concern for many parties who are interested in U.S. education.

Unlike many of these examples, the fair use doctrine is an expansive (rather than a restrictive) doctrine in the context of legal rights in schools. Consequently, compliance with the fair use doctrine by school staff in their use of copyrighted materials in schools is an appropriate limitation. Evidence that fair use is an expansive doctrine begins with the statutory language of the Copyright Act of 1976, which specifically includes "teaching (including multiple copies for classroom use), scholarship, or research" in its classification of lawful purposes of use of copyrighted material without the owner's permission. Teaching, scholarship, and research are at the core of every educational institution's mission. The intentional inclusion of these central functions of education in the statute demonstrates the breadth of fair use in an educational context as compared with other settings.

Additionally, one of the four factors used in the fair use determination focuses on educational usage of copyrighted material. In deciding whether or not the use of copyrighted materials is lawful or an infringement, a court must look to "the purpose and character of the use, including whether such use is of a commercial nature or is for nonprofit educational purposes." Although they must also evaluate the three other factors, courts have often found commercial usage of copyrighted materials, as opposed to that of nonprofit educational usage, to be an influential factor in the determination that use of copyrighted materials is an infringement. In other words, courts are more expansive in finding fair use when the use of copyrighted materials is for nonprofit educational purposes. Because the fair use doctrine is an expansive (rather than a restrictive) doctrine in the context of legal rights in schools, it is an appropriate limit for school staffs' usage of copyrighted materials without the owners' permission.

FAIR USE: A DOCTRINE THAT PROVIDES APPROPRIATE GUIDANCE FOR SCHOOLS' LAWFUL USAGE OF COPYRIGHTED MATERIALS

The fair use doctrine does not specifically enumerate the number of words that a non-copyright owner may use of another's work before it crosses the line from fair use to copyright infringement. Regardless, the fair use doctrine does provide appropriate guidance for schools' lawful usage of copyrighted materials. It is important to keep in mind that the fair use doctrine does not exist in a vacuum, that it has been construed by many courts, and that it has generated interpreting guidelines that provide school staff direction on what is (and what is not) fair use.

The fair use doctrine was initially developed by the courts. The Copyright Act of 1976 codified this doctrine, and it has been construed by many courts since the passage of this federal statute. The substantial number of judicial opinions that outline what conduct falls within the fair use defense enable school staff to understand what is considered lawful usage of copyrighted material. Additionally, the instructive nature of the fair use doctrine encourages school staff to maintain good relationships with legal counsel that specializes in the area of intellectual property law.

Further, interpreting guidelines of the fair use doctrine, although not expressly binding as law, have been established by Congress to help educators in their use of copyrighted materials in schools. Congress and other administrative agencies have produced a variety of guidelines that interpret the fair use doctrine as a way to provide additional guidance for educators. Although many school staffs may not be aware of these guidelines, it is the responsibility of schools to make educators aware of these parameters as a way to avoid copyright infringement. These guidelines, along with court opinions construing the fair use doctrine, demonstrate that this doctrine is an appropriate limit for school staffs' usage of copyrighted materials without the owners' permission.

THE TEACH ACT: USE OF COPYRIGHTED MATERIALS IN DISTANCE LEARNING

With the evolution of technology comes novel legal issues. The innovations in online education have presented additional legal complications regarding the use of copyrighted materials by school staff in virtual classrooms. However, Congress has passed the TEACH Act, which supplements the fair use doctrine in that it provides an important legislative solution to the use of copyrighted materials in the new technologies that are present in distance learning and teaching. This statute counters any type of assertion that there should be no limits on school staffs' use of copyrighted materials that are delivered via the Internet.

The TEACH Act, which became law in 2002, allows greater latitude for teachers in the use of copyrighted materials in distance learning environments. However, before teachers can be granted these rights, the educational institution must meet several criteria, including the retention of accredited, nonprofit educational status; maintenance of copyright policies; provision of copyright information and notice of copyright to students; implementation of technological safeguards to protect the copyrighted material from external dissemination; and limitations of use of the copyrighted materials to reasonable and limited mediated instructional use for a class session and the students enrolled therein. The inclusion of these requirements within the TEACH Act serve as an appropriate limit on school staffs' usage of copyrighted materials as they balance educational access and intellectual property rights. Finally, the TEACH Act only supplements the fair use doctrine, upon which educators can always rely no matter the nature of the classroom—be it traditional or online.

CONCLUSION

In the U.S. educational system, the ideals of fairness and balance are taught in many courses and at many levels. These same values are inherent in the question of whether there should be limits on how school staff can use copyrighted materials and intellectual property in schools. An appropriate solution to this query is one that provides proper attention to educational access to works of authorship and to the intellectual property rights of those authors. Schools, like all other individuals and entities, should act within the scope of the law when using copyrighted materials. Fortunately, educational institutions have the guidance of the fair use doctrine and the TEACH Act, which each provide increased amounts of protection for the use of copyrighted materials to schools, when making decisions as to this use in the traditional and virtual classroom. The limits established by Congress and the courts in copyright law are appropriate, fair, and balanced limits that help reinforce some of the foundational tenets of U.S. education.

FURTHER READINGS AND RESOURCES

Bonner, K. M. (Ed.). (2006). *The Center for Intellectual Property handbook.* New York: Neal-Schuman.

Donner, I. (1992). The Copyright Clause of the U.S. Constitution: Why did the framers include it with unanimous approval? *The American Journal of Legal History, 36*(3), 361–378.

Heins, M., & Beckles, T. (2005). *Will fair use survive? Free expression in the age of copyright control: A public policy report.* New York: Brennan Center for Justice at NYU School of Law, Democracy Program, Free Expression Policy Project.

Lipinski, T. A. (2006). *The complete copyright liability handbook for librarians and educators.* New York: Neal-Schuman.

Mawdsley, R. D. (2009). The tangled web of plagiarism litigation: Sorting out the legal issues. *Brigham Young University Education and Law Journal, 2009,* 245–268.

Russell, C. (2002, December). *New copyright exemptions for distance educators: The Technology, Education and Copyright Harmonization (TEACH) Act.* Syracuse, NY: ERIC Clearinghouse on Information and Technology. Retrieved from http://www.eric.ed.gov/PDFS/ED470984.pdf

Simpson, C. (2005). *Copyright for schools: A practical guide.* Worthington, OH: Linworth.

Simpson, C. A. (2008). *Copyright for administrators.* Columbus, OH: Linworth.

Simpson, C. A. (2010). *Copyright for schools: A practical guide* (5th ed.). Columbus, OH: Linworth.

U.S. Copyright Office. (2009). *Circular 21: Reproduction of copyrighted works by educators and librarians.* Washington, DC: Author. Retrieved from http://www.copyright.gov/circs/circ21.pdf

Westbrook, S. (Ed.). (2009). *Composition & copyright: Perspectives on teaching, textmaking, and fair use.* Albany: SUNY Press.

Court Cases and Statutes

Clark v. Crues, 260 Fed. Appx. 292 (Fed. Cir. 2008).

Copyright Act of 1976, 17 U.S.C. §§ 101 *et seq.*

Copyright Term Extension Act (CTEA), 17 U.S.C. §§ 101 *et seq.*

Marcus v. Rowley, 695 F.2d 1171 (9th Cir. 1983).

Pavlica v. Behr, 397 F. Supp. 2d 519 (S.D.N.Y. 2005).

Technology, Education and Copyright Harmonization (TEACH) Act, 17 U.S.C. 101 §§ 110, 112, and 802.

West Publishing Co. v. Mead Data Center, 799 F.2d 1219 (8th Cir. 1986).

Should schools have the authority to require students to wear uniforms?

POINT: Richard Fossey, *University of North Texas*

COUNTERPOINT: Todd A. DeMitchell,
University of New Hampshire

OVERVIEW

Requiring students to wear school uniforms has long been the policy in Roman Catholic and an array of other nonpublic schools. Historically, public school boards have not had uniform policies in place for their students. To date, no state has enacted a statute calling on local public school boards to enact mandatory uniform policies for their students. Even so, state laws and regulations typically afford local boards the authority to devise uniform policies. Yet, as noted in the now archived *Manual on School Uniforms* (n.d.), in which the U.S. Department of Education voiced its support for uniforms in public schools, states such as California, Florida, Georgia, Indiana, Louisiana, Maryland, New York, Tennessee, Utah, and Virginia have promulgated regulations calling for uniforms for students. Accordingly, increasing numbers of public school boards have relied on their discretionary authority to implement occasionally controversial student uniform policies based on an array of rationales.

Among the most often cited rationales justifying uniform policies are that they promote school safety by forbidding students to wear "gang clothes" to school; foster a more disciplined atmosphere that helps students focus, thereby improving learning outcomes; help with discipline by avoiding distracting "fashion shows"; reduce stereotypes about specific groups of students; allow school personnel to recognize outsiders in facilities easily; level the playing field by eliminating clothing that indicates a student's socioeconomic class; save parents money on clothing; allow students to be easily recognized outside of school; and make it easier for students and parents when children are getting dressed for school.

Critics of mandatory school uniforms raise an array of concerns. Critics oppose school uniforms because they stifle individual speech, expression, and creativity by students; parents may not be able to afford uniforms; not all students look good in uniforms; and uniforms made of durable fabrics ordinarily do not adapt to the weather, so they may be too warm in hot weather but fail to offer enough protection when it is cold outside.

Not surprisingly, given a lack of consensus regarding the appropriateness of mandating uniforms for students in public schools, a growing body of litigation has emerged. Courts typically uphold school uniform policies that direct what students can wear (or, for that matter, dress codes that identify what students cannot wear, a distinction that is discussed further in the following debates), as long as they meet five important requirements. First, when boards devise dress code policies, they must establish that the rules are rationally related to legitimate pedagogical concerns in support of the schools' educational missions (*Blau v. Fort Thomas Public School District*, 2005). Second, boards must enact content-neutral policies, meaning that they do not distinguish between different points of view and are not designed to suppress student speech (*Canady v. Bossier Parish School Board*, 2001). Third, these policies must be narrowly tailored to achieve an important governmental interest such as safety (*Jacobs v. Clark County School District*, 2008). Fourth, uniform policies must be neither vague nor overbroad, meaning that they must clearly identify what students can wear to school (*Canady v. Bossier Parish School Board*, 2001). Fifth, officials must apply their policies consistently (*Littlefield v. Forney Independent School District*, 2001).

Relying in part on some of the litigation addressed in this overview, the essays in this chapter reach differing conclusions on the appropriateness of policies requiring students in public schools to wear uniforms. In his point essay, Richard Fossey, University of North Texas, maintains that school board officials should have the authority to enact mandatory dress code policies in public schools because they are effective. More specifically, Fossey posits that to the extent that boards have created viewpoint-neutral policies that advance important governmental interests such as school safety and improving learning environments in a way that does not suppress student expression, then educational officials should have the authority to operate their schools as they see fit by requiring students to wear uniforms even if academicians do not agree about uniforms' overall effectiveness in achieving stated goals.

Conversely, the counterpoint essay by Todd DeMitchell, University of New Hampshire, retorts that educational leaders should not have the power to require students in public schools to wear uniforms because uniform policies are not as effective as their supporters claim. In his analysis, he takes the position that little data support the effectiveness of uniform policies, and that they act as little more than "quick fixes" that fail to offer long-term chances for success at improving schooling. DeMitchell thus concludes that boards should not have the ability to require students to wear uniforms to school.

As you read these debates about school uniforms, ask yourself the following questions. First, do you think that school uniform policies in public schools are effective in achieving their stated goals? Second, do you support policies requiring students in public schools to wear uniforms? Third, if you favor school uniforms, what should students wear to school?

Charles J. Russo
University of Dayton

POINT: Richard Fossey
University of North Texas

Not long ago, school uniforms were associated with exclusive private institutions or Catholic schools. Thus, school uniforms symbolize one of two things—wealth and privilege or a rigorous, religion-based education. Today, however, more and more public school boards are adopting uniform policies for their students, especially in inner-city schools where the need to maintain order and discipline is most apparent. In light of these developments, this point essay relies primarily on the arguments contained in federal circuit court cases in taking the position that schools should be permitted to require students to wear uniforms because they promote safety and improved school environments. In reviewing the judicial analyses in some detail, this essay argues that the courts have adopted the correct position in not "second-guessing" educational leaders. The courts have appropriately demonstrated judicial deference to the perspectives of educators who have better understandings of the needs of their local communities than they do and have not imposed their views about the wisdom, effectiveness, or justness of uniform policies for students as officials seek to create safe and effective learning environments.

SCHOOL UNIFORM POLICIES AND THE FEDERAL COURTS

School boards that introduce uniform policies often run into opposition from parents and their children. In at least four recent cases, in three different federal circuits, parents and their children unsuccessfully sued school boards arguing that the implementation of uniform policies violated the constitutional rights of students.

A review of these cases provides a good overview of the constitutional issues pertaining to uniform policies in public schools. Further, these cases outline the reasons that school boards gave in defense of their uniform policies. In addition, the rationales in these cases summarize the policy justifications that boards have articulated for adopting school uniform policies for their students. In general, the boards adopting student uniform policies did so to get better academic outcomes and improve school discipline.

LITIGATION INVOLVING SCHOOL UNIFORM POLICIES
Fifth Circuit

Canady v. Bossier Parish School Board

The Fifth Circuit has resolved two cases involving school uniform policies in public schools. In *Canady v. Bossier Parish School Board* (2001), a board in Louisiana adopted a uniform policy for 16 of its schools with the goal of determining whether doing so would have a beneficial effect on their learning environments. Apparently concluding that it did, the board later adopted a uniform policy for all of its schools. The typical uniform consisted of a choice of two colors of polo or oxford shirts and navy or khaki pants. Officials notified parents by letter of the new student dress rules and provided them with a list of local vendors that supplied the required clothing. In adopting its uniform policy, the board acted in accordance with a state law permitting boards to adopt mandatory uniform policies for students as long as officials sent parents written notice explaining the dress requirements.

Not long after the board implemented its new uniform policy, parents and students filed suit to enjoin its enforcement on the grounds that "the dress code violated their children's First Amendment rights to free speech, failed to account for religious preferences, and denied their children's liberty interest to wear clothing of their choice in violation of the Fourteenth Amendment" (p. 439). A federal trial court granted the board's motion for summary judgment on the basis that the policy did not violate students' constitutional rights.

On appeal, the Fifth Circuit affirmed in favor of the board although it disagreed with the trial court's view that clothing choices are entitled to constitutional protection. Nevertheless, the court pointed out that the uniform policy was viewpoint-neutral and that it had not been enacted to suppress a particular student point of view. The court found that it had no choice but to uphold the policy because it furthered an important or substantial governmental interest and was no more restrictive on First Amendment activities than was necessary to facilitate its interests.

In the Fifth Circuit's view, "Improving the educational process is undoubtedly an important interest of the Bossier Parish School Board" (p. 443). Actually, the school board had enacted the policy to further its goal of increasing student-achievement test scores and reducing disciplinary problems. To this end, the board submitted statistical evidence showing that student test scores increased and discipline problems diminished after the board implemented its uniform policy. The parents challenging the policy presented no evidence to the contrary, so there was no fact issue before the court regarding whether the uniform policy improved the quality of education in the district.

The court next rejected the plaintiffs' claim that the policy's mandating parents to buy uniforms created a large financial burden while depriving some students of the right to obtain a free public education. The court responded,

> Because uniforms are available at inexpensive retail stores, it is hard to imagine how the purchase of uniforms consisting of a certain color of shirt and pants could be any more expensive than the normal cost of a student's school clothes. (p. 444)

Littlefield v. Forney Independent School District

In *Littlefield v. Forney Independent School District* (2001), the Fifth Circuit upheld a uniform policy implemented by a school board in Texas. As in *Canady*, the board enacted its uniform policy to improve the learning environment in its schools. After educational officials reviewed studies on the efficacy of school uniforms, conferred with officials in other districts, and sought input from parents, the board adopted a uniform policy that was even more specific than the one in *Canady*. This policy required that all students dress in solid color polo-type shirts with collars, oxford-type shirts, or blouses with collars in one of four colors (white, yellow, red, or navy blue). The shirts could be either short- or long-sleeved but must be tucked in at all times. Students could also wear either blue or khaki colored pants, shorts, skirts, or jumpers. The shorts and skirts had to be of appropriate size and length (no shorter than three inches above the knee) (p. 280).

At the same time, the policy forbid students from wearing denim, leather, suede, or vinyl, or any clothing that suggests gang affiliation, could conceal contraband, or could create a distraction. Certain other clothing items were also banned, such as open-heeled sandals, flip-flops, military boots, overalls, athletic pants, spandex, baggy clothing, and sleeveless shirts (p. 280).

As required by Texas law, the policy contained an "opt-out" provision exempting students from wearing the prescribed uniform if their parents had a religious or philosophical objection to their children wearing a school uniform. Apparently, the board also exempted some students from wearing school uniforms based on medical reasons.

Parents who objected to the uniform policy filed suit in federal court asserting three separate challenges. First, the parents argued that the policy violated their children's First Amendment rights because wearing uniforms constituted "coerced speech" that prevented students from conveying messages that they wished to communicate. Second, the parents claimed that the policy interfered with their constitutionally protected right to control the upbringing and education of their children. Third, the parents alleged that the policy's opt-out provision impermissibly delved into their families' religious beliefs and favored established religions over others.

After a federal trial court granted the board's motion for summary judgment, the Fifth Circuit affirmed in its favor. Following the reasoning of *Canady*, the *Littlefield* court upheld the policy in rejecting all of the plaintiffs' constitutional arguments. The court held that the uniform policy was a viewpoint-neutral policy enacted to further important and substantial governmental interests. In particular, the court noted that the policy was adopted "to improve student performance, instill self-confidence, foster self-esteem, increase attendance, decrease disciplinary referrals, and lower drop-out rates" (p. 286). The court rejected the parents' claim that the policy was enacted to coerce or suppress student speech. Nor, in the court's view, did the policy infringe on the parents' constitutional right to direct the education and upbringing of their children. The court observed both that parental rights are not absolute in the public school context and that the policy did not infringe on any of their constitutionally protected interests. Finally, the court rejected the parents' religion-based claims as having no merit because it did not violate either the Establishment or Free Exercise Clauses of the First Amendment.

Sixth Circuit

Blau v. Fort Thomas Public School District

In a case that originated in Kentucky, the Sixth Circuit upheld a board policy regarding student clothing in *Blau v. Fort Thomas Public School District* (2005). Although the court referred to the policy as a "dress code" rather than a uniform policy, the code was fairly restrictive in the clothing students could wear to school. The code, as modified after litigation was filed, forbade students from wearing blue jeans to school but permitted them to wear pants, shorts, or skirts of any solid color and to wear tops that were striped or patterned.

A father who was an attorney sought to enjoin the uniform policy both on its face, meaning as it was written, and as it applied to his daughter. The plaintiffs did not argue that the policy restricted the student from conveying a particular message or that it conflicted with her religious beliefs. Instead, in its analysis, the court rejected the student's claim, as well as one espoused by her father who expressed his full support for her stance that the 12-year-old had the right to wear clothing that allowed her to like the way that she looked and feel good about herself in and that also allowed her some vague feelings of expressing herself as an individual.

The plaintiffs argued that the dress code violated their constitutional rights, arguments that the Sixth Circuit rejected in their entirety. As to the student's free speech claim, the court surveyed Supreme Court jurisprudence, positing that the plaintiffs failed to prove that the student's wish to achieve what the Sixth Circuit described as "her middle-class individuality" in "looking nice" and "feeling good" (p. 390) about what she wore was of paramount importance. The court thus indicated that the plaintiffs' challenges to the uniform policy were not entitled to the protection of the First Amendment. Nor, in the court's view, had the board violated the student's right to substantive due process by prohibiting her from wearing blue jeans. Disposing of another constitutional claim, the court determined that the dress code had not infringed on the father's constitutional right to direct the upbringing of his daughter.

Reasoning much like the Fifth Circuit in the *Canady* and *Littlefield* cases, the Sixth Circuit concluded that the dress code had not been promulgated to suppress student expression and that it furthered an important and substantial governmental interest. The court went on to enumerate these governmental interests in detail:

> They include: bridging socioeconomic gaps between families within the school district, focusing attention on learning, increasing school unity and pride, enhancing school safety, promoting good behavior, reducing discipline problems, improving test scores, improving children's self-respect and self-esteem, helping to eliminate stereotypes and producing a cost savings for families. (*Blau*, 2005, p. 391)

The Sixth Circuit appeared satisfied with the evidence that the school board presented to show that the dress code furthered its governmental interests. The court also pointed out that the student had various means of expression available to her during school hours and that the board had not shut off all means of student expression by enacting its dress code.

Ninth Circuit

Jacobs v. Clark County School District

In a case from Nevada, *Jacobs v. Clark County School District* (2008), the Ninth Circuit upheld the constitutionality of a policy that created a standard dress code for all of its students while establishing a process for officials in individual schools to adopt more stringent dress policies. The board enacted its policy in accordance with a state statute that gave boards the authority to implement mandatory uniform policies for students. At issue was a policy from a high school that called for students to wear "solid khaki-colored bottoms and solid-colored polo, tee, or button-down shirts (blue, red or white) with or without [school] logos" (p. 423).

An 11th grader who repeatedly violated the dress code was suspended five times for a total of 25 days of school. Officials provided the student with educational services while she was suspended; her grade point actually improved during the time she was under suspension. Nevertheless, the student filed suit claiming that she

> missed out on classroom interactions, suffered reputational damage among her teachers and peers, had a tarnished disciplinary record, and was unconstitutionally deprived of her First Amendment rights to free expression and free exercise of religion because of [the school's] enforcement of its mandatory school uniform policy. (p. 423)

Other parents and students joined the plaintiff in her unsuccessful suit, including a peer who alleged that the policy at his middle school violated his right to free exercise of religion. This latter student sought an exemption from his school's uniform policy on the basis that his religion "teaches its members to embrace their individuality and further teaches that . . . no one can force uniformity onto a person" (p. 424). Apparently, school officials at the middle school denied the student's request for an exemption without explanation.

Adopting an analysis similar to the Fifth Circuit's rationale in *Canady*, the Ninth Circuit affirmed that the dress code policy was a content-neutral and viewpoint-neutral policy that advanced important governmental interests. Those interests, as articulated by the school board, were as follows:

1. "Promot[ing] safety by reducing the ability to hide weapons, drugs or alcohol"

2. "Allow[ing] students and staff to focus more attention to increasing student achievement"

3. "Eliminat[ing] dress differences that emphasize different income levels"

4. "Simplify[ing] daily school preparation and maintenance for families" (p. 432)

Moreover, the court upheld the policy because it was convinced that the uniform policy advanced the school board's important governmental interests in ways that had a minimal effect on the free expression rights of students.

In its analysis, the Ninth Circuit, like the Fifth and Sixth Circuits, accepted the testimony of school board officials as evidence that the dress code policy advanced important governmental interests. In addition, the court recognized the U.S. Department of Education's *Manual on School Uniforms* (n.d.), which acknowledged the efficacy of school uniforms in advancing the interests of boards in promoting safety, increasing student achievement, and creating positive school environments.

One of the plaintiffs specifically argued that the mandatory student-uniform policy had the effect of compelling him to symbolically express support for conformity, a viewpoint with which he disagreed. The Ninth Circuit emphatically rejected this argument. According to the court, a uniform policy is not a form of compelled speech. The court explained that the board "does not force [the student] to communicate any message whatsoever—much less one expressing support for conformity or community affiliation—simply by requiring him to wear solid-colored tops and bottoms mandated by its uniform policy" (p. 438).

Finally, the Ninth Circuit disposed of the two remaining constitutional claims in short order. The court ruled that the uniform policy had not violated any plaintiff's right to free exercise of religion. The court added that it was neutral policy of general applicability and that the plaintiffs had no right under the Free Exercise Clause to a religious exemption. Nor, in the court's view, had the board infringed on students' due process rights by implementing the policy. Although the board had not followed its own parent survey procedures before implementing the policy, the court did not think that this lapse amounted to a violation of due process.

CONCLUSION

To date, the three federal circuits that have addressed the issue have approved uniform policies, finding them to be viewpoint-neutral policies that were adopted to advance important governmental interests and not to suppress student expression. In addition, a federal trial court in Arkansas, in a case discussed and analyzed extensively in an article by Todd DeMitchell and Mark Paige (2010), upheld a student-uniform policy based on reasoning that closely followed the analysis of the Fifth and Sixth Circuits (*Lowry v. Watson Chapel School District*, 2007). In all of the circuit court opinions discussing the merits of uniform policies, then, the panels accepted the arguments brought by defendant school boards that their policies helped foster better student academic performance and improve discipline. In other words, the courts are deferring to local educational leaders in allowing them to set uniform policies of their own making that are crafted to meet the needs of their communities rather than engaging in second guessing about the wisdom and effectiveness of such an approach.

As reflected in the counterpoint essay, it is true that not all scholarly research agrees with this view that school uniforms improve school environments. Some researchers have found that school uniforms have no significant impact on academics or discipline. Yet, the courts seem content to accept the testimony of educational officials that uniforms improve overall school environments. Indeed, this essay fully supports the Fifth's Circuits pointedly stated position that school officials are in a better position to evaluate the benefits of uniform policies than are the federal courts.

To date, school boards have prevailed against constitutional challenges to their uniform policies that have been brought in federal courts. As a matter of public policy, this trend is a good thing. Many educational officials believe these policies help promote better school environments for academics and safety. Moreover, schools with uniform policies in place avoid never-ending battles with students about the appropriateness of particular pieces of clothing or specific messages on T-shirts. Schools with uniform policies in place can avoid having to make day-by-day subjective decisions about students' choice of clothing and simply enforce clear-cut uniform policies that help to ensure safe and orderly learning environments. Allowing educators to enact such policies will allow students and teachers to focus on academics—their reason for being there—rather than on what children are wearing to school.

COUNTERPOINT: Todd A. DeMitchell
University of New Hampshire

The argument for wearing uniforms is straightforward. Proponents of mandatory school uniforms, including the U.S. Department of Education and former President William Jefferson Clinton, assert that school uniforms can reduce discipline problems, increase safety at school, and enhance learning. In addition, school boards, when faced with challenges to their uniform policies, claim that such approaches help reduce violence and theft of such items as expensive sneakers, help parents and students resist peer pressure to wear the latest clothes by eliminating "label competition," help children concentrate on their school work, help administrators recognize intruders, and foster school pride and unity. This is a tall order for just a change of clothes.

The praise of their supporters notwithstanding, including the point essay, school uniform policies promise more than they can deliver. Who knew that students' early morning decisions to wear khaki pants and blue polo shirts rather than T-shirts and jeans would have such positive effects on their education—or do they?

Uniform policies are different from dress codes. Dress codes state what cannot be worn, but uniform policies dictate what must be worn. Dress codes contract the universe of clothing options for students, but mandatory uniform policies define the universe of clothing options. Under dress code policies, students are free to wear clothes that are not proscribed by the code; under uniform policies, they can wear only the clothes prescribed by the policies, usually a combination of khaki and blue and khaki and white. Public school uniform policies overwhelmingly do not require students to wear plaids or other types of clothing often associated with Catholic and other private schools.

This counterpoint essay explores, and ultimately rejects, the policy reasons underlying the rationale for requiring students to wear uniforms to schools. The basic argument for adopting uniforms is that a change of clothes will bring about desired behavioral and academic student outcomes; that uniforms transform individuals appears to be at the heart of the argument. Yet, does just wearing a uniform bring about changes in behavior? Does the research support the policy goals of a mandatory school uniform policy, and can practical problems of implementation be overcome? However, before examining these issues and rejecting the notion that students should be required to wear uniforms to school, this counterpoint essay first reviews whether such mandatory policies violate the free speech rights of students.

SCHOOL UNIFORMS AND FREE SPEECH

The major legal challenge to school uniforms is that mandatory school uniform policies infringe on the First Amendment free speech rights of students. In *Tinker v. Des Moines Independent Community School District* (1969), a case dealing with students' wearing black armbands to protest the Vietnam War, the Supreme Court held that under the U.S. Constitution, students are persons possessing fundamental rights including free speech. According to *Tinker*, a student's right to free speech inside the schoolhouse gate can be abridged by school officials only if it can be shown, or reasonably forecast, that the speech will create a material and substantial disruption or will collide with the rights of others. The *Tinker* standards provide students significant discretion in expressing their points of view. *Tinker* sought to protect students from becoming "closed-circuit recipients" who receive only that which schools choose to communicate. Pursuant to *Tinker*, the desire of school officials to avoid uncomfortable topics cannot form the basis for restrictions on speech.

The Supreme Court subsequently reduced *Tinker*'s reach. Seventeen years later, in *Bethel School District No. 403 v. Fraser* (1986), the Court decided that educational officials could sanction a high school student for using lewd, vulgar, or offensive sexual metaphors during a political speech at a school assembly. The Court found that public education inculcates the habits and manners of civility. Even with these restrictions on student speech, student speech at school retains a certain amount of vitality.

When the free speech rights of students are applied to wearing mandatory school uniforms, complaining students assert that their choice of clothing has expressive rights attached to their choices. What students choose to wear in the morning to school may be a form of speech and expression that reflects their feelings. The Fifth Circuit, in *Canady v. Bossier Parish School Board* (2001), acknowledged that color patterns or styles may constitute speech if worn with intent to express a particular message. Then again, the choice of what to wear may be based on what is clean or what is on the top of the pile of clothes.

Consequently, given that students have the right to free speech at school as long as it does not create material and substantial disruptions, does not collide with the rights of others, and is not lewd, vulgar, or offensive, do they have the right to wear whatever clothes they want to school? Essentially this is the claim made by students when they contest the imposition of mandatory uniform policies.

DRESS CODES AND THE COURTS

The arguments against school uniform policies are similar to the one that students bring against dress codes. A variety of federal trial courts recognized the right of school officials to proscribe the wearing of apparel advertising alcoholic beverages or proclaiming that "Drugs Suck" on a T-shirt. Another court noted that wearing sagging pants did not constitute speech for First Amendment purposes, thereby sustaining a school board's dress code. However, dress codes have also failed to pass constitutional muster. For example, one court struck down a ban on a Jeff Foxworthy "Redneck" T-shirt as unconstitutional, and another invalidated a policy against wearing rosaries as a potential gang symbol because they had been used as gang symbols in other places, although not in the school the student attended.

One legal commentator, Rob Killen, argues that the "Achilles' heel" of dress codes is the difficulty of defining proper dress at school without violating the constitutionally protected free speech rights of students. Dress code litigation tends to look more like a potpourri than a unified, articulated body of case law. Unanimity on the issue of the constitutionality of dress codes has not been achieved, leaving a large degree of judicial uncertainty. Given this uneven legal outcome for dress codes, have uniform challenges encountered similar results in the courts?

LEGAL CHALLENGES TO SCHOOL UNIFORM POLICIES

Though there have been many cases regarding dress codes, there are only six major school uniform cases. As discussed earlier, dress code cases do not have a clear, consistent outcome, with some T-shirt restrictions being upheld and others found unconstitutional. In contrast, in all six school uniform cases, uniform policies have been upheld as constitutional in both state and federal courts. Although dress codes are less restrictive than mandatory school uniforms, the more restrictive uniform policies have passed constitutional muster in both federal and state courts. In other words, the more restrictive clothing policy, school uniforms, which compels what students must wear prevails while the less restrictive dress code policy, which states only what cannot be worn, is a mixed bag.

What accounts for this consistency of legal opinions regarding school uniforms and the lack of consistency in dress code litigation? The students in both dress code and uniform cases use *Tinker* as authority for their opinions. The difference may lie in the case authority the courts use. Although *Tinker* is applied in dress code cases, it is not cited in school uniform litigation. In fact, in all six school uniform cases, the courts did not use *Tinker*; instead, they used the nonschool standard of *United States v. O'Brien* (1968). In *O'Brien*, the Supreme Court declared that although burning draft cards to protest the Vietnam War implicated the First Amendment, such actions could nonetheless be proscribed because the government had a substantial interest separate from the suppression of expression.

The first prong of this three-part test involving governmental policies asks whether the disputed policies on school uniforms are unrelated to the suppression of ideas. Although students must wear uniforms while at school, they are not required to wear them after school, on weekends, during holidays, or during vacations. The second prong asks whether policies further important governmental interests. A federal trial court in Arkansas (*Lowry v. Watson Chapel School District*, 2007) applied this prong to a school uniform policy in finding that it furthered important governmental policies such as bridging socioeconomic gaps between families in the school system, focusing attention on learning rather than fashion, and improving school security. The third part of the test requires that a policy is written as narrowly as possible to not burden more speech than necessary. In other words, the school uniform policy does not foreclose all the means of communication available to students while they are in school.

The bottom line under *O'Brien* is that uniform policies must be content-neutral—that is, they cannot single out any particular speech to suppress. Insofar as uniforms basically suppress all speech associated with clothing by requiring specific colors, all speech is treated the same. Because all speech associated with clothing is banned, the uniform policies do not target any particular speech; they are neutral toward speech.

School uniform litigation to date has produced consistent wins for school boards. The paradox is that students have had some success contesting the lesser restrictions of dress codes but no success in contesting the more restrictive mandatory school uniform policies.

So far, one of the arguments against school uniforms, that they violate student free speech rights, has not prevailed. Uniforms have passed constitutional muster. Are there other reasons for not adopting school uniform polices? This is addressed in the next section.

SCHOOL UNIFORM POLICIES: GOOD POLICY?

Constitutionally firm policies are not the same as educationally sound policies. That policies do not infringe on students' constitutional rights does not mean that such policies should be adopted and implemented. If anything, the fact that school uniform policies have passed all six of the legal tests that they have faced gives one pause to ask why more school boards have not adopted uniforms as a reform that brings safety and security to their campuses and provides environments in which attendance improves, student learning reaches new heights, and parents and students no longer have to engage in label competition for the latest and typically more costly fashion. If all of this can be done simply by requiring students to change their clothes, why are school boards not rushing to adopt policies that have such great outcomes with so little effort? For example, the author's state of New Hampshire, perhaps atypical of the national trend in which support seems to be growing if the number of states with permissive language is any indication, as reflected in the U.S. Department of Education's *Manual on School Uniforms* (n.d.), does not have a single school board with a mandatory uniform policy. Something else is at work that causes superintendents and boards to hesitate even though there do not appear to be legal obstacles.

Donna Kerr (1976) argues that educational policies must pass four evaluative tests if they are to qualify as justifiable or normatively rational polices.

According to Kerr, the following logical conditions must be met to judge any policy as acceptable. An acceptable policy must be

- desirable (accomplish appropriate educational goals),
- effective (the desired results are actually achieved by the policy),
- just (the policy must seek purposes that are morally right), and
- tolerable (the cost of the policy should not be "out of proportion" to its effectiveness).

School uniform policies seek desirable goals, which may also be just in the minds of their developers. The question is whether such policies are effective and tolerable.

ARE SCHOOL UNIFORM POLICIES EFFECTIVE?

Most research studies supporting school uniforms are small in scale and are often perception studies. An often quoted study of 755 principals conducted by the National Association of Elementary School Principals (2000) found in phone interviews that significant percentages (60% plus) reported that school uniforms had a positive effect on the school's image in the community, classroom discipline, peer pressure, the school, concentration on schoolwork, and student safety. However, only 29% of the principals actually had student uniform policies on which their perceptions could be based. Moreover, a national study by Todd DeMitchell, Richard Fossey, and Casey Cobb (2000) found that principals were more likely to support dress codes than to support school uniform policies. The study also reported that high school principals did not support mandatory uniforms.

Empirical research, especially as reported in large-scale national studies, has failed to uncover support for the notion that school uniforms achieve the desired goals touted by their proponents. For example, David Brunsma and Kerry Rockquemore (1998) found in their large national data set study that school uniforms did not have a direct effect on behavioral or academic outcomes of students. They concluded that policies adopting school uniforms were largely symbolic gestures. Similarly, Ryan Yeung (2008), in a study also using robust large-scale national data sets reported that there was little evidence that uniforms improve achievement in schools. He maintained that insofar as uniforms appear to have had little to no effect on the achievement scores of students in public schools on mathematics achievement, it seems that they do not offer the solution for what ails U.S. education.

At this point, there does not seem to be clear evidence that school uniforms achieve the results articulated in the rationale for their implementation. Educational policymakers must thus approach uniform policies with a healthy skepticism to avoid the lamentable and frequent situations in which educational leaders chase the newest reform. In an era characterized by the need for data-driven decision making, there is little data to support the adoption of school uniforms.

ARE SCHOOL UNIFORM POLICIES TOLERABLE?

To pass the tolerability test, school uniform policies must not have negative unintended consequences, and the effort expended in pursuit of their enforcement must be proportional to the desired outcome. Uniform policies have questionable outcomes that question whether they have met the tolerability portion of Kerr's policy justification test. This section discusses four of the tolerability questions.

First, on the surface it seems that school uniform policies should be easy to implement. It also appears that there are few to no expenditures of resources to enact these policies. Yet, the surface sometimes hides what is beneath. Will school uniform policies demand more resources than having dress code policies or no policies at all covering student dress? It can be argued that with dress codes, educators can be selectively blind to dress that may push the envelope of dress codes. Given the large variation in dress on any given day, students may just melt into the crowd, thus not implicating the protection that *Tinker* might provide in allowing pupils to express their individuality However, if there is uniformity in student appearances, all khaki and blue, a Hawaiian shirt will stand out and require a response. Failure to respond undermines the policy in a visible way. How much time must teachers and administrators expend on enforcement?

Second, most uniform policies include some form of waivers or opt-out provisions. On what basis should waivers be granted, and to what extent should provisions of the uniform policy be waived? How much time must be dedicated to keeping track of the specifics of waivers and who has them? In addition to waivers, what accommodations for religion or other forms of protected expression will be allowed? Officials must develop accommodations, keep them on file, and implement them uniformly. This adds another level of complexity to the policies.

Third, if uniform policies are district-wide, does the grade level of a school make a difference? Is it easier to implement school uniform policies at the elementary school level than in a high school? In the DeMitchell, Fossey, and

Cobb study cited, high school principals had negative views of school uniforms. The desired goals cut across all grade levels, so can uniform policies be implemented consistently across elementary, middle, and high schools?

Fourth, deep and sustained school change is difficult and time consuming. Do educators run the risk of acting as legislators, believing that because they have adopted school uniform policies, then no more heavy lifting is necessary? The historical short attention span of many legislators allows easy bumper sticker solutions to replace the difficult work of real reform. It is easier to mandate changes of clothes than to review the many interrelated and complex components that go into implementing and sustaining systemic change. This is similar to our penchant for the quick fix for financing schools through devices such as lotteries rather than by employing sustained efforts aimed at prioritizing society's needs and consequent resource allocation.

Do school uniforms solve problems or divert resources into enforcement? Will a focus on what students wear divert attention from the student activities that matter most? Reform is hard work. A change of clothes alone will not work.

CONCLUSION

The heart of the uniform argument appears to be that wearing uniforms transforms individuals and improves schooling. Is it really that simple? If so, then this is the proverbial free lunch: a strategy requiring no real sustained effort, but excellent, which achieves desired results through just a change of clothes.

Student behavioral change, school cultural change, and higher achievement, all for little or no cost, must be the holy grail of school remedies. Yet, will the bromide of only a change of clothes bring about these desired outcomes? Right now, it appears that school uniforms as a reform strategy offer a vain hope and false promise. Thus, students should not be required to wear uniforms to school.

FURTHER READINGS AND RESOURCES

Brunsma, D. L. (2004). *The school uniform movement and what it tells us about American education: A symbolic crusade.* Lanham, MD: Rowman & Littlefield Education.

Brunsma, D. L., & Rockquemore, K. A. (1998, September/October). The effects of student uniforms on attendance, behavior problems, substance use, and academic achievement. *The Journal of Educational Research, 92*(1), 53–62.

Daugherty, R., Peltier, G. L., & Imle, R. M. (2004). The U.S. Department of Education's exemplary school uniform programs: A status report. *Education Law Reporter, 187*, 397–404.

DeMitchell, T. A. (2001). School uniforms and the Constitution: Common dress in an uncommon time. *Education Law Reporter, 156,* 1–19.

DeMitchell, T. A. (2004). The law and student clothing. In D. L. Brunsma, *The school uniform movement and what it tells us about American education: A symbolic crusade* (pp. 51–73). Lanham, MD: Rowman & Littlefield Education.

DeMitchell, T. A. (2006, December 14). Commentary: School uniforms: There is no free lunch. *Teachers College Record.* Retrieved from http://www.tcrecord.org/Content .asp?ContentId=12891

DeMitchell, T. A., Fossey, R., & Cobb, C. (2000). Dress codes in the public schools: Principals, policies, and precepts. *Journal of Law and Education, 29*(1), 31–49.

DeMitchell, T. A., & Paige, M. A. (2010). School uniforms in the public schools: Symbol or substance? A law & policy analysis. *Education Law Reporter, 250,* 847.

Kerr, D. H. (1976). *Educational policy: Analysis, structure, and justification.* New York: David McKay.

Killen, R. (1999). The Achilles' heel of dress codes: The definition of proper attire in public schools. *Tulsa Law Journal, 36,* 459–486.

National Association of Elementary School Principals. (2000, February). *Survey of school principals reports positive effects of school uniforms.* Retrieved December 3, 2006, from http://www.naesp.org/ContentLoad.do?contentId=929

U.S. Department of Education. (n.d.). *Manual on school uniforms.* Retrieved from http://www.ed.gov/updates/uniforms.html

Walker, K. (2007, February 26). *Research brief: School uniforms.* Retrieved September 8, 2011, from http://educationpartnerships.org/pdfs/SchoolUniforms.pdf

Wenkart, R. D. (2008). School uniform policies, school dress codes and the First Amendment: A fourth category of student speech? *Education Law Reporter, 238,* 17–26.

White, K. A. (2000, February). Do school uniforms fit? *School Administrator, 57,* 36–40.

Yeung, R. (2008). Are school uniforms a good fit? Results from the ECLS-K and the NELS. *Educational Policy, 23,* 847–874.

Zernicke, K. (2002, September 13). Plaid's out again, as schools give up requiring uniforms. *The New York Times,* p. A1. Retrieved from http://www.nytimes.com/2002/ 09/13/us/plaid-s-out-again-as-schools-give-up-requiring-uniforms.html

COURT CASES AND STATUTES

Bethel School District No. 403 v. Fraser, 478 U.S. 675 (1986).

Blau v. Fort Thomas Public School District, 401 F.3d 381 (6th Cir. 2005).

Canady v. Bossier Parish School Board, 240 F.3d 437 (5th Cir. 2001).

Jacobs v. Clark County School District, 526 F.3d 419 (9th Cir. 2008).

Littlefield v. Forney Independent School District, 268 F.3d 275 (5th Cir. 2001).

Lowry v. Watson Chapel School District, 508 F. Supp 2d 713 (E.D. Ark. 2007).

Tinker v. Des Moines Independent Community School District, 393 U.S. 503 (1969).

United States v. O'Brien, 391 U.S. 367 (1968).

Should students be subject to random drug testing?

POINT: Robert C. Cloud, *Baylor University*

COUNTERPOINT: Luke M. Cornelius, *University of North Florida*

OVERVIEW

In *New Jersey v. T.L.O.* (1985), the Supreme Court ruled that the Fourth Amendment applied to schools to protected students from unreasonable searches and seizures, even as it upheld a search of a student conducted by officials on the basis of "reasonable suspicion." Three years later, a dispute from Indiana became the first case directly addressing the then novel question of drug testing of student-athletes. After five baseball players tested positive for having smoked marijuana, the school board implemented a random drug testing policy for student-athletes and cheerleaders. The Seventh Circuit affirmed the validity of testing on the basis that testing was reasonable under the Fourth Amendment and that school officials instituted sufficient safeguards to protect student privacy (*Schaill v. Tippecanoe County School Corp.*, 1988). As the heart of its rationale, the court explained that insofar as student-athletes and cheerleaders gained enhanced prestige in the community from their roles in extracurricular activities, it was not unreasonable to require them to submit to drug testing.

Since the 1990s, a growing body of litigation has addressed drug testing of students. The courts generally uphold rules preventing drug use and allowing testing of student-athletes, regardless of whether infractions occur on campus, on the ground that taking part in extracurricular activities is a privilege rather than a right (*Palmer v. Merluzzi*, 1989). These controversies culminated in two Supreme Court cases upholding the constitutionality of drug tests of student-athletes in *Vernonia School District 47J v. Acton* (1995a, b) and *Board of*

Education of Independent School District No. 92 of Pottawatomie County v. Earls (2002a, b).

At the same time, in the limited number of cases where school officials have sought to subject students to across-the-board testing for drugs, the courts have been unwilling to permit them to do so. For example, the Supreme Court of Colorado prohibited random testing of members of a school band, including those who participated for academic credit rather than as an extracurricular activity, because they had greater expectations of privacy under the state constitution than did members of the sports teams that were subject to this policy (*Trinidad School District No. 1 v. Lopez*, 1998). Further, a federal trial court in Texas struck down a policy under which educational officials sought to drug test all students in junior and senior high school (*Tannahill ex rel. Tannahill v. Lockney Independent School District*, 2001). The court invalidated the policy as unreasonable even though testing imposed a low level of intrusion on the students' rights to privacy. The court explained that officials lacked a compelling interest outweighing the privacy interests of students insofar as drug use in the school was actually lower than in other schools in the state.

The following two essays address the legal and policy considerations associated with drug testing. However, before turning to these debates, it is worth keeping in mind the current statistics on drug use among students. The database of the National Institute on Drug Abuse (2011) reports statistics that are alarming. These data reveal that the percentage of students who admit to "any illicit drug use" has generally grown during each year from 2007 through 2010. Among 8th graders, the rate rose from 19.0 to 19.6 to 19.9 to 21.1. For 10th graders, the 2007 rate of 35.0 slipped to 34.1 in 2009 but increased to 36.0 in 2009 and to 37.0 in 2010. Among seniors, the rate went from 46.8 to 47.4, declined to 46.7 in 2009 but jumped to 48.2 in 2010. Clearly, these data help confirm that drug use in school remains a serious problem.

Against this backdrop, the essays in this chapter rely on largely the same body of case law dealing with the Fourth Amendment in school settings but reach divergent outcomes on whether students should be subjected to random drug testing. The point essay of Robert C. Cloud, Baylor University, stands for the proposition that given the special custodial duties of public school officials, they have the duty of maintaining safe and orderly learning environments. In balancing the need to protect the many in school communities who may be at risk because of the few who present risks of harm to others, Cloud maintains that educational officials should have the authority to subject all students to random drug testing to help keep schools safe.

In the counterpoint essay, Luke M. Cornelius, University of North Florida, responds that random drug testing is a bad idea. He raises an assortment of questions about the applicability of the Supreme Court cases on the Fourth Amendment. Cornelius also voices concerns about the potential costs of testing, both financial and nonfinancial, and about the ways school officials can use test results that come back as positive for drug use. Given these considerations, he concludes that school officials should not have the power to subject students to testing.

As you read these debates about drug testing, ask yourself the following questions. First, do you think that wide-scale random drug testing accomplishes anything? Second, do you support random drug testing of all students? If so, what legal standard would you apply before students could be tested? Third, what actions should school officials take when students test positive for drugs? Put another way, would you call for approaches that are more rehabilitative or more punitive in nature?

Charles J. Russo
University of Dayton

POINT: Robert C. Cloud
Baylor University

The far-reaching problems associated with drug abuse in today's society are a major concern of officials in public schools, especially because schools are microcosms of the general society. Given this ongoing concern, this point essay addresses whether educational leaders in U.S. public schools should have the authority to compel all students to submit to random drug testing. At first blush, such authority seems to violate the Fourth Amendment rights of students to freedom from unreasonable searches and seizures because children do not shed their constitutional rights at the schoolhouse gate (*Tinker v. Des Moines Independent Community School District*, 1969, p. 506). Still, given the grave situation in many schools and the wide U.S. society, this is a question that deserves thoughtful consideration.

As early as 1925 in *Pierce v. Society of Sisters*, the U.S. Supreme Court held that states have a compelling interest in ensuring school safety. Without a doubt, ensuring the safety of children is a priority of educational officials in every community. In fact, concern for student health and safety is basic to the schools' caretaking duties. Moreover, it is undeniable that drug use in and near schools by students (and others) poses serious health risks for children (*Board of Education of Independent School District No. 92 of Pottawatomie County v. Earls*, 2002).

Maintaining order in the schools has never been easy, but in recent years, school disorder has taken particularly ugly forms. As the Supreme Court noted in its first case on the Fourth Amendment and schools, *New Jersey v. T.L.O.* (1985), wherein it permitted a search of a student, drug use and violent crime in the schools have become major social problems (p. 339). Relying on such precedent, preventing drug abuse by students of all ages is a compelling interest of public school officials because the "public expects its schools not simply to teach the fundamentals, but 'to shoulder the burden of feeding students breakfast and lunch, offering before and after school child care services, and providing medical and psychological services,'" in a school environment that is safe and encourages learning (*Earls*, p. 840, quoting National School Boards Association *Amici Curiae*, pp. 3–4).

At the same time, educational leaders must combat the rise in drug-related violence and disruption in classrooms and across the campuses because "the effects of a drug-infested school are visited not just upon the users, but upon the entire student body and faculty, as the educational process is disrupted" (*Vernonia School District 47J v. Acton*, 1995a, p. 662). Accordingly, public schools have the custodial responsibility to maintain order and control drug abuse by the few to protect the interests of the many (*Acton*, p. 653).

As the Supreme Court noted in *Earls* (2002a, p. 831),

> Without first establishing discipline and maintaining order, teachers cannot begin to educate their students. And apart from education, the school has the obligation to protect pupils from mistreatment by other children, and also to protect teachers themselves from [drug-induced] violence by the few students whose conduct in recent years has prompted national concern. (citing *New Jersey v. T.L.O.*, 1985, p. 350)

In other words, drug abuse by a small number of students can and does interfere with the right of the majority to receive a quality education.

Clearly, the authority of officials in public schools to subject students to drug testing is an issue ripe for litigation. Drug tests that are mandated by educational leaders, including the collection of urine samples, are searches under the law. Insofar as these searches invade bodily functions traditionally shielded by complete privacy, they implicate the Fourth Amendment rights of students. However, school officials are obligated legally and ethically to maintain safe learning environments. In recent years, federal courts have tried to balance these conflicting interests.

As of this writing, the Supreme Court has upheld random drug testing by public school officials for two classes of students, those involved in athletics and in other extracurricular activities (*Acton*, 1995; *Earls*, 2002). Yet, albeit in nonbinding dicta, the Court has rejected mass, suspicionless drug testing of all students as a violation of their Fourth Amendment rights. In *Acton* (1995a, p. 665), for example, the Court cautioned "against the assumption that suspicion-less drug testing will readily pass constitutional muster in other contexts" (i.e., universal testing of all students). Still, given the serious problems that drug use presents, this point essay stands for the proposition that the broad custodial responsibilities of public schools create special and unique needs that justify random drug testing of all students when necessary.

RANDOM SEARCHES OF PUBLIC SCHOOL STUDENTS: OVERVIEW

The Fourth Amendment to the U.S. Constitution restrains the actions of governmental officials by guaranteeing "the right of the people to be secure in their persons, houses, papers, and effects, against unreasonable searches and seizures." As the wording of the Fourth Amendment indicates, the reasonableness of searches by government agents determines whether they pass constitutional muster. In other words, as a rule, "reasonableness" requires proof of individualized suspicion and a showing of probable cause before judges or magistrates agree to issue search warrants (*Chandler v. Miller*, 1997). Ultimately, the reasonableness of searches is judged by balancing the intrusion on the privacy rights of the individuals being searched against the promotion of legitimate governmental interests such as safety (*Acton*, 1995a, pp. 652–653).

In *New Jersey v. T.L.O.* (1985), the Supreme Court established a legal framework for public school searches that continues to guide judicial deliberations to this day. First, the Court pointed out that the Fourth Amendment prohibits unreasonable searches by public school officials (p. 325). Second, the Court noted that students have reduced expectations of privacy when compared with members of the general population. To the *T.L.O.* Court, it was simply unrealistic to think that students have the same subjective expectations of privacy or other rights as the general population has (p. 348). Third, the Court observed that the freedom of students from unreasonable search must be balanced against the special needs of school officials to maintain order and ensure safety in the closed confines of schools where there are generally fairly large numbers of children but relatively few adults to provide supervision.

Fourth, the Supreme Court was of the opinion that school officials are not required to demonstrate probable cause or secure search warrants before initiating searches of students or their property. The *T.L.O.* court explained that strict adherence to the probable cause standard that applies in police searches would undercut the substantial need of teachers and administrators to maintain order in the schools (pp. 340–341). Fifth, the Court asserted that students can be searched if school officials have good reason to suspect that they are concealing drugs, weapons, stolen property, or other contraband. "Reasonable suspicion," then, which must be more than a mere hunch, is defined as a belief based on the facts in a given situation. Again, reasonable suspicion is a lower standard than the probable cause standard that is required for police to secure a search warrant. Sixth, the Court indicated that the area that officials search must be reasonable in terms of what they are looking for.

Although less stringent than the probable cause standard, reasonable suspicion does require creditable evidence of wrongdoing before any search of students. Therefore, under *T.L.O.*, school searches cannot be random or suspicionless. After *T.L.O.*, the legality of school searches depended on their reasonableness, under all circumstances. In so ruling, the *T.L.O.* Court granted public school officials substantial discretion to operate safe and efficient schools.

Four years after its decision in *T.L.O.*, the Supreme Court held that urinalysis drug tests that are administered by governmental agents are searches within the meaning of the Fourth Amendment. The Court reached this judgment in companion cases involving testing of engineers who were involved in railway accidents (*Skinner v. Railway Labor Executives' Association*, 1989) and employees of the U.S. Customs Service who applied for promotions or transfers to drug interdiction—positions that would have required them to carry firearms (*National Treasury Employees Union v. Von Raab* (1989). With these two cases as a backdrop, it should come as no surprise that the Court went on to determine that drug testing of public school students implicates their Fourth Amendment rights just as any other search. Under other circumstances, school officials would be required to show probable cause before drug testing a student. However, in light of *T.L.O.* and subsequent rulings in *Acton* (1995) and *Earls* (2002), the Court declared that individualized suspicion and probable cause are not necessary in school drug testing or other searches because of the special needs existing in the schools.

Reflecting on its 1985 opinion in *T.L.O.*, the Supreme Court reiterated in *Acton* that probable cause and a warrant are unnecessary in the public school context because such requirements "would unduly interfere with the maintenance of the swift and informal disciplinary procedures needed in the schools" (*Acton*, 1995, p. 653, quoting *T.L.O.*, p. 340). Therefore, the Court concluded that an inquiry about reasonableness cannot disregard the schools' custodial and tutelary responsibility to protect children. Clearly, since 1985, the Supreme Court has acknowledged that the special duty of public school leaders to maintain order reduces some of the concerns associated with the Fourth Amendment.

NECESSITY OF RANDOM DRUG TESTING TO ENSURE SAFETY FOR ALL

In the years since *T.L.O.*, and as the Supreme Court noted in *Earls* (2002a, p. 834), the nationwide drug epidemic has made drug use and its consequences a pressing concern in every school in the United States. Earlier, in *Acton* (1995a, p. 661), the Court asserted that deterring drug use in U.S. schools is now at least as important as controlling the illegal flow of drugs across our borders. As the war on drugs has escalated and concern for school safety has increased accordingly, the Court's thinking and perspective on the Fourth Amendment have evolved to favor the custodial authority of the schools over the constitutional rights of students under certain circumstances. As noted—in *Acton* and *Earls*, for example—the Court permitted school officials to conduct random, suspicionless drug tests of two classes of students to the chagrin of constitutional purists everywhere.

In *Acton*, the Supreme Court upheld the random drug testing policy that a school board in Oregon enacted for athletes against a claim that it violated their rights to privacy. The Court ruled that the board had shown that its athletes were immersed in the local drug culture and that officials had demonstrated a special need to ensure that student leaders such as athletes were not using drugs. "Not only were student athletes included among the drug users but, as the district court found, athletes were the leaders of the drug culture" (*Acton*, 1995a, p. 649). The Court added that the athletes had a reduced expectation of privacy because they volunteered to represent the school through athletics, an activity that required them to give up a significant measure of personal privacy. Finally, the Court was satisfied that the school board had shown good faith by minimizing the intrusiveness of its drug testing program through the following policies: ensuring maximum student privacy when collecting urine samples, maintaining the confidentiality of the test results, mentoring drug abusers, and refraining from reporting positive test results to law enforcement authorities.

Seven years after its decision in *Acton* (1995), the Supreme Court considered another case involving drug testing of a particular class of public school students (*Earls*, 2002a). In *Earls*, the Court extended the authority of public school officials to conduct random drug tests on a larger population than that addressed in *Acton*. The Court approved the policy of a school board in Oklahoma that required all students who participated in competitive extracurricular activities to submit to random drug testing. After reviewing the board's policy and the reasons cited for its implementation, the Court agreed that the students affected by it had a limited expectation of privacy comparable with that of the student athletes in *Acton*. According to the Court, "Students who participate in competitive extracurricular activities voluntarily subject themselves to the same intrusions on their privacy as do athletes" (*Earls*, p. 831). Therefore, the Court decided that it was reasonable to apply the same level of scrutiny here as it used in permitting testing of student athletes in *Acton*.

As part of its rationale in *Earls*, the Supreme Court pointed out that the drug test results at issue did not lead to unreasonable disciplinary action or academic suspension, and they were not released to law enforcement authorities. The Court observed that the only consequence of a failed test was to limit the student's privilege of participating in extracurricular activities (*Earls*, 2002a, p. 833). Under the policy, the Court acknowledged that students could test positive for drugs twice and continue to participate in extracurricular activities (*Earls*, p. 833). The Court explained that only after a third positive test were students suspended from extracurricular participation for the remainder of the school year, or 88 school days, whichever was longer. Given the minimally intrusive nature of the drug tests and the limited uses of the test results, the Court concluded that the invasion of students' privacy was not significant. While upholding the drug policy, the Court stressed that school officials are not required to demonstrate that there is an identifiable drug abuse problem among a sufficient number of students before implementing aggressive and preventive measures such as random drug testing.

In reviewing the arguments of the counterpoint essay, the issue of cost, not directly addressed in either *Action* or *Earls*, merits a brief response. Even in conceding that drug testing can be costly, does this mean that school officials should not do all that they can to help protect students? If anything, it is worth keeping in mind that if the use of drug testing can help avoid even one unnecessary death of a student in a school system, then district officials would have to count their program as a success.

In summary, Supreme Court decisions in *T.L.O., Acton, Earls,* and related cases reiterate that public school students do not shed their constitutional rights at the schoolhouse gate. Even so, the nature of those rights is what is appropriate for children in schools. The cases all agree that the constitutional rights of students in schools must be balanced against the special need of school officials to maintain order and discipline. Clearly, Fourth Amendment rights, like First and Fourteenth Amendment rights, are different in public schools than elsewhere. The decisions in *Acton* and *Earls*, in particular, suggest that because the needs of officials in public schools to maintain safe and orderly learning environments are increasingly important in an era when drugs and accompanying violence threaten all students and staff, then random drug testing should be a permissible means to achieve this compelling governmental interest.

CONCLUSION

No reasonable person would question the necessity of the Fourth Amendment in a free society or that students in public schools, like all citizens, should have the right to privacy and freedom from unreasonable searches and seizures (*Tinker*, 1969; *T.L.O.*, 1985). Yet, officials in public schools have custodial responsibilities to ensure safety and orderly learning environments for all students (and staff). Moreover, school officials cannot meet their duties without having the authority to implement aggressive and preventive measures to secure their campuses via drug testing.

Without doubt, the conflicting interests of the rights of students to privacy and the duty of school officials to maintain safety pose a dilemma for both educational leaders and the courts. Clearly, the interests of both students and school officials are precious and must be protected. However, during a time when drugs and the accompanying deadly weapons increasingly threaten the safety of school children, public school leaders must have the authority to compel students to submit to random drug testing to help ensure safety. Otherwise, school officials will be hard-pressed to protect the rights of all students from the irresponsible and illegal behavior of the few who threaten the well being of the many.

COUNTERPOINT: Luke M. Cornelius
University of North Florida

When someone writes a history of "things that sounded like good ideas at the time," random drug testing of students will probably be featured prominently. After all, because few issues affect U.S. youth more seriously than illicit drug use and abuse in and around schools, it seems as if almost any tool that appears relevant to solving the problem should be embraced. Yet, on more thorough analysis, drug testing of students becomes much more problematic. Testing can be expensive and cumbersome, and one must wonder what the process might achieve. In light of the two preceding concerns, and others discussed herein, this counterpoint essay argues that educational officials should not have the authority to subject students in public schools to random drug testing.

THE LITIGATION

As a matter of first impression, student drug testing, under at least some circumstances, is generally constitutional under *Vernonia School District 47J v. Acton* (1995a, b) and *Board of Education of Independent School District No. 92 of Pottawatomie County v. Earls* (2002a, b). However, it should be noted that in these cases, the Supreme Court addressed only drug testing related to voluntary participation in school athletics and extracurricular activities. Applying analysis ranging from student safety to role modeling, the Court decided that participants in extracurricular activities, especially athletes, have a lower expectation of privacy than others have. This justification is further extended by the voluntary nature of the activities. The Court's reasoning here was that drug testing, much like pre-activity physicals, is warranted by the assertion that extracurricular activities are privileges, not rights. If they wish to avoid the intrusions or searches, students can simply refrain from taking part in the activities.

The arguments that the point essay makes aside, neither *Acton* nor *Earls* can be relied on to support a generalized scheme of random or suspicionless drug testing. *Acton* is almost completely inapplicable to this issue because it involved both a suspicion, albeit a vague and nonspecific one, and the limitation that the drug testing applied only to students who, with full notice of its requirement, voluntarily subjected themselves to it by participating in extracurricular programs. Nothing in *Acton* suggests support for a less voluntary and suspicionless regime of general student drug testing. Indeed, the strictures of *Acton* almost appear to contravene such testing of the general student population.

Earls presents a slightly stronger case, at least for suspicionless testing. In *Earls*, the Supreme Court relied on circumstantial evidence that drugs had been present on campus and that one extracurricular participant had been caught with drugs. In his majority opinion, Justice Clarence Thomas went so far as to indicate that safety concerns related to schools and extracurricular activities could justify suspicionless testing for after-school programs far removed from athletics and student leadership. In the same opinion, Justice Thomas rationalized that the fact that athletes often disrobed together in common locker rooms before contests was sufficient to overcome the inherent Fourth Amendment privacy concerns of student participants to drug testing.

Even in its tortured and highly attenuated reasoning of *Earls*, the Supreme Court stopped short of suggesting a case for the involuntary testing of the student body at-large. As with *Acton*, the Court stressed two critical issues that precluded widespread testing. First, the Court ruled that the voluntary activities subject to testing, unlike the general education program, did not create any rights of participation. Hence, students who are excluded from clubs or teams for refusing to take drug tests could not claim the loss of constitutionally protected liberty or property interests. Second, despite essentially permitting suspicionless drug testing of students involved in extracurricular activities, the Court again retained the essential distinction that all such testing was premised on the students' voluntary participation programs and their awareness of the testing requirement. Nowhere in *Earls* is there any suggestion that testing can be predicated merely on compulsory attendance.

The Supreme Court's recent school search ruling in *Safford v. Redding* (2009) tends to affirm that there are limits to the search and seizure powers of public school officials even when some reasonable and particular suspicion exists with regard to testing of students incident to general compulsory educational programs. Incorrectly, proponents of more general drug testing appeal to the landmark precedent of *New Jersey v. T.L.O.* (1985). However, this is an appeal to a false analogy. Although *T.L.O.* did establish the lower suspicion standard for school searches and seizures as opposed to probable cause for criminal law, it upheld the rights of students to be free from unreasonable searches and seizures. Moreover, the Court rejected the proposition that educators may conduct searches absent reasonable and particularized suspicion. Again, the reasonable suspicion standard makes *T.L.O.* a precedent that stands against any argument that might be made for random, suspicionless, student drug testing.

Even if *T.L.O.* did imply some wide-ranging authority for officials to conduct highly intrusive searches under the rubric of "student safety," *Safford* considerably limited this power. To reiterate: In *Safford*, the Supreme Court noted that there are limits to the search and seizure powers of school officials even when they have some reasonable and particularized suspicion with regard to students in general compulsory educational programs.

Safford involved a drug search, although this time the drugs were allegedly hidden on the person of a 13-year-old girl. Even though the source of the "suspicion" that the student had drugs—the one who borrowed the day planner— was also a known troublemaker in the school, an assistant principal required the girl to strip down to her underwear in a failed search for prescription and over-the-counter medications. In *Safford*, the Supreme Court held that the school officials went too far beyond the limit of *T.L.O.*, ruling that such a personal and degrading search, based on a less than reliable source and allegations of limited drug possession, exceeded their authority. The Court was especially concerned with the effects of such searches on young people when the immediate threat to the school community was considered fairly low. The Court also questioned the application of *T.L.O.* to strip and other highly invasive searches, even when reasonable suspicion existed. Given the recent limitations imposed by *Safford* on suspicion-based searches, it exceeds logic to assume that any Supreme Court precedent supports highly personal and degrading drug tests based on little more than the general presumption that "some" students use drugs.

Returning to *Acton* for a moment, it is important to note that the facts giving rise to the dispute there were predicated on the belief of school officials that a "drug culture" was emerging among student-athletes, a condition that was neither universal nor predominant in the school as a whole. It is reasonable to presume that in many schools, "drug cultures" might well exist among non-involved students as they choose to avoid testing by electing not to participate in extracurricular activities. Clearly, the Supreme Court has not ruled in favor of drug testing, either random or universal, for student bodies at large. Therefore, extracurricular drug testing may, at best, only segregate student drug users from well-defined student groups and activities.

OTHER CONCERNS WITH REGARD TO TESTING
Lack of Precedent

Other legal concerns remain. First, not every state high court has interpreted its own search and seizure clause as permissively as the U.S. Supreme Court has done with the Fourth Amendment. For example, Colorado's highest court rejected random suspicionless drug testing in public schools. Additionally, the U.S. Supreme Court has only addressed urine testing, which it has held, at least in the context of locker rooms, to be less intrusive. Other types of testing, including blood, saliva, and hair samples, have been addressed only by lower courts, if at all. Although some school boards have attempted to expand the scope of drug testing to student bodies as a whole, such exercises currently lack substantial legal support.

Cost

Drug testing also has a financial aspect as well. Some drug tests, in particular basic urinalysis, can be conducted at a deceptively low price, even as low as $15 per student by reputable and established labs. Less intrusive procedures can be significantly more expensive. Yet, for even modest sports programs, this basic testing can result in several thousand dollars in additional costs per season. In larger programs, or if nonathletic activities are added, the costs can soar even higher. At the same time, even these costs are deceptively low. For testing to remain effective, it must be maintained, every season or semester. To some extent, of course, costs can be mitigated by using random testing, but this carries the price of reduced effectiveness. Additionally, the general protocol for drug testing, especially low-cost initial tests, is that all positives must be retested for false positives and then confirmed through more extensive, and expensive, testing such as blood tests. Further, although members of school staff are generally competent to supervise the integrity of urine testing, other methods of testing and advanced blood tests generally require the involvement of outside technicians. In one study involving a single U.S. school, a complete round of testing of the entire student body ultimately resulted in $35,000 in expenses and in a grand total of 11 confirmed drug users. These costs excluded the expenditures related to positive outcomes such as alternative schooling, counseling programs, and due process activities.

Nonmonetary Costs

There are also nonmonetary costs and considerations to drug testing. General suspicionless testing, for extracurricular participants or the student body as a whole, changes the dynamic between educators and students, particularly when nonathletes must be observed for urine testing. Although small-scale testing may only involve a school nurse or some coaching personnel, testing of students in other extracurricular activities or the student body as a whole will, of necessity, involve many more staff in activities that many employees and innocent students, not to mention parents, may well find distasteful, at best. As noted, such testing either involves school staff supervising the bodily functions of their pupils, or the expensive involvement of outside professionals. Other options may include less intimate, but more costly and inaccurate procedures, such as the testing of hair, sweat, and saliva. These techniques require more skilled collection methods, and they have other limitations. For example, some of these tests only detect certain substances if ingested within as little as 24 hours. Also, hair testing is especially difficult since the scope of testing is limited by the length of a hair sample. Subjects of testing who have had recent haircuts or, even worse, have shaved their heads completely, may be able to evade detection completely for even fairly recent drug (and alcohol) use.

Use of Test Results

Another issue with student drug testing is what school personnel can or should do with the results. To the uninitiated, a simple drug test is just that: Once a positive result is received, officials can move on to an appropriate response. Yet, the truth about drug testing is considerably more complicated and less determinative than many assume. As noted, the immediate consequence is not some affirmative action but, rather, more extensive and expensive testing to eliminate false positives or produce a more specific report. This phase requires noticeably more outlay and usually requires considerably more time for analysis. It is not inconceivable that, as is the case with many Olympic, professional, and amateur athletes, the results of preseason drug testing may not even be known until after the competitive season is completed. Even then, final lab results are far from the end stage of the process. School officials must notify students and their parents of the results while conducting due process procedures to determine not merely the accuracy of tests but also alternate explanations for any positive results. This is likely to include a review of family medical history, recent prescriptions, and possibly even the home drug cabinet.

All of the preceding items pose significant challenges for school officials. For instance, although the popular belief that ordinary poppy seeds can result in a positive test for opiates is somewhat dated given the recent improvements in testing, many other legal substances can produce positive results. In most foreign countries, including neighboring Canada and Mexico, aspirin and acetaminophen (paracetamol) with codeine can be purchased over the counter and, generally, are legal to import and possess, thus creating a particular problem with immigrant families and communities near international borders. Likewise, children with chronic allergy and sinus conditions are likely to test positive for steroids.

Alcohol is a particular problem in school settings. It is so common in numerous non-recreational applications, from household medicines and mouthwash to solvents and topical treatments that, unless students are discovered intoxicated while at school, positive results for alcohol are probably worth nothing in testing and disciplinary regimes. Likewise, marijuana, though an easily detectable illicit substance, can be so easily absorbed into the bloodstream from second-hand and external sources that positive test results can easily be produced among nonusers who have attended concerts or other events where cannabis was being consumed.

Even if school officials are able and willing to invest the staff hours necessary to verify and evaluate confirmed positive results, the question of what actual value testing achieves remains. The Supreme Court has been clear that the results of testing can be used to restrict student participation in extracurricular activities. As such, drug testing advocates claim the real value of drug testing is less in its catching and sanctioning users, than in its usefulness as a deterrent. Yet, in a U.S. Department of Education study released in 2010, researchers found only a modest decrease in reported drug use among extracurricular participants in schools with regular testing program (16.5% vs. 21.9%). Even worse, the study concluded that there was no spillover deterrent effect of drug testing on non-extracurricular participants. The same study also found that drug testing had no effect on students' long-term and post-scholastic drug use.

CONCLUSION

Beyond their limited and minor preventative effects, the operational value of the results of positive drug tests is debatable. Certainly, it is appropriate, based on both safety and fair play to exclude athletes from training and competition if they are using dangerous or performance-enhancing drugs. It is also allowable, under the Supreme Court precedent, to exclude drug-abusing students from other extracurricular activities as both a punishment and as an example for others. Yet, aside from these actions, the legal and administrative limits of drug testing become more apparent.

Activity-based suspicionless drug tests do not meet the "reasonable suspicion" standard for search and seizure established in *T.L.O.*, so their results are of no value for law enforcement purposes. Indeed, the release of these results might well violate federal and state laws regarding the confidentiality of student and health records. It is even legally debatable whether school officials can impose additional punishments or consequences on students beside their exclusion from specified activities. If anything, it can be argued that the lack of reasonable suspicion may bar schools from taking additional actions against student drug users. Even where courts may conclude, as a general matter of law, that school officials can pursue additional disciplinary options for student drug users, it may be a moot issue unless educators can prove that the drug use or intoxication occurred while the students were at school. Otherwise, educational officials may have a difficult time convincing courts that their interest in preventing drug use in general should allow them to extend their authority over drug use that may have occurred well off-campus and maybe even outside the academic term.

Ultimately, educators must consider whether student drug testing, in any context or population, is worth the effort or expense. Like many other social welfare agendas, drug testing represents even at its best a diversion from the primary missions of schools. School leaders need to address whether the resources of time, money, and effort are truly worth spending on drug screening compared with other, more academically focused activities to deter drug use, and they should not have the authority to require students to submit to drug testing.

FURTHER READINGS AND RESOURCES

Einesman, F., & Taras, H. (2007). Drug testing of students: A legal and public health perspective. *Journal of Contemporary Health Law and Policy, 23*(2), 231–271.

Gerada, C., & Gilvarry, E. (2005). Random drug testing in schools. *British Journal of General Practice, 55*(516), 499–501.

LaCroix, T. (2008). Student drug testing: The blinding appeal of in loco parentis and the importance of state protection of student privacy. *Brigham Young University Education and Law Journal, 2008*, 251.

Mawdsley, R. D., & Russo, C. J. (2003). Drug testing for extracurricular activities. *Education Law Reporter, 173*, 1–15.

McKinney, J. R. (2006). The effectiveness and legality of random student drug testing programs. *Education Law Reporter, 205*, 19–31.

National Institute on Drug Abuse, National Institutes of Health, U.S. Department of Health and Human Services. (2011). *High school and youth trends.* Retrieved from http://www.drugabuse.gov/infofacts/HSYouthtrends.html

Russo, C. J., & Gregory, D. L. (1999). Legal and ethical issues surrounding drug testing in schools. *Law Review of Michigan State University–Detroit College of Law, 1999*, 611–644.

Russo, C. J., & Mawdsley, R. D. (2008). *Searches, seizures and drug testing procedures: Balancing rights and school safety* (2nd ed.). Sarasota, FL: LRP.

Schimmel, D. (2002). Supreme Court expands random drug testing: Does the Fourth Amendment still protect students? *Education Law Reporter, 170*, 15–25.

Stuart, S. P. (2010). When the cure is worse than the disease: Student random drug testing & its empirical failure. *Valparaiso University Law Review, 44*(4), 1055–1082.

Turner, J. K. (2007). A "capricious, even perverse policy": Random, suspicionless drug testing policies in high schools and the Fourth Amendment. *Missouri Law Review, 72*, 931–946.

Court Cases and Statutes

Board of Education of Independent School District No. 92 of Pottawatomie County v. Earls, 536 U.S. 822 (2002a), *on remand*, 300 F.3d 1222 (10th Cir. 2002b).

Chandler v. Miller, 520 U.S. 305 (1997).

National Treasury Employees Union v. Von Raab, 489 U.S. 656 (1989).

New Jersey v. T.L.O., 469 U.S. 325 (1985).

Palmer v. Merluzzi, 868 F.2d 90 (3d Cir. 1989).

Pierce v. Society of Sisters of the Holy Names of Jesus and Mary, 268 U.S. 510 (1925).

Safford Unified School District v. Redding, 129 S. Ct. 2633 (2009).

Schaill v. Tippecanoe County School Corp., 864 F.2d 1309 (7th Cir. 1988).

Skinner v. Railway Labor Executives' Association, 489 U.S. 602 (1989).

Tannahill ex rel. Tannahill v. Lockney Independent School District, 133 F. Supp. 2d 919 (N.D. Tex. 2001).

Tinker v. Des Moines Independent Community School District, 393 U.S. 503 (1969).

Trinidad School District No. 1 v. Lopez, 963 P.2d 1095 (Colo. 1998).

Vernonia School District 47J v. Acton, 515 U.S. 646 (1995a), *on remand*, 66 F.3d 217 (9th Cir. 1995b).

Should teachers be subject to drug testing?

POINT: Robert C. Cloud, *Baylor University*

COUNTERPOINT: Richard Fossey, *University of North Texas*

OVERVIEW

Drug and alcohol abuse is a widespread problem in society today. According to the U.S. Department of Health and Human Services, in 2004, approximately 8% of the nation's population over the age of 12 used illicit drugs, and drug and alcohol abuse contribute to more than 120,000 deaths annually. Drug and alcohol testing of employees, particularly those in safety-sensitive positions in both the private and public sectors, is controversial as the courts reach mixed results.

Courts have ruled that school boards may order employees to take drug and alcohol tests when they have evidence of abuse as long as their suspicions are grounded in reasonable suspicion. In one case, the Eleventh Circuit upheld a teacher's dismissal for insubordination when she refused to allow her vehicle to be searched after marijuana was discovered in her car (*Hearn v. Board of Public Education*, 1999). Conversely, a federal trial court in Missouri rejected claims that a teacher's difficulty in getting along with her peers was an adequate basis for subjecting her to drug testing (*Warren v. Board of Education of St. Louis*, 2001). In yet another case, the Sixth Circuit upheld a policy allowing a school board to test employees whose job performance or behavior may have been affected by the use of illegal drugs (*Knox County Education Association v. Knox County Board of Education*, 1998). The court noted that the policy's detailed provisions required reasonable cause and individualized suspicion before testing. Courts have upheld drug testing policies when evidence indicates a drug problem among the staff (*Crager v. Board of Education of Knott County*, 2004) and when it is minimally intrusive (*Aubrey v. School Board of Lafayette Parish*, 1998).

Suspicionless drug testing of school employees is more controversial, with most courts agreeing that teachers' privacy rights trump school boards' authority to implement random drug testing policies. Although many argue that boards should be able to subject teachers to suspicionless testing because of the nature of their positions where they are entrusted with the care and safety of children, not all courts agree.

As the discussions in both the point and counterpoint essays demonstrate, boards failed to demonstrate compelling reasons to carry out suspicionless drug testing in most cases. The Sixth Circuit, in *Knox County*, stands as a lone exception. Here, the court, declaring that teachers hold safety-sensitive positions, affirmed that part of the policy requiring candidates who were offered jobs was to take drug tests. The court acknowledged the board's duty to ensure the safety and security of children entrusted to it while recognizing that teachers have a diminished privacy interest in not being tested. Other courts disagreed that teachers occupy safety-sensitive positions (*American Federation of Teachers v. Kanawha County Board of Education*, 2009; *Jones v. Graham County Board of Education*, 2009).

Courts are also reluctant to endorse drug testing that targets a particular class of employees without reasonable suspicion or a compelling governmental interest. For example, courts have struck down policies allowing testing absent individualized suspicion of drug use (*United Teachers of New Orleans v. Orleans Parish School Board*, 1998) or reasonable suspicion or evidence of a drug problem (*Patchogue-Medford Congress of Teachers v. Board of Education of the Patchogue-Medford Union Free School District*, 1987). In the latter decision, the court explained that searches conducted by a government entity without reasonable suspicion are allowed only when the implicated privacy interests are minimal, the government's interest is substantial, and safeguards are in place to protect individuals' reasonable expectation of privacy. Thus, when boards want to test all employees, they must identify a compelling governmental interest, and the interest in maintaining a drug-free workplace may not always be sufficient (*Georgia Association of Educators v. Harris*, 1990).

In the point essay, Robert C. Cloud, Baylor University, argues that public school boards should have the authority to require random drug testing of teachers because of their duty to ensure student safety. Cloud insists that teachers should not expect the same privacy rights as employees in other fields have because of the special nature of their jobs. Positing that teachers' unique duties amount to a sacred trust to protect students, Cloud asserts that teachers cannot honor that trust while under the influence of drugs. Richard Fossey, University of North Texas, takes the opposite view, maintaining that random drug testing of teachers intrudes on their reasonable expectations of privacy and is not justified by any special need. Citing recent court decisions, he argues that such policies violate the Fourth Amendment rights of teachers and are not justified by safety concerns. In essence, Fossey agrees with those courts that contend that teachers are not in safety-sensitive positions.

As the previous discussion, coupled with the point and counterpoint essays in this chapter, demonstrate, drug and alcohol testing of teachers remains controversial. As you read these essays, it might be helpful to reflect on the following questions: Should drug testing be allowed when school boards have a reasonable suspicion that an individual employee is using illegal drugs or is under the influence of alcohol? Should suspicionless testing of teachers be allowed when there is a special need for the testing such as when there is evidence of a drug problem among a particular group? Are teachers in safety-sensitive positions because of their influence on impressionable children, and if so, is suspicionless drug testing warranted?

Allan G. Osborne, Jr.
Principal (Retired), Snug Harbor Community School,
Quincy, Massachusetts

POINT: Robert C. Cloud
Baylor University

Should public schools have the authority to adopt policies compelling teachers to submit to random drug testing? At first glance, such policies would seem to violate the Fourth Amendment rights of teachers to privacy and freedom from unreasonable search and seizure. Yet, the question deserves a second look, and the answer is "yes."

Because of the unique and special nature of U.S. public schools, courts have approved random drug testing of some educational employees in specified "safety-sensitive" positions. The courts have defined these jobs as "those positions where a single mistake by such employee can create an immediate threat of serious harm to students and fellow employees" (*Knox County Education Association v. Knox County Board of Education*, 1998, p. 367). For example, the District of Columbia Circuit Court of Appeals ruled in *Jones v. McKenzie* (1987) that the school board could require drug testing of bus drivers because of obvious concerns for the safety of school children. It is thus worth noting that many school boards require all employees who drive school buses to submit to random drug testing, not just full-time bus drivers.

Subsequently, the Fifth Circuit upheld the policy of a school board in Louisiana requiring a school custodian to submit to random drug testing because he used chemical solvents, worked with electricity, and lit natural gas pilot lights in an elementary school, activities that could endanger children if not properly handled (*Aubrey v. School Board of Lafayette Parish*, 1998). In addition, at least one other federal appellate court, the Sixth Circuit, ruled that drug testing of teachers is permissible because they occupy safety-sensitive positions (*Knox County*).

At the same time, the Supreme Court permitted random drug testing of public railway employees for drugs and alcohol after serious accidents, even without showings of individualized suspicion, in *Skinner v. Railway Labor Executives' Association* (1989) and of drug enforcement agents in *National Treasury Employees Union v. Von Raab* (1989), cases discussed as follows. The Court also upheld drug testing of public school students who participated in competitive extracurricular activities, concluding that participants should expect less privacy than nonparticipants and that schools are not required to document serious drug problems before implementing testing procedures (*Board of Education of Independent School District No. 92 of Pottawatomie County v. Earls*, 2002).

Clearly, the authority of public school boards and officials to control drug abuse by employees (and students) is an issue ripe for litigation. At this writing, the constitutionality of drug testing for teachers has been considered in only five cases, and in four of those decisions, courts ruled that random testing of teachers violates their Fourth Amendment rights. However, this point essay presents the argument that public school boards should have the authority to develop policies requiring random drug testing of teachers because of their unique duty to ensure student safety.

RANDOM DRUG TESTING OF PUBLIC EMPLOYEES: AN OVERVIEW

The Fourth Amendment to the U.S. Constitution restrains government actions by guaranteeing "the right of the people to be secure in their persons, houses, papers and effects, against unreasonable searches and seizures." Therefore, governmental searches must be based on individualized suspicion as authorities must show probable cause before obtaining search warrants (*Chandler v. Miller*, 1997). Even so, the Supreme Court has approved random and suspicionless drug testing of public employees in limited and special circumstances.

Given increasing levels of drug abuse and violence in the general society, the Supreme Court has permitted testing of public employees in safety-sensitive positions where the use of drugs can threaten public safety. For instance, in *Skinner v. Labor Railway Executives' Association* (1989), the Court decided that the government's compelling interest in railroad safety constituted a special need justifying a deviation from the normal probable cause and warrant requirements of governmental searches. The Court concluded that railway employees had diminished privacy expectations because they had accepted employment in an industry "that is regulated pervasively to ensure safety" (p. 627).

In another case on drug testing, the Supreme Court reasoned that the government could require the random testing of U.S. Customs agents seeking promotion or transfer to positions directly involved in the interdiction of illegal drugs. Customs agents in those positions were privy to highly classified information, they were armed, and they used deadly force when necessary to apprehend drug-trafficking criminals. The Court described the Customs Service as the "nation's first line of defense against one of the greatest problems affecting the health and welfare of our population" and found it "readily apparent" that the government has a compelling interest in ensuring unimpeachable integrity and judgment among its customs agents (*National Treasury Employees Union v. Von Raab*, pp. 668–670). In the end, the Court determined that the government's interest in efficient and effective drug law enforcement took precedence over the agents' constitutional right to privacy (*Von Raab*).

RANDOM DRUG TESTING OF TEACHERS AND SAFETY

As early as 1925 in *Pierce v. Society of Sisters of the Holy Names of Jesus and Mary* (p. 510), the Supreme Court recognized that states have a compelling interest in school safety. Indeed, few governmental interests are more important to communities than ensuring the safety of their children. Classroom teachers who serve in loco parentis, literally in the place of the parent, a topic that is the subject of a debate in the volume on school discipline and safety, are responsible for securing order and protecting students.

Teachers are expected to identify drug-related and other suspicious activities and report prohibited behavior immediately. While safeguarding school environments, teachers are expected to model exemplary behavior for their students through word and deed. This dual role places unique and special duties on teachers that few other professionals confront. Teachers are ethically and legally obligated to carry out assigned duties free from the debilitating influence of drugs, and schools should have the right to compel their compliance with law and policy through random drug testing. To paraphrase the Supreme Court in *Skinner* (1989), public school teachers should not expect the same privacy rights as employees in other fields because of the unique and special nature of their calling. However, to date, most federal courts have held that random drug testing violates teachers' privacy rights under the Fourth Amendment.

Patchogue-Medford Congress of Teachers v. Board of Education of Patchogue-Medford Union Free School District (1987) was the first case in which a state court of last resort addressed drug testing of teachers. At issue was a local school board policy requiring all probationary teachers to pass a urinalysis drug test before being granted tenure. When the local union sued, alleging violation of the teachers' right to privacy, the board responded that the urinalysis was not a search because it was not intrusive. New York's highest court considered the dispute under both the state constitution and the U.S. Constitution prohibitions against unreasonable searches and seizures, finding unanimously that the testing plan was unconstitutional. First, the court wrote that the act of discharging urine is an intensely private and intimate act and that urine contains information that reveals private information about bodily integrity. Therefore, in the court's view, requiring teachers to submit to a urinalysis constituted a search in violation of both state and federal constitutions. Second, the court pointed out that the board was not required to show probable cause and obtain a warrant before initiating a search. In certain circumstances, the court determined, less than probable cause and no warrant are acceptable in schools. *Reasonable suspicion*, the court explained, is the appropriate standard when searches of students are involved. Similarly, the court observed that reasonable suspicion is the appropriate standard when school authorities suspect teachers of drug abuse. The board presented no evidence of significant drug abuse among teachers that would justify universal testing, so the court ruled that the drug testing protocol violated teachers' Fourth Amendment rights (Russo, 1987).

Eleven years later in *United Teachers of New Orleans v. Orleans Parish School Board* (1998), the Fifth Circuit ruled that two school boards in Louisiana violated the Fourth Amendment rights by requiring school employees, including teachers, who were involved in accidents to submit to drug testing without regard to the circumstances. Because the test required production of a urine sample, the court maintained that it was a governmental search requiring individualized suspicion of wrongdoing. Testimony in the case revealed that a primary purpose of the drug testing was to support the state's interest in denying particular types of workman's compensation claims. The court commented that under state law, boards were not required to compensate employees who were injured while under the influence of alcohol or other drugs. In the end, the court thought that because the drug tests were not based on individualized suspicion and that the boards had not demonstrated the existence of widespread drug abuse among teachers, it was unconstitutional.

Not long thereafter, the Sixth Circuit upheld the policy of a school board in Tennessee that mandated drug testing for teachers in two specific circumstances (*Knox County*, 1998). First, the policy required suspicionless testing of all employees, including teachers, who applied for, transferred to, or were promoted into safety-sensitive positions. Second, the policy required testing for any employee if school officials had a reasonable suspicion that the person's job performance was compromised by drug abuse.

In upholding the policy, the Sixth Circuit described teachers as "front-line observers in providing for a safe school environment" with the special duty to report matters that endanger life, health, and safety (*Knox County*, pp. 375, 378). To the court, teachers served in a unique setting where "even a momentary lapse of attention can have disastrous consequences" (p. 378). Because teachers occupied safety-sensitive positions, the court was convinced that public interest in drug testing outweighed the privacy interests of teachers not to be tested because of the circumscribed and narrowly tailored nature of the testing (p. 384). Finally, the court concluded that teachers, like railway employees, also serve in a heavily regulated profession and that they have a diminished expectation of privacy.

In 2009, two courts agreed that random drug testing of schoolteachers was unconstitutional. In *American Federation of Teachers v. Kanawha County Board of Education* (2009), plaintiffs sued a school board in West Virginia over its policy requiring employees in safety-sensitive positions to submit to random drug testing. The policy included teachers, building principals, and the superintendent among 47 safety-sensitive job categories. During trial proceedings, the superintendent testified that the school board implemented drug testing of the 47 employee categories out of a general concern for student safety. Concern for students, he testified, also led the board to install cameras, ban knives and guns, and remove shrubbery outside of school buildings. The board's concern for student safety notwithstanding, a federal trial court ruled that teachers did not occupy safety-sensitive positions and that the board failed to demonstrate a special need justifying drug testing of its teachers. Differing with the outcome in Knox County, discussed earlier, the court was of the opinion that the teachers did not have a diminished expectation of privacy.

Later in 2009, an appellate court in North Carolina invalidated another random testing policy for teachers and other school employees who ostensibly occupied safety-sensitive positions (*Jones v. Graham County Board of Education*, 2009). School employees affected by this policy included coaches, principals, assistant principals, and the superintendent. A teacher and others sued the board claiming that the policy violated the state constitution's prohibition against suspicionless searches. In reversing an earlier grant of summary judgment in favor of the board, an appellate court ruled that the state's constitutional search provision, by definition, could not be viewed to accord lesser rights than those guaranteed by the Fourth Amendment because, according to *Jones*, "the United States Constitution is binding on the states. . . ." In the end, the appellate court ruled that the school board's drug testing policy was not only unnecessary and intrusive but that it did little or nothing to reduce the risk of harm to students and staff.

According to the court, then, because the drug testing policy had to comply with the Fourth Amendment, but did not, it was unconstitutional.

CONCLUSION

Should public schools have the authority to compel teachers to submit to random drug testing? School boards that have implemented such programs often cite concerns for student safety as the motivating factor in their actions. Legitimate concerns for safety aside, most of the courts to date have answered no to the question.

In the five published court decisions addressing drug testing for teachers between 1987 and 2009, four of the school boards were unable to demonstrate a pervasive drug problem that justified random testing. Only the Sixth Circuit upheld a board policy of engaging in suspicionless drug testing of teachers, and even this policy was limited to the testing of teachers who were hired, promoted, or transferred into safety-sensitive positions. Alone among the courts, the Sixth Circuit found drug testing of teachers to be constitutional. At this point, the message from the courts is loud and clear: Teachers' Fourth Amendment rights overcome the schools' interest in monitoring teachers' use of chemical substances.

No thinking person would question the necessity of the Fourth Amendment in a free society, and teachers, like all citizens, have the right to privacy and freedom from unreasonable search. Yet a dilemma remains for school officials in their efforts to secure school environments. Public schools can be dangerous places, and educational officials have legal and ethical responsibilities to ensure the safety of all. Teachers occupy frontline positions in the continuing effort to secure the schools. Indeed, teachers' special and unique duty to protect children amounts to a sacred trust in the minds of many.

Teachers simply cannot honor that trust and do their duty while under the influence of drugs. Trying to fulfill a teacher's duties while physically or mentally impaired by drugs is unethical, unthinkable, and unacceptable. The counterpoint essay's arguments aside, school boards should thus have the right to ensure that teachers comply with high ethical standards through drug testing or other measures that are compatible with the U.S. Constitution. Time will tell whether a reasonable balance can be found between the compelling interests of educational officials to maintain schools as safe and orderly learning environments while safeguarding the constitutional rights of teachers to be free from unreasonable drug searches. In the meantime, it is better to be "safe than sorry," by testing teachers to keep potential drug users out of these important jobs.

COUNTERPOINT: Richard Fossey
University of North Texas

Should school boards have the constitutional authority to compel public school teachers to submit to random drug testing? The short answer is "no." The U.S. Supreme Court has already approved random drug testing of student athletes. Further, in a 1998 opinion, the Fifth Circuit upheld a school board's random drug testing policy for custodians (*Aubrey v. School Board of Lafayette Parish*). At the same time, the Sixth Circuit sustained a board policy calling for drug testing of teachers who are new hires or who are promoted to or transferred from jobs within the district into what it described as "safety-sensitive" positions, meaning that they either work directly with students or have positions that affect the well-being of children (*Knox County Education Association v. Knox County Board of Education*, 1998). Given these decisions, many ask why courts should not approve random drug testing for all public school teachers.

As is reflected in the point essay, one can make a reasonable case that school boards should have the legal authority to require teachers to submit to random drug testing. Even so, this counterpoint essay argues that such policies would violate teachers' right to be free from unreasonable searches under the Fourth Amendment. So far, as noted both here and in the point essay, only five published cases have addressed the constitutionality of suspicionless drug testing of public school teachers. In four of these cases, courts agreed that such testing violates teachers' constitutional rights.

LEGAL STATUS OF RANDOM DRUG TESTING OF PUBLIC EMPLOYEES

In *Skinner v. Railway Labor Executives' Association* (1989), the U.S. Supreme Court ruled that a urinalysis drug test of railway employees following accidents that are administered by a governmental entity or one of its agents is a search under the Fourth Amendment. The Court interpreted blood testing for alcohol by a governmental agent as a search, involving as it did, "compelled intrusions of the body . . . through penetration of the skin and subsequent chemical analysis to discover physiological data about an individual" (*Schmerber v. California*, 1966).

According to the Supreme Court, drug testing by urinalysis is a search for the purposes of Fourth Amendment analysis, even though collection of urine does not involve a physical intrusion into the body. "It is not disputed," the Court wrote in *Skinner*, "that chemical analysis of urine, like that of blood, can reveal a host of private medical facts about an employee, including whether he or she is epileptic, pregnant, or diabetic" (p. 617). In addition, the Court pointed out, "The process of collecting the sample to be tested, which may in some cases involve visual or aural monitoring of the act of urination, itself implicates privacy interests" (p. 617). Indeed, the Court observed, "There are few activities in our society more personal or private than the passing of urine. Most people describe it by euphemisms if they talk about it at all. It is a function traditionally performed without public observation; indeed, its performance in public is generally prohibited by law as well as social custom" (p. 617, internal citation omitted).

Generally, governmental searches require individualized suspicion to pass muster under the Fourth Amendment (*Chandler v. Miller*, 1997). Nevertheless, the Supreme Court upheld random drug testing of governmental employees without individualized suspicion in limited circumstances. In *Skinner* (1989), for example, the Court determined that the government's interest in regulating the conduct of railroad employees to ensure safety presented "'special needs' beyond the normal needs of law enforcement" that justified a departure from the usual warrant and probable-cause requirements that applied to searches conducted in criminal investigations (p. 620). Moreover, the Court noted, the railway employees who were subject to random drug testing had diminished privacy expectations because they worked in an industry "that is regulated pervasively to ensure safety" (p. 627).

On two occasions, the Supreme Court has also upheld random drug testing by public school authorities for two classes of students. In *Vernonia School District 47J v. Acton* (1995), the Court upheld the random drug testing policy of a school board in Oregon for varsity athletes against a challenge that the policy violated the athletes' right to privacy under the Fourth Amendment. Likewise in *Board of Education of Independent School District No. 92 of Pottawatomie County v. Earls* (2002), the Supreme Court approved the policy of a school board in Oklahoma requiring all students who participated in the district's competitive extracurricular activities to submit to random drug testing.

In *Earls* (2002a), the Supreme Court stressed that school boards have a duty to combat drug use by young people and that officials were not required to quantify a specified level of student drug abuse before implementing random drug testing programs. Essentially relying on the test from *Acton* (1995a), the Court upheld the policy because the students had minimal privacy expectations, the testing was minimally intrusive, and the nature and immediacy of the government's interest was such that the policy was constitutional.

At the same time, lower courts have upheld school board policies for randomly drug testing certain classes of school employees. For instance, in *Aubrey*, the Fifth Circuit ruled that a board policy requiring a school custodian to submit to random drug testing did not violate his Fourth Amendment right to privacy. The court reasoned that insofar as the custodian worked in close proximity to elementary school children while using dangerous machinery and cleaning supplies containing hazardous chemicals, the policy was constitutional.

Likewise, the federal circuit court for the District of Columbia upheld suspicionless drug testing of school bus drivers based on obvious safety concerns, a practice that is almost universal in U.S. school systems (*Jones v. McKenzie*, 1987). As with custodians, the court was satisfied that the school board had a special need to ensure that its bus drivers were not under the influence of drugs while transporting students to and from school.

RANDOM DRUG TESTING AS AN UNJUSTIFIED INTRUSION ON EXPECTATIONS OF PRIVACY

As noted, to date, only five published opinions have addressed the constitutionality of suspicionless drug testing of public school teachers. In *Patchogue-Medford Congress of Teachers v. Board of Education of Patchogue-Medford Union Free School District* (1987), a school board in New York sought to require all tenure-eligible teachers to submit to a drug test by urinalysis, with urine samples to be collected by the school nurse. The board's purpose in conducting the tests was to evaluate whether any probationary teachers were using illegal drugs, informing those who refused to participate that they would not be recommended for tenure.

New York's highest court rejected the school board's argument in favor of suspicionless drug testing of probationary teachers. First, the court ruled, requiring teachers to submit to drug testing by urinalysis is a severe intrusion into their personal privacy such that it constituted a search for constitutional purposes. Although the court found that the board was not required to obtain a warrant to conduct drug testing of its workforce, it had to proceed only on reasonable suspicion that drug testing would have turned up evidence of drug use. Yet, the court indicated that the board was unable to produce evidence of a problem with drug abuse among its teaching staff. Accordingly, the court struck down the policy requiring all tenure-eligible teachers to submit to urinalysis drug testing as violating their Fourth Amendment right to privacy.

Conversely, 11 years later, in *Knox County* (1998), the Sixth Circuit upheld a policy from a school board in Tennessee that required teachers to submit to drug testing under two specific conditions. First, the court acknowledged that the suspicionless drug testing was to be conducted on all teachers (and other employees) who applied for, transferred to, or were promoted into safety-sensitive positions with the district. Second, the court explained that the policy called for drug testing of any school employee if school officials had "reasonable suspicion" that the person's performance was affected by illegal use of drugs or alcohol.

In upholding the board's policy for suspicionless drug testing, the court basically determined that teachers occupy "safety-sensitive positions because "even a momentary lapse of attention can have disastrous consequences" (*Knox County*, p. 378, internal citation omitted). Further, tracking the analysis of *Skinner* and other Supreme Court precedents, the Sixth Circuit decided that teachers have a diminished expectation of privacy by virtue of their working in a heavily regulated profession.

In contrast to the *Knox County* decision, the Fifth Circuit ruled that two school boards in Louisiana violated teachers' Fourth Amendment privacy rights by requiring individuals who were involved in accidents to submit to drug testing (*United Teachers of New Orleans v. Orleans Parish School Board*, 1998). In the court's view, the school boards had not justified their policy of drug testing teachers involved in accidents without regard to the circumstances. The court pointed out that the school boards had not presented evidence of a drug use problem among teachers.

Patchogue-Medford Congress of Teachers, Knox County, and *United Teachers of New Orleans* were the only published opinions on suspicionless drug testing of teachers until 2009. In 2009, then, two courts agreed that requiring teachers to submit to random, suspicionless drug testing was unconstitutional.

In *American Federation of Teachers v. Kanawha County Board of Education* (2009), two teacher unions sued a school board in West Virginia to stop it from implementing a policy of requiring all employees in safety-sensitive positions—including teachers, principals, and the district superintendent—to submit to random drug testing. Altogether, the school board had identified 47 of the school board's job descriptions as safety sensitive as it contemplated testing 25% of its safety-sensitive employees each year.

A federal trial court in West Virginia enjoined the school board from implementing its drug testing program on the ground that it had not shown a "special need" to randomly drug test teachers. Critical to the court's holding was its emphatic conclusion that teachers did not occupy safety-sensitive positions. The court declared that "[a] train, nuclear reactor, or firearm in the hands of someone on drugs presents an actual concrete risk to numerous people. . . . The same cannot be said for a teacher wielding a history textbook" (*American Federation of Teachers*, p. 903). Nor in the court's view could the teachers be said to have a diminished expectation of privacy because of the nature of their jobs that would justify the program of randomly collecting their urine for drug testing. It was true, the court acknowledged, that teachers were required to be certified, but the purpose of this certification was to ensure that individuals had the necessary teaching skills. In other words, the court did not think that state certification had anything to do with regulating teachers for safety purposes. In the end, the court specifically disagreed.

Finally, in *Jones v. Graham County Board of Education* (2009), an intermediate appellate court in North Carolina struck down a suspicionless drug testing policy for teachers that a school board had enacted. The policy called for random drug testing of employees who occupied safety-sensitive positions, including teachers, athletic coaches, principals, assistant principals, and the superintendent. A teacher and the state's Association of Educators sued the school board to enjoin implementation of the policy on the ground that it violated the North Carolina constitution's prohibition against governmental searches conducted "without evidence of the act committed" (p. 177).

On further review of a grant of summary judgment in favor of the school board, finding that there was no constitutional violation, an appellate court reversed in favor of the plaintiffs. According to the court, the state's constitutional search provision could not have been interpreted as affording individuals fewer rights than are guaranteed by the Fourth Amendment of the federal constitution. Thus, the court analyzed the school board's random drug testing policy to determine whether it violated the Fourth Amendment, noting that if it did, then it would automatically violate the state constitution as well.

Drawing on federal court precedents, the court remarked that the school board had not demonstrated a special need to conduct suspicionless drug testing of its employees under a policy the court described as "remarkably intrusive" (*Jones*, p. 180). Striking down the policy, the court observed that the board's employees had no reduced expectation of privacy simply because they worked for a public school system. Moreover, the court pointed out that the board had admitted that there was "no evidence in the record of any drug problem among its employees" (p. 180). Finally, the court flatly rejected the board's contention that its employees occupied safety-sensitive positions that made drug use a special concern. "In fact," the court maintained emphatically, there was "absolutely no evidence in the record that any Board employee whose body contains 'a detectable amount of an illegal drug or of alcohol' increases the risk of harm to anyone" (p. 182). The court thus concluded that the board's random drug testing policy violated its employees' right to be free from unreasonable searches under the state constitution.

CONCLUSION

In the five published court cases involving suspicionless drug testing of teachers, none of the school board defendants established that they had significant and concrete problems with drug use by their teaching employees. As such, one can only wonder why boards continue to adopt such policies. Although the Sixth Circuit ruled in *Knox County* that a suspicionless drug testing policy could be applied to teachers who were hired, promoted, or transferred into safety-sensitive positions, the more skeptical approach to suspicionless drug testing by four other courts is more persuasive insofar as it protects the privacy rights of teachers and other school employees.

In particular, the opinion in *American Federation of Teachers* argues sensibly that teachers simply do not occupy "safety-sensitive" jobs justifying suspicionless drug testing programs like those approved for people working in jobs where safety is a legitimate concern. Moreover, in *Jones*, the court agreed that the teachers were not safety-sensitive employees with reduced expectation of privacy justifying their submission to random drug testing.

This counterpoint essay argues that because the two 2009 opinions, in particular, are well reasoned, they should govern the thinking of educational decisionmakers about suspicionless drug testing of public school teachers. In sum, such suspicionless drug testing policies simply violate the Fourth Amendment of the U.S. Constitution absent concrete safety concerns that were not present in any of the reported cases. Although no one wants to see drug users employed in public schools, and the point essay's arguments notwithstanding, absent individualized suspicion, there is no reason to submit public school teachers to suspicionless drug testing.

Further Readings and Resources

Fossey, R. (2009). Do schools have a legal right to collect teachers' urine for random drug testing? Let's hope not! *Teachers College Record.* Available from http://www .tcrecord.org (ID Number: 15653)

Russo, C. J. (1987). Drug testing of teachers: *Patchogue-Medford Congress of Teachers* revisited. *Education Law Reporter, 40*(2), 607–614.

Russo, C. J., & Mawdsley, R. D. (2008). *Searches, seizures and drug testing procedures: Balancing rights and school safety* (2nd ed.). Sarasota, FL: LRP.

U.S. Department of Health and Human Services. (2006, January 13). *Fact sheet: Substance abuse—A national challenge: prevention, treatment and research at HHS.* Retrieved September 8, 2011, from http://www.hhs.gov/news/factsheet/subabuse .html

Court Cases and Statutes

American Federation of Teachers v. Kanawha County Board of Education, 592 F. Supp. 2d 883 (S.D.W.Va. 2009).

Aubrey v. School Board of Lafayette Parish, 148 F.3d 559 (5th Cir. 1998).

Board of Education of Independent School District No. 92 of Pottawatomie County v. Earls, 536 U.S. 822 (2002), *on remand*, 300 F.3d 1222 (10th Cir. 2002b).

Chandler v. Miller, 520 U.S. 305 (1997).

Crager v. Board of Education of Knott County, 313 F. Supp. 2d 690 (E.D. Ky. 2004).

Georgia Association of Educators v. Harris, 749 F. Supp. 2d 1110 (N.D. Ga. 1990).

Hearn v. Board of Public Education, 191 F.3d 1329 (11th Cir. 1999).

Jones v. Graham County Board of Education, 677 S.E.2d 171 (N.C. Ct. App. 2009).

Jones v. McKenzie, 833 F.2d 335 (D.C. Cir. 1987).

Knox County Education Association v. Knox County Board of Education, 158 F.3d 361 (6th Cir. 1998).

National Treasury Employees Union v. Von Raab, 489 U.S. 656 (1989).

Patchogue-Medford Congress of Teachers v. Board of Education of Patchogue-Medford Union Free School District, 517 N.Y.S.2d 456 (N.Y. 1987).

Pierce v. Society of Sisters of the Holy Names of Jesus and Mary, 268 U.S. 510 (1925).

Schmerber v. California, 384 U.S. 757, 767–768 (1966).

Skinner v. Railway Labor Executives' Association, 489 U.S. 602 (1989).

United Teachers of New Orleans v. Orleans Parish School Board, 142 F.3d 853 (5th Cir. 1998).

Vernonia School District 47J v. Acton, 515 U.S. 646 (1995), *on remand*, 66 F.3d 217 (9th Cir. 1995).

Warren v. Board of Education of St. Louis, 200 F. Supp. 2d 1053 (E.D. Mo. 2001).

Are the disciplinary standards under the Individuals with Disabilities Education Act fair to all students?

POINT: Allan G. Osborne, Jr., *Principal (Retired),*
Snug Harbor Community School, Quincy, Massachusetts

COUNTERPOINT: Robert J. Safransky,
Nova Southeastern University

OVERVIEW

The federal special education statute now known as the Individuals with Disabilities Education Act (IDEA) was adopted and signed into law in 1975 as the Education for All Handicapped Children Act, largely in response to successful suits that were filed on behalf of students with disabilities seeking equal educational opportunities. In an early case, *Pennsylvania Association for Retarded Children v. Pennsylvania* (1971, 1972), a trial court established some of the basic due process rights for students with disabilities—such as they could not have their placements changed without parental input—that later made their way into the IDEA. A year later, in *Mills v. Board of Education of the District of Columbia* (1972), another federal trial court ruled that because as many as 18,000 students, many of whom had behavioral problems, were completely excluded from the public schools, the board had to admit them to classes. Three years later, the IDEA described its main purpose in its preamble: to provide students with disabilities access to a free appropriate public education (FAPE).

A FAPE consists of any special education and related services that students with disabilities require. The cornerstone of a FAPE is an individualized education program (IEP) developed by school personnel in concert with parents. In its first case interpreting the IDEA, *Board of Education of Hendrick Hudson Central School District v. Rowley* (1982), the Supreme Court held that a FAPE is designed to confer educational benefits on students and was developed in conformance with the procedures spelled out in the IDEA.

The IDEA contains a number of procedural safeguards designed to protect the rights of students with disabilities. An important aspect of the law, which at the time of the IDEA's enactment was somewhat unique, is that it provides for parental involvement every step of the way. In enacting the IDEA, Congress envisioned parents as equal partners with school officials in the development of the IEPs for students. Thus, school officials must seek parental permission before initially evaluating children and placing them in special education settings. Another important provision of the law prohibits educators from arbitrarily changing the educational placements of students without parental consent. This section of the IDEA, known as the status quo or stay put provision, mandates that while administrative hearings or judicial proceedings are pending, children with disabilities must remain in their then current placements unless their parents and school officials agree otherwise (IDEA, 20 U.S.C. § 1415(j)).

A glaring omission in the early versions of the IDEA was that it failed to contain explicit language regarding discipline. Not surprisingly, some of the earliest litigation contested disciplinary actions imposed on students with disabilities. These disputes culminated in a 1988 Supreme Court case, *Honig v. Doe*, which helped clarify the rights of students with disabilities who are subject to discipline.

Following *Honig*, a growing body of case law developed prompting Congress to amend the IDEA in 1997 to add disciplinary provisions to the statute. Congress further refined these provisions in 2004. The 1997 amendments added the requirement that students with disabilities cannot be expelled or subjected to long-term suspensions if their misconduct is a manifestation of their disabilities. These amendments also obliged school personnel to complete functional behavioral assessments and implement behavior intervention plans under specified circumstances, such as when they determine that students' misconduct is a manifestation of their disabilities. In 2004, Congress amended the definition of a *manifestation* while simplifying its overall related procedures. The amendments also addressed the status of students who bring weapons or drugs to school or present threats of serious bodily harm to themselves or others.

The two following essays examine the IDEA's disciplinary provisions and whether they create unfair standards for students who are disabled and their peers who are not disabled. In the point essay, Allan G. Osborne, Jr., a retired principal (Snug Harbor Community School, Quincy, Massachusetts), argues that the IDEA does not create different disciplinary standards for students with disabilities. Rather, he notes that the IDEA just affords students with disabilities additional procedural rights before they can be subjected to serious disciplinary sanctions such as long-term suspensions and expulsions. Although these additional safeguards add steps to the disciplinary process for students with disabilities, Osborne stresses that they are both necessary and understandable given the history of discriminatory treatment toward children with disabilities. Osborne believes that the IDEA's disciplinary procedures strike an appropriate balance between the need for school officials to maintain safe, orderly schools and the rights of students with disabilities to a FAPE.

In the counterpoint essay, Robert J. Safransky (Nova Southeastern University), another former principal, responds that the impact of the IDEA is that school officials unfairly cannot discipline students with disabilities to the same degree as their peers who are in regular educational settings. Rather, he posits that insofar as students with IEPs receive special discipline and exceptions to the rules, an approach that teaches them to disrespect authority, they should be held responsible for their own behavior. Safransky argues that students with special educational needs should be treated the same as all children, meaning that they must be made responsible for their own behavior so that they can benefit from their rights to FAPEs as delineated in the IDEA.

As you read these essays, ask yourself the following questions. First, which essay makes the stronger argument? In other words, does the IDEA create unfair disciplinary standards for students depending on whether they have disabilities or are the different procedures justified? Second, given your answer to the first question, would you modify the law, and if so, how?

Charles J. Russo
University of Dayton

POINT: Allan G. Osborne, Jr.
Principal (Retired), Snug Harbor Community School, Quincy, Massachusetts

The Individuals with Disabilities Education Act (IDEA) affords students with disabilities additional procedural protections when facing serious disciplinary sanctions. Yet, the IDEA did not originally create disciplinary standards for students with disabilities. In fact, the courts initially crafted procedural safeguards before Congress enacted later statutory changes that were put in place to prevent school officials from excluding students for misconduct that was caused by their disabilities. The IDEA was originally enacted in 1975 as the Education for All Handicapped Children Act, later reauthorized as the IDEA, to end the long history of exclusion of students with disabilities from educational systems. Unfortunately, many of the students who were excluded exhibited behaviors that were difficult for school personnel to handle. The IDEA's disciplinary procedures were developed so that school boards could not use disciplinary processes to avoid their legal responsibilities for educating students with disabilities.

Although the IDEA did not include disciplinary provisions before 1997, courts applied its general procedural protections to the disciplinary process. Essentially, early courts ruled that students with disabilities could not be deprived of their rights to receive free appropriate public education (FAPE) as a consequence of school discipline, particularly when the offending conduct was a manifestation of, or caused by, their disabilities. The courts did not prevent school authorities from disciplining students with special needs but required personnel to observe all of the IDEA's procedural protections before imposing sanctions that effectively deprived students of the FAPEs they were guaranteed. Insofar as this case law formed the basis for the disciplinary provisions that are now part of the IDEA, this point essay briefly reviews the early litigation as background for understanding why these procedures are fair to all students.

EARLY LITIGATION

In *Stuart v. Nappi* (1978), a federal trial court ruled that an expulsion was a change in educational placement that school personnel could not carry out unless they followed the IDEA's procedures. However, the court acknowledged that students with disabilities could be temporarily suspended or moved to more restrictive settings if educators complied with the act's procedures. The following year, another federal trial court added that administrators could not expel students with disabilities whose misconduct was caused by their disabilities (*Doe v. Koger*, 1979). In *S-1 v. Turlington* (1981), the Fifth Circuit broadened the manifestation of the disability doctrine, as it became known, pointing out that the determination of whether misconduct was a manifestation of a child's disability had to be made by a specialized and knowledgeable group of persons, essentially an individualized education program (IEP) team. Thus, the emerging case law indicated that students with disabilities could be suspended or transferred to more restrictive settings but could not be expelled for misbehaviors that were manifestations of their disabilities because expulsions would deprive them of a FAPE.

The Supreme Court weighed in on the issue in *Honig v. Doe* (1988), a dispute that began when school officials attempted to expel two special education students whose misconduct clearly was a manifestation of their disabilities. The Court held that students could not be expelled for misbehavior that was related to their disabilities. Further, the Court noted that Congress intentionally limited the power of school officials to exclude students with disabilities, even for disciplinary purposes, when it enacted the IDEA. Even so, the Court did not leave school officials without remedies because it allowed officials to suspend students with disabilities for as long as 10 days if the students posed immediate threats to the safety of others. The Court emphasized that during this 10-day "cooling off" period, educators had to try to reach agreements with parents for alternate, possibly more restrictive, placements for disruptive children. If parents adamantly refused to consent to changes in placements, the Court suggested that officials could seek judicial relief where, in appropriate cases, courts could issue temporary injunctions preventing dangerous students from attending school.

In the years following *Honig*, but before the enactment of the 1997 IDEA Amendments, courts continued to resolve disciplinary issues, making it clear that short-term suspensions were not changes in placement subject to the IDEA's procedural protections. At the request of school officials, courts granted injunctions allowing them to exclude dangerous or extremely disruptive students from regular classroom settings temporarily while they worked out other educational arrangements.

The 1997 and 2004 disciplinary amendments to the IDEA are arguably the most far-reaching changes to the statute since it was enacted. As noted, many of these provisions codified case law, and others clarified gray areas that remained. The net result is that the IDEA now contains comprehensive guidelines for school officials who deal with students with disabilities. The IDEA's major disciplinary provisions are outlined as follows.

IDEA'S DISCIPLINARY PROCEDURES

Functional Behavioral Assessments and Behavior Intervention Plans

The IDEA obligates school officials to conduct functional behavioral assessments (FBAs) and implement behavior intervention plans (BIPs), if they have not already done so, or review such assessments and plans that are already in place whenever they impose disciplinary sanctions that may result in changes in placements for students with disabilities (IDEA, 20 U.S.C. § 1415(k)(1)(D)(ii)). In this way, FBAs and BIPs are required when educators intend to impose actions such as suspensions of more than 10 days, expulsions, or transfers to interim alternative settings for as long as 45 days. One federal trial court explained that because the quality of a student's education is linked to the child's behavior, an effective evaluation should identify behavioral problems (*Harris v. District of Columbia*, 2008). The court posited that an FBA is essential to addressing a student's behavioral difficulties and plays an integral role in the development of an IEP.

Manifestation Determination

A key requirement of the IDEA is that school officials must determine whether misconduct results from a student's disability before changing the placement of a student with disabilities who violates school rules. This evaluation, which is made in conjunction with parents, is referred to as a manifestation determination. The 2004 IDEA amendments state that those making the manifestation determination must decide "if the conduct in question was caused by, or had a direct and substantial relationship to, the child's disability" or "if the conduct in question was the direct result of the local educational agency's failure to implement the IEP" (IDEA, 20 U.S.C. § 1415(k)(1)(E)(i)). If the answer to either of these inquires is "yes" then the misconduct must be considered to have been a manifestation of the children's disabilities. In making manifestation determinations, IEP teams must consider all relevant information in students' files, including their IEPs, teacher observations, and germane information provided by the parents. If teams decide that offending behaviors were not manifestations, the students may be disciplined in the same manner as classmates who do not have disabilities except that the delivery of a FAPE may not be terminated (IDEA, 20 U.S.C. § 1415(k)(1)(C), 20 U.S.C. § 1412(a)(1)(A)). In such a case, students may be expelled from their current educational settings but officials must offer alternative means of providing FAPEs when the misconduct is not a manifestation of their disabilities.

As expected, courts have been asked to settle disputes over the manifestation determination because parents do not always agree with the results. Overall, the judiciary has supported the actions of manifestation determination teams. In one case, a federal trial court agreed that a manifestation was not present for a student who sold marijuana at school, concluding that he understood the rules and that his actions were not compulsive (*Farrin v. Maine School Administrative District No. 59*, 2001). Similarly, the Fourth Circuit upheld a finding that a student's misconduct—persuading a peer to place a threatening note in a third student's computer file—was not a manifestation of his emotional disability (*AW ex rel. Wilson v. Fairfax County School Board*, 2004). The court observed that the student was aware of the consequences of his actions and even anticipated them by recruiting another student to place the note. More recently, another federal trial court held that the behavior of a student who was involved in an incident where he and peers drove by the school three times one afternoon in order to shoot paintballs at the building and vehicles in the parking lot was not a manifestation of his disabilities (*Fitzgerald v. Fairfax County School Board*, 2008). The court specifically credited the facts that the student planned the incident and that it took place over several hours. The court added that the IDEA's emphasis on parental involvement did not give parents the right to veto or block officials' ability to discipline their son.

Interim Alternative Placements

The IDEA gives school officials the explicit authority to transfer students with disabilities to appropriate interim alternative educational settings for as many as 45 school days, regardless of whether their infractions were manifestations of their disabilities, for violations involving weapons or drugs or infliction of serious bodily injury (IDEA, 20 U.S.C. § 1415(k)(1)(G)). Placements made under this section must allow students to progress in general education curricula and continue to receive their special education services (IDEA, 20 U.S.C. § 1415(k)(1)(D)(i)).

As in other areas, courts support school officials who make interim alternative placements as long as they follow all proper procedures. For example, one federal trial court maintained that school officials were justified in transferring a student who ripped the pants off of a female peer to an alternative educational program, recognizing that the behavior called for stern and aggressive remedial action (*Randy M. v. Texas City ISD*, 2000). In another case, the Eighth Circuit held that officials acted justifiably in repeatedly suspending a student with disabilities whose infractions included bringing a knife to school, fighting, and assaulting other students and staff (*M.M. ex rel. L.R. v. Special School District No. 1*, 2008). The court commented that when a student commits such egregious acts of misbehavior, school administrators have the authority to impose suspensions, particularly when they have no other options because the parents have rejected other alternatives.

Knowledge of a Disability

School officials must extend the IDEA's protections to students who have not been classified as having disabilities if they knew, or should have known, that students had disabilities before their misbehavior occurred (IDEA, 20 U.S.C. § 1415(k)(5)). The IDEA provides that educators have such knowledge when parents have expressed written concern that the students may require special education or made requests for evaluations, or school personnel specifically expressed concerns about the students' patterns of behavior.

Courts support parental contentions that educators knew their children had disabilities under the circumstances enumerated in the IDEA. In one such case, a federal trial court recognized that officials had knowledge that a student who vandalized a school bus had a disability because his parents expressed concern over his poor performance and had requested evaluations (*J.C. v. Regional School District No. 10*, 2000). Similarly, in another case parents of a student who was expelled successfully argued that educators knew that their daughter may have had a disability because she had failed all of her courses (*S.W. and Joanne W. v. Holbrook Public Schools*, 2002). Thus, when courts find sufficient evidence that school officials reasonably should have suspected that a child had a disability, but failed to evaluate the child as required by the IDEA, the statute's disciplinary provisions apply. In other words, school officials cannot ignore signs of a possible disability and then mount the defense that they were unaware of the child's disability.

Expedited Hearings and Court Injunctions

In *Honig*, the Supreme Court explained that school officials could seek court injunctions to exclude dangerous students with disabilities from general educational settings. Congress added another avenue in the form of an expedited due process hearing that grants hearing officers the authority to issue orders changing students' placements to interim alternative settings if school officials can show that the students pose a danger (IDEA, 20 U.S.C. § 1415(k)(3)). Congressional insertion of the expedited hearing provision in the IDEA does not replace the right of educators to go directly to courts to seek injunctions to exclude students they consider truly dangerous. Regardless of whether educators choose to seek change in placement orders from hearing officers or injunctions, they bear the burden of showing that such actions are necessary. Parents also have the right to seek expedited due process hearings when they disagree with decisions regarding placement for disciplinary purposes or manifestation determinations.

The IDEA does place some limitations on the authority of hearing officers. The IDEA basically gives hearing officers two options: to return students to their previous educational placements or transfer them to interim alternative educational settings for as many as 45 school days. Even though hearing officers have the power to fashion appropriate relief, they do not necessarily have the right to override the specific sanctions meted out by school administrators as long as personnel followed proper procedures and the disciplinary penalties do not deprive the students of FAPEs.

CONCLUSION

Students with disabilities are subject to the disciplinary process and the same rules as their peers when they misbehave. The IDEA entitles students with disabilities to a FAPE, so additional due process is required when disciplinary sanctions can cause substantial losses of educational opportunities. Unfortunately, because archaic attitudes still exist, absent these provisions, many students whose disabilities cause them to behave in an inappropriate manner would be excluded from schools as they were in the days before the IDEA was implemented.

The counterpoint essay suggests that students with disabilities cannot be disciplined to the same degree as other students. However, the IDEA allows educators to suspend, and even expel or transfer, students with disabilities to more restrictive settings as long as they follow proper procedures. Admittedly, those procedures add steps to the process, but they do not prevent officials from disciplining students with disabilities to the same extent as their peers and certainly do not, as the counterpoint essay suggests, exempt them from the rules. Unfortunately, absent the IDEA's disciplinary procedures, officials could use the disciplinary process to rid themselves of difficult-to-educate students while denying children with disabilities the FAPE they are entitled to by law.

It is important to differentiate between what the IDEA requires and what may be done by incompetent administrators. For example, the counterpoint essay describes a situation where students with disabilities are essentially wreaking havoc in a regular classroom by moving about the room, screaming, yelling, and refusing to obey the teacher. The IDEA does not in any way condone such behavior, and no court has ever ordered a school to put up with such actions. If situations such as this occurred, it is because administrators, and teachers, failed to take proper actions to rectify them. The IDEA allows officials to remove students who are disruptive or dangerous and place them in more restrictive, and more appropriate, environments. The counterpoint essay raised the question: "Why should a school teacher or administrator not fairly and equitably enforce the student code of conduct for all students including students with disabilities when they break the rules?" The answer is that nothing in the IDEA prevents school officials from fairly and equitably enforcing the rules for all students, including students with disabilities, as long as they follow proper procedures. When educators fail to do so, it is either because they choose not to act or they completely misunderstand the IDEA and its requirements.

The counterpoint author also suggests that students with disabilities need to be responsible for their behavior. The reason why we need the IDEA's disciplinary provisions is that many students, because of their disabilities, are unable to control or be responsible for their behavior. The IDEA's procedures allow for students with disabilities whose behavior is not a manifestation of their disabilities to be disciplined in the same manner as their peers. In other words, they can be suspended and even expelled if their misconduct was not caused by or directly and substantially related to their disabilities. Further, the counterpoint essay misses the point that many students with disabilities are disruptive because they are in inappropriate environments or their needs are not properly being met. Again, the IDEA's disciplinary provisions are needed to make sure that these students are not excluded from schools because of the manifestations of their disabilities but, rather, are given the services they need. Once again, it is important to recognize the distinction between the requirements of the IDEA and the actions of incompetent administrators who fail to do what is required.

The disciplinary sections of the IDEA, coupled with case law, strike an appropriate balance between the rights of students with disabilities to a FAPE and administrators' need to maintain safe, orderly school settings. Officials may take disciplinary actions against students with disabilities by following the IDEA's procedures. This balance allows administrators to discipline misbehaving students while safeguarding them from being deprived of educational opportunities for behavior that stems from their disabilities and over which they may not have control. As long as school personnel follow all procedures and make responsible decisions, they will be successful if litigation ensues.

In sum, it is important to recall that many students with disabilities exhibit inappropriate behaviors as a consequence of their impairments. In this respect, educators need to remember that an original meaning of the word *discipline* is "to teach." Thus, when students with disabilities exhibit offensive behaviors as manifestations of their disabilities, they need to be taught appropriate behaviors. Punitive measures are not always the appropriate response. Rather, when students with disabilities continuously misbehave, officials need to review and make adjustments to their programs to address the conduct. This is what Congress intended in passing the IDEA. Educators need to understand that all students have a right to an appropriate education, even those who may be difficult to teach.

COUNTERPOINT: Robert J. Safransky
Nova Southeastern University

Two early cases in federal trial courts, *Pennsylvania Association for Retarded Children v. Pennsylvania* (1972) and *Mills v. Board of Education of the District of Columbia* (1972) helped pave the way to the enactment of the Education for All Handicapped Children Act (EAHCA).

Signed into law in 1975 by President Gerald Ford, the EAHCA afforded explicit educational rights to students with disabilities and their parents. The EAHCA, revised and updated by Congress, is now known as the Individuals with Disabilities Education Act (IDEA). The IDEA was most recently revised in 2004, and its implementing regulations were promulgated in 2006.

Perhaps the most controversial elements in the IDEA, safeguards that were not present in the original version of the law, address the rights of students with disabilities who are subject to discipline for their misbehavior in schools. However, before discussing the implications of the revised IDEA and regulations for educators, this counterpoint essay must first review a Supreme Court case that affected students with special needs because it sought to clarify their rights when being subjected to discipline for breaking school codes of conduct.

In its only case on point, *Honig v. Doe* (1988), the Supreme Court ruled that students with disabilities could not be suspended from school for more than 10 days if their behavior was related to their disabilities. The *Honig* Court certainly took steps to protect the rights of students with disabilities. Yet, the Court's failure to address and resolve all of the legal issues surrounding the steps that educators must follow in disciplining students with disabilities led to additional litigation and eventual modifications in the IDEA. This counterpoint essay contends that in light of *Honig* and subsequent modifications to the IDEA and its regulations in 1997 and 2004, students have learned that they can break school rules and not be punished for their actions because of their disabilities.

Almost needless to say, *Honig* and the disciplinary provisions in the IDEA and its regulations have handcuffed school officials, thereby making discipline of students with disabilities a contentious, and more difficult than necessary, issue. Accordingly, this counterpoint essay disagrees sharply with the point essay and maintains that the implementation of *Honig*, coupled with the 1997 and 2004 revisions of the IDEA, and its implementing regulations relating to the discipline of students with disabilities have contributed to a breakdown of respect for law in U.S. society. The remainder of this counterpoint essay, then, explicates its position that because these provisions simply do not treat all children fairly insofar as they afford students with disabilities with rights that their peers simply lack, the IDEA should be amended to remove these special protections.

THE IDEA GENERALLY

According to the IDEA and its regulations, children with disabilities are entitled to a free appropriate public education (FAPE) in the least restrictive environment. At the same time, the IDEA provides students and their parents with a wide array of additional substantive and procedural due process rights that children in regular educational placements do not receive. There are a variety of possible placements ranging from the goal of full inclusion in general education programs to self-contained placements in a special education setting to being served in residential facilities, all of which are provided at public expense.

Placing students with disabilities in regular educational environments has led to difficult situations wherein teachers must instruct their regular classes while trying to deal with children who will not or cannot restrain their behavior. These children exhibit misbehavior in a variety of ways such as by displaying their tempers, screaming, yelling, moving about the rooms, and refusing to obey any and all commands of the teachers or the teacher aides. In these circumstances, the rights of children with disabilities are raised higher than those of their regular education peers in classrooms who cannot learn when classmates with disabilities cannot or will not control their outbursts, and teachers must stop teaching as they attempt to restore order. When this occurs, it seems that initial evaluations of individualized education programs (IEPs) that teams developed to place these children in regular classrooms were in error. If IEP teams and schools follow the law, there could be changes in placement of these students with disabilities who misbehave.

These situations are exacerbated because many students with disabilities know that school officials cannot discipline them to the same degree as their peers in regular education. Thus, some students with disabilities flaunt their misbehaviors by telling administrators or teachers that they cannot be disciplined for their actions in the same manner as their peers in regular education. This attitude can easily spread from one student to the next and causes increased disciplinary problems for teachers.

DISCIPLINE UNDER THE IDEA

Insofar as this material was covered in depth in the point essay, this counterpoint essay finds it unnecessary to engage in a detailed analysis of the IDEA's discipline provisions because there is little dispute over the text of the law itself. Even so, this counterpoint essay reviews key elements of the IDEA that are relevant to its position. Moreover, since both essays have adopted significantly different positions on whether the provision of additional rights for students with disabilities is fair to all children, this counterpoint essay continues to argue that the IDEA should be revised to make it more equitable for all children.

Somehow, the members of Congress and the authors of the IDEA's newest regulations heard the concerns of teachers, administrators, regular education students, and others whose learning environments were disrupted by the inappropriate behavior of their peers with disabilities. As a result, the IDEA and its regulations have been revised to afford school officials more control over the disruptive behavior of students with disabilities in school settings. Even so, these changes have not gone far enough and the regulations as they currently stand still leave school administrators hamstrung.

When the behavior of a student with disabilities impedes that child's learning or that of others, IEP teams must consider the use of positive behavior interventions and supports and other strategies to address the behavior (34 C.F.R. § 300.324(a)(2)(i)). Additionally, IEP teams may address the behavior through annual goals in IEPs (34 C.F.R. § 300.320(a)(2)(i)). IEPs may include modifications in the programs of students, support for their teachers, and related services necessary to achieve those behavioral goals (34 C.F.R. § 300.320(a)(4)). If children need behavior intervention plans (BIPs) to improve their learning and socialization skills, the BIP can be included in their IEPs and aligned with the goals of the latter.

Pursuant to the IDEA, educational officials must follow specific guidelines in considering whether misconduct is related to the disabilities of students (IDEA, 20 U.S.C.A. § 1415(k)). Still, educators can regulate the inappropriate behavior of the students with disabilities by using specific procedures to subject them to the IDEA's discipline provisions.

If it is unclear whether the actions of students with disabilities are manifestations of their disabilities, then school officials must convene IEP teams, including their parents, to evaluate whether, on "case-by-case determinations" misconduct is related to their disabilities. The IDEA defines manifestations as conduct that was caused by or had a direct and substantial relationship to the disabilities of students or was the direct result of the failure of school officials to implement IEPs properly (IDEA, 20 U.S.C. § 1415(k)). In reviewing the appropriateness of placements, IEP teams must apply the same standards that they used in prospectively evaluating whether proposed placements were appropriate.

In the event that IEP teams interpret misconduct as either manifestations of students' disabilities or as the result of improperly implemented IEPs, children may not be expelled or suspended for more than 10 days and school officials must reconsider their current placements. In making manifestation determinations, IEP teams must consider all relevant information, including evaluations and diagnostic results as well as student observations (IDEA, 20 U.S.C.A. § 1415(k)).

At the same time, officials must conduct functional behavioral assessments (FBAs) and implement BIPs, if they have not already done so, or review such assessments and plans that are already in place whenever they impose disciplinary sanctions that may result in changes in placements for students with disabilities (IDEA, 20 U.S.C. § 1415(k)(1)(D)(ii)). Thus, FBAs and BIPs are required when educators intend to impose actions such as suspensions of more than 10 days, expulsions, or transfers to interim alternative settings for as long as 45 days. In doing so, educational leaders must convene IEP meetings to evaluate whether the misbehaviors of students were manifestations of their disabilities.

If IEP teams decide that the misbehaviors of students with disabilities are not manifestations of their disabilities, then children may be suspended or disciplined in the same manner as their peers in regular education by following through in applying the appropriate punishments under their school codes of conduct. Yet, in an area that leads to inequitable results, the IDEA addresses whether school officials can discontinue services for children who are properly expelled for misconduct that is not disability-related. In codifying a federal policy that directed officials to provide services for a student who was excluded for misbehavior that was not disability-related, the IDEA essentially obviated a case from Virginia wherein the Fourth Circuit rejected the argument that would have allowed for a complete cessation of services (*Commonwealth of Virginia, Department of Education v. Riley*, 1997).

Regardless of whether misbehaviors are related to their disabilities, the IDEA now requires school officials to provide appropriate educational placements for all children with disabilities, including those who have been expelled from school (IDEA, 20 U.S.C.A. §§ 1412(a)(1)(A), 1415(k)(1)(D) (i)). In other words, even if students are expelled for disciplinary infractions that are unrelated to their disabilities, they must be provided with services that allow them to progress toward achieving their IEP goals (34 C.F.R. § 300.530(d)(i)), typically in the form of homebound instruction for 5 hours per week. Even conceding, for the sake of argument, that students with disabilities may not have engaged in misbehaviors intentionally, it is difficult at best to try to argue that such an approach treats all children fairly.

Another inequity that the point essay seems to gloss over is that IDEA has since clarified the status of students who misbehaved, were not yet assessed for special education, but claimed to have been covered by the IDEA. As reflected by at least one case (*J.C. v. Regional School District No. 10*, 2000, 2002), the IDEA directs school officials to apply the law's protections to students if they knew that children were disabled before they misbehaved (IDEA, 20 U.S.C.A. § 1415(k)(8)). Again, how this is fair or equitable remains to be seen.

Another issue that needs to be kept in mind is that the IDEA requires states, through local school boards, to provide a FAPE for students with disabilities through the age of 21 if need be, essentially until the day before they reach their 22nd birthday. Yet, as they go through school, all students, including those with disabilities, must have their parents agree to and sign their IEPs until they reach the age of 18, at which time they are considered to be adult and have the appropriate privileges and responsibilities. This issue can arise when students with disabilities leave school, regardless of the age. Put another way, what happens when these former students with disabilities misbehave after they leave the cozy confines of their schools? Does law enforcement overlook their breaking of the law? It does not seem that it does.

As a reflection of this reality, the discipline provisions in the IDEA do not prohibit school officials from reporting student crimes to the proper authorities or impeding law enforcement and judicial authorities from carrying out their duties (IDEA, 20 U.S.C.A. § 1415(k)(6)(A). Under this provision, if officials do report crimes, they must make copies of students' special education and disciplinary records available to appropriate authorities (IDEA, 20 U.S.C.A. § 1415(k)(6)(B). Consequently, requiring students with disabilities to live up to the same rules as their peers while in school may save them from harsh realities once they complete their FAPEs.

AN UNANSWERED QUESTION

A question that has not been answered is why teachers or administrators should be unable to enforce student codes of conduct fairly and equitably for all children, including those with disabilities when they break the rules. Why do students and parents want to use every stratagem available to avoid complying with codes of conduct and use the fact that they have IEPs and are in special education placements as defenses? When considering the actions of students with disabilities who are entitled to apply these special discipline deals, why have they not improved their behavior? Somehow, all of the concern for students with disabilities to be included fully in regular classes where they can associate with peers who are not disabled does not follow them when they are sent to the assistant principal's office for discipline in that they cannot be subject to the same disciplinary rules as others.

If anything, administrators must afford students with disabilities additional protections in the form of special discipline because they have disabilities or other conditions that cause them to act out in classes or in response to requests from teachers to modify their behavior. After all, they are students who must be given an exception to the rules. It might be their behavior and scofflaw attitudes that have led to the breakdown of discipline in public schools across this country. In a particular application, educational leaders, not to mention parents, in many urban school districts are concerned about their rising discipline rates in major categories of disrespect, assault, battery, and disruption of the learning environment. Perhaps these rates would go down if there were uniform codes of conduct that were applied fairly and equitably to all students, including those with special educational need.

RESPONSE TO POINT ESSAY

The concluding paragraph of the point essay is a perfect summation of its entire argument because it claims that it is not the behavior of students that needs to be corrected. Rather, the point essay asserts that it is the responsibility of school officials who need "to review and make adjustments to their programs to address the conduct." Nowhere in the point essay is there any word about responsibility of students to change their behaviors so that they can benefit from their right to a FAPE. The point essay also fails to speak about IEPs not being carried out or not making positive changes in the behavior of students with disabilities. Further, the point essay does not make any mention of the fact that the misbehavior of the students with disabilities may well deprive their peers of their right to an education.

It is interesting that the point author states, "An original meaning of the word *discipline* is 'to teach.'" At no time and no place did the author mention that students with disabilities would respond appropriately to any of the accommodations made by their IEP teams. Why do students with disabilities have rights but no responsibilities to respond to their teacher and to respect the rights of their peers in learning environments? Why does the point essay find so many court cases to substantiate the rights of students with disabilities but makes no mention of the responsibility of students to respond to the learning programs? It seems that for too many, it is always the fault of teachers, schools, or IEP teams that students are not responsible for their behavior because of misdiagnosis, or their misbehavior is the result of their disabilities, over which they have no control.

The other question is this: How will students with disabilities respond to corrective actions when they leave the sheltered environs of their public schools and their right to a FAPE? If legislators, educators, and others truly care about the long-term well-being of students with disabilities, then they will work to support changes in the IDEA requiring that these children be subject to the same disciplinary sanctions as their peers, especially when their actions are not related to their disabilities. The failure to make such modifications in the IDEA and its regulations is likely to have harmful effects on students with disabilities when they learn the hard way that they are no longer subjected to privileged treatment once they leave school. To adopt any other position is simply not consistent with the U.S. notion of justice and fairness under the law for all students.

FURTHER READINGS AND RESOURCES

Daniel, P. T. K. (2001). Discipline and the IDEA reauthorization: The need to resolve inconsistencies. *Education Law Reporter, 142,* 591–607.

Dayton, J. (2002). Special education discipline law. *Education Law Reporter, 163,* 17–35.

Osborne, A. G., & Russo, C. J. (2007). *Special education and the law: A guide for practitioners* (2nd ed.). Thousand Oaks, CA: Corwin.

Osborne, A. G., & Russo, C. J. (2009). *Discipline in special education.* Thousand Oaks, CA: Corwin.

Zirkel, P. A. (2007). "Stay-put" under the discipline provisions: What is new? *Education Law Reporter, 214,* 467–471.

Zirkel, P. A. (2008). Discipline of students with disabilities: A judicial update. *Education Law Reporter, 235,* 1–10.

Court Cases and Statutes

AW ex rel. Wilson v. Fairfax County School Board, 372 F.3d 674 (4th Cir. 2004).

Board of Education of Hendrick Hudson Central School District v. Rowley, 458 U.S. 176 (1982).

Code of Federal Regulations, as cited.

Commonwealth of Virginia, Department of Education v. Riley, 106 F.3d 559 (4th Cir. 1997).

Doe v. Koger, 480 F. Supp. 225 (N.D. Ind. 1979).

Education for All Handicapped Children Act of 1975, 20 U.S.C. § 1401 *et seq.*

Farrin v. Maine School Administrative District No. 59, 165 F. Supp. 2d 37 (D. Me. 2001).

Fitzgerald v. Fairfax County School Board, 556 F. Supp. 2d 543 (E.D. Va. 2008).

Harris v. District of Columbia, 561 F. Supp. 2d 63 (D.D.C. 2008).

Honig v. Doe, 484 U.S. 305 (1988).

Individuals with Disabilities Education Act, 20 U.S.C. §§ 1400 *et seq.*

J.C. v. Regional School District No. 10, 115 F. Supp. 2d 297 (D. Conn. 2000), *reversed and remanded on other grounds*, 278 F.3d 119 (2d Cir. 2002).

Mills v. Board of Education of the District of Columbia, 348 F. Supp. 866 (D.D.C. 1972).

M.M. ex rel. L.R. v. Special School District No. 1, 512 F.3d 455 (8th Cir. 2008).

Pennsylvania Association for Retarded Children v. Pennsylvania, 334 F. Supp. 1257 (E.D. Pa., 1971), 343 F. Supp. 279 (E.D. Pa. 1972).

Randy M. v. Texas City ISD, 93 F. Supp. 2d 1310 (S.D. Tex. 2000).

S-1 v. Turlington, 635 F.2d 342 (5th Cir. 1981).

Stuart v. Nappi, 443 F. Supp. 1235 (D. Conn. 1978).

S.W. and Joanne W. v. Holbrook Public Schools, 221 F. Supp.2d 222 (D. Mass. 2002).

Are school boards adequately meeting the IDEA's requirement of providing a free appropriate public education for all students with disabilities?

POINT: Timothy E. Morse, *University of Southern Mississippi Gulf Coast*

COUNTERPOINT: Margie W. Crowe, *University of Southern Mississippi*

OVERVIEW

Before the passage in 1975 of the Education for All Handicapped Children Act, now known as the Individuals with Disabilities Education Act (IDEA), students with disabilities were routinely excluded from public schools or were denied educations appropriate to their needs. The rights of students with disabilities dramatically changed for the better as a result of early court decisions mandating that they be given equal educational opportunities. Two of those cases, *Pennsylvania Association for Retarded Children v. Pennsylvania* (1972) and *Mills v. Board of Education of the District of Columbia* (1972), provided a backdrop for the passage of the federal special education legislation by essentially ordering local school boards to provide students with disabilities with appropriate educational services. Even so, providing the free appropriate public education (FAPE) mandated by the IDEA is increasingly complicated and continues to serve as a source of much litigation.

The IDEA requires states and, by delegation, local school boards to provide students with disabilities with a FAPE, consisting of needed special education and related services. The IDEA defines students with disabilities as those who have at least one of any number of identified impairments and who need special education and related services because of their conditions. However, since the IDEA does not establish substantive standards by which the adequacy of services can be measured, it has been left to state legislatures and courts to set the benchmarks. The IDEA requires that school boards provide students with disabilities specially designed instruction in conformance with their individualized education programs (IEPs). The Supreme Court, in its first case interpreting the IDEA, *Board of Education of Hendrick Hudson Central School District v. Rowley* (1982), ruled that students with disabilities are entitled to personalized instruction with support services sufficient to permit them to benefit from the education they receive. Even though the Supreme Court cautioned lower courts not to impose their views of preferable educational methods on school personnel, hearing officers and judges are continuously asked to determine what level of services is required to meet the IDEA's minimum standards.

The IDEA's regulations oblige school boards to offer a "continuum of alternative placements" to meet the needs of students with disabilities for special education and related services (Assistance to the States for the Education of Children With Disabilities, 34 C.F.R. § 300.115). This continuum ought to range from placements in general education to private residential facilities while including homebound services. Even so, the placements selected for all students must be in the least restrictive environment (LRE) for each child and removal from general education can occur only to the extent necessary to provide special education and related services.

Under the IDEA, all placements must be made at public expense and must meet state educational standards. IEP teams, consisting of school personnel and parents, are required to review all placements at least annually and make revisions when necessary. In *Rowley*, the Supreme Court maintained that an appropriate education is one that is developed in compliance with the IDEA's procedures and is reasonably calculated to enable the child to receive educational benefits. Although states are directed to adopt policies and procedures consistent with the IDEA, they have the option of providing greater benefits than those outlined in the federal statute. When states do establish higher standards, courts consider those standards when judging the appropriateness of challenged IEPs.

The debate in this chapter centers on the inclusion movement flowing out of the IDEA. During the past 2 decades, as noted by the point and counterpoint authors, courts have ordered school boards to educate students with disabilities, even those with severe disabilities, in settings alongside their peers. The courts have agreed that placements in general education should be the setting of choice and that school boards are required to provide whatever supplementary aids and services are required to make the placements successful. In this respect, courts have allowed the removal of students with disabilities from general education environments only when school boards have shown that children could not be educated in such settings even with significant accommodations and a full array of supplemental aids and services.

In the point essay, Timothy E. Morse, University of Southern Mississippi Gulf Coast, suggests that school officials need to use the continuum of placements that the IDEA requires school boards to offer to provide an appropriate education. He asserts that in the current era of inclusion—the philosophy whereby students with disabilities are educated alongside their peers who are not disabled—pullout programs are still very much needed, particularly for students whose disabilities are such that they cannot appropriately be educated in the mainstream. He points out that using pullout programs, when necessary, is supported by both the IDEA and case law. Thus, Morse makes the case that in many instances school boards are meeting the IDEA's requirement of providing a FAPE in the least restrictive environment even when students are placed in pullout programs.

The author of the counterpoint essay, Margie W. Crowe, University of Southern Mississippi, maintains that the question is not one of inclusion, but rather the degree and quality of inclusion. Noting that a general education classroom is the natural setting for students, she suggests that every effort must be made to provide students with disabilities with the services and instructional attention they need in that setting. Crowe agrees that there are reasons why students sometimes need to be removed from general education settings, but that this must be done only when it is in the best interests of the students. Thus, she concludes that pullout settings often are not the most effective setting for many students and that school boards are failing to meet the IDEA's requirements in all instances where pullout placements are used.

Insofar as most children with disabilities will benefit from some degree of interaction with their peers who do not have disabilities, in reading these essays one should think about the situations in which mainstreaming or inclusion is best for children and, just as importantly, when it is not. Readers also may want to consider situations in which it may be best to place students with disabilities in settings that provide them with increased opportunities for socialization even at the expense of academic benefit.

Allan G. Osborne, Jr.
Principal (Retired), Snug Harbor Community School,
Quincy, Massachusetts

POINT: Timothy E. Morse
University of Southern Mississippi Gulf Coast

The Individuals with Disabilities Education Act (IDEA), the federal statute addressing the provision of special education services for children with disabilities, most of whom attend public schools, directly deals with the issue of the location where these children are to be educated. In fact, some have argued that the primary intent of the IDEA—which was titled the Education for All Handicapped Children Act when first enacted in 1975—has been to provide students with disabilities the opportunity to access our nation's public education system while receiving meaningful benefit from the instruction presented therein.

On its passage, the IDEA unknowingly set into motion what has been referred to as the "integration to inclusion movement," whereby more than a million students with the most significant disabilities were, at first, integrated into the public school systems to which they were denied entry. These students were subsequently provided with opportunities to be integrated fully in general education classrooms alongside their same-age peers who were not disabled. Yet, this movement failed to abolish the concept of a continuum of alternative placements for special education students that was established through the IDEA's least restrictive environment (LRE) requirement. The LRE requirement consistently called for both general and special education placements to be made available to special education students.

Some have crafted a philosophical position, referred to as *inclusion*, that circumvents the IDEA's LRE requirement by calling for every special education student to be educated in a general education classroom. Yet, many valid reasons remain in support of a continuum of alternative placements that, in some instances, involves special education students being removed from general education classrooms and educated in segregated settings, namely pullout programs. These reasons include the validation of this continuum resulting from the process that is followed to craft the IDEA and its accompanying regulations, the inherent characteristics of some special education students' disabilities, guidance from case law, resource availability and deployment, perceived student competence and preference, the proliferation of nontraditional schooling options, nonschool community integration opportunities, and the evidence-based practice movement. Accordingly, this point essay enumerates and discusses these reasons in making the case that a range of placements must be made available to special education students to enable them to receive an appropriate education.

VALIDATION OF PULLOUT PROGRAMS VIA THE IDEA DEVELOPMENT PROCESS

Perhaps the strongest argument in favor of pullout programs for special education students is the legislative process that resulted in the IDEA, its LRE requirement and, later, the concept of a continuum of alternative placements for special education students. The IDEA's LRE requirement states that, to the maximum extent appropriate, children with disabilities must be educated in general education classrooms alongside their peers who are not disabled with the use of supplementary aids, services, and supports as necessary. Yet, this provision adds that when such placements are inappropriate for children, a range of special education options such as a continuum of alternative placements must be considered and made available. Hence, under the IDEA, general education classroom placements in neighborhood schools are to be considered the default placements for special education students. Even so, given valid reasons for doing so, these students could be educated in other special education placements.

Noteworthy with respect to the LRE requirement and all other central concepts in the IDEA is that every affected constituency, including parents of children with disabilities, school personnel, disability rights advocacy groups, and teacher unions, is afforded an opportunity to petition the legislators who write the law and the executive agencies that promulgate the regulations to include the content these constituencies believe should be included in implementing special education in schools. Given this circumstance, one can conclude that the product that results from the process is necessarily valid—a form of expert validity. Clearly, the consensus opinion is that pullout programs for special education students are needed.

CHARACTERISTICS OF STUDENTS WITH DISABILITIES

The reason for this consensus debatably rests on special education students' incredibly diverse needs arising from their various disabling conditions and the concomitant fact that every general education classroom cannot be configured to address meaningfully all of their needs. Put another way, the inherent nature of some disabling conditions requires the configuration of specialized settings where the students' needs can be addressed.

General education teachers focus their efforts on teaching core academic content, such as reading/language arts, mathematics, and science, that is emphasized on statewide assessments of student achievement in accordance with the No Child Left Behind Act (NCLB). Still, these teachers can readily include in their classrooms special education students whose goal is to master these curricula. Teachers in general education can, and do, make accommodations and modifications in their lessons while working with support specialists as needed, to enable certain special education students, particularly those with mild disabilities, to participate in them. However, these teachers are not able to address adequately the more divergent academic and unique nonacademic needs of other students who are more significantly disabled and are candidates for placements in this setting. In a number of instances, the inherent natures of some disabilities demand that educators rely on alternative settings to meet and adequately address the needs of students.

For example, both students who have been identified as mentally retarded and those diagnosed with autism demonstrate inherent needs to be taught numerous nonacademic tasks. By definition, persons who are mentally retarded exhibit significant deficits in their acquisition of adaptive behaviors, otherwise known as activities of daily living, such as grooming skills, toileting, and meal preparation. Core characteristics of autism include qualitative impairments in social interaction and communication skills. Hence, although these students do need to master as much of the academic content that comprises the general education curriculum as they can, the IDEA dictates that they also must be taught a relevant curriculum that includes the aforementioned nonacademic skills. Further, these skills must be taught in atypical settings such as kitchens or bathrooms that are specifically structured to account for students' underlying characteristics, such as unusual resistance to change, distractibility, and nonprint literacy skills.

GUIDANCE FROM CASE LAW

Case law, particularly the Fifth Circuit's decision in *Daniel R.R. v. State Board of Education* (1989), supports the use of pullout programs and provides guidance to school personnel for doing so. Not surprisingly, this guidance accounts for the issues that have been raised to this point. In *Daniel R.R.*, the Fifth Circuit established a two-part test to be used by courts and school personnel to determine whether the IDEA's LRE provision has been met in a given situation. The first part of the test asks whether education in the regular classroom, with supplementary aids and services, can be achieved satisfactorily. If not, and special education must be provided, the second part of the test asks whether the school has mainstreamed the child to the maximum extent appropriate.

In *Daniel R.R.*, the Fifth Circuit validated the use of pullout programs for some students in special education settings. Additionally, the court identified issues that school personnel must consider as they apply the two-part test, including the ability of students to grasp the general education curriculum, the nature and severity of their disabilities, their overall experience in general education settings, the effect that their presence would have on the functioning of general education classrooms, and the amount of exposure the special education students would have to children who were not disabled. The Third (*Oberti v. Board of Education of the Borough of Clementon School District*, 1993) and Ninth (*Sacramento City Unified School District Board of Education v. Rachel H.*, 1994) Circuits reached similar outcomes.

RESOURCE AVAILABILITY AND DEPLOYMENT

The inherent nature of some students' disabilities, which has been recognized in case law and was discussed at length previously, as well as the relatively small number of students with disabilities that are characterized as being significant, supports an additional argument in favor of pullout programs, namely that they allow for the consolidation of the specialized services. More specifically, students with significant disabilities require direct, intensive instruction throughout entire school days to be able to master, maintain, and generalize their curricular content. To ensure that they receive meaningful benefit from their special education services, every moment at school must be seen as a teachable moment. Further, as a result of these students' presenting needs, professionals from across disciplines such as speech-language pathologists, occupational therapists, and school psychologists need to coordinate their work. If only a small number of students across entire school districts warrant these services and are placed in general education classrooms that are spread across schools, they are unlikely to be able to receive needed specialized, intensive services.

PERCEIVED COMPETENCE AND STUDENT PREFERENCE

Ultimately, educating select special education students in pullout programs enables them to learn how to function in ways allowing them to be viewed as competent and able by others. Some argue that the mere act of placing special education students in segregated settings is problematic because they automatically are negatively stigmatized. Yet, an argument in favor of these placements is they disallow some special education students to be viewed negatively by their same-age peers who are not disabled when they demonstrate that they either cannot independently perform skills that are being taught in general education classrooms or else can perform content areas skills, but at much lower levels.

A related matter is the development of the self-esteem of some special education students who report that they are constantly humiliated in general education classrooms when they are required to exhibit their skill deficiencies in front of their peer groups. Pullout programs afford these students opportunities to work on appropriate instructional level skills in nonthreatening settings. Teachers can also configure important variables so that they enhance students' academic achievement. These variables include, but are not necessarily limited to, pupil to teacher ratios, instructional strategies, pacing of instruction, number of opportunities for active students responding with immediate feedback, and the use of attentional prompts. Consideration of variables such as these highlights the fact that the location where instruction is presented to special education students is only one of a multitude of variables that affect student achievement of the skills targeted for instruction.

PROLIFERATION OF NONTRADITIONAL SCHOOLS

When one acknowledges that the location where instruction is presented is only one of a number of instructional variables that must be considered for special education students to receive an appropriate education, one quickly becomes aware of the number of locations that are now available to educate all students in this country. In addition to traditional public schools are religious schools, charter schools, magnet schools, special day schools, residential facilities, and home schools. Hence, given the options available to the broader population, it is apparent that universal agreement does not exist with respect to a location where all students should be educated.

Particularly given the growing charter school movement, it is increasingly difficult to support the original argument in favor of the creation of a public school system that would serve, in part, as a mechanism for assimilating the various microcultures that exist within a multiethnic society like that of the United States. As traditional public schools are directed to place more emphasis on teaching core academic content, teachers in general education classrooms will have less time for teaching peripheral topics such as the academic and nonacademic skills some special education students need to learn or even the civics content that is intended to result in a more coherent, seamless society. This circumstance enhances arguments in favor of pullout programs in public schools for special education students.

NONSCHOOL COMMUNITY INTEGRATION OPPORTUNITIES

An examination of the role of public schools within all of society highlights that they are not the only venue where students with and without disabilities can learn to coexist. In other words, all children can be integrated in nonschool environments such as Sunday School, Little League athletic events, Boy and Girl Scouts, and various social clubs. When placed in this broader context, public schools can be viewed as one of a large number of locations in which all children can be taught how to interact as the mission of public schools can be more clearly defined, perhaps as the location where core academic content is emphasized for most students but nonacademic content is emphasized—as is appropriate—for others. Under these conditions, it is easier to make an argument in favor of pullout programs because there can be an acknowledgement that the critical issue of integration, and how to teach it, can be addressed in the numerous nonschool environments that are frequented by children. Since typical children spend just under 10% of their school-aged years attending school, a detailed examination of what they do during this time is arguably more important than where they spend their time in school settings.

EVIDENCE-BASED PRACTICE MOVEMENT

Finally, the evidence-based practice movement that is emerging in education as a result of calls for the use of scientifically based interventions via pertinent federal laws, such as the IDEA and NCLB Act, support the use of pullout programs. This movement, as applied to special education, refers to a three-part process in which peer-reviewed research, consumer preference, and ongoing data collection and analysis are considered for crafting an appropriate program for a special education student.

Considering the arguments that have been put forth above in favor of pullout programs, it is reasonable to think that, in some instances, the personnel who construct students' special education programs and follow the evidence-based practice process will conclude that children can only receive an appropriate education in a pullout program. Since limited research supports the effectiveness of an inclusion model for all students, the need for individualized education program teams to demonstrate that children with disabilities have received meaningful benefit from the special education services that they received while employing evidence-based practice will, logically, lead these teams to explore the use of a continuum of alternative placements and to employ them.

RESPONSE TO THE COUNTERPOINT ESSAY

Some statements in the counterpoint essay, such as that general education classrooms are the default placements for all special education students and a continuum of alternative placements is supported by legislation and case law, are factually correct. However, issues that were raised in the counterpoint essay need to be addressed to refine the argument in support of a continuum of alternative placements for special education students.

First, the evidence-based practice movement in special education runs counter to the claims that "Good teaching is good teaching," and there is no magic to specialized instruction for special education students. Recently, organizations such as the National Professional Development Center on Autism Spectrum Disorders have spent considerable time analyzing research to identify effective interventions for students with autism. One reason for this work is the realization that traditional instructional approaches used in many general education classrooms, with teachers presenting instruction primarily via verbal language to large groups, has not been effective with students with autism.

Second, the availability of resources is always a factor in addressing how and where school-based services are provided. Judges have ruled that, with respect to planning for and implementing special education programs for students, school boards can be somewhat justified in adopting utilitarian perspectives. Courts recognize that boards have finite amounts of resources at their disposal that inhibits their abilities to provide optimal programs. Arguably, because boards are required to ensure that special education students realize meaningful benefits from their individualized education programs (IEPs) rather than maximizing their potential is recognition that available resources drive service provision and placement decisions.

Third, just as race and disability are unalterable characteristics that cannot be used as bases for segregating students, a related arbitrary distinction is the concept of age-appropriate placements. Children master skills as a result of a host of instructional variables that have nothing to do with their chronological age, and a detailed examination of these variables should drive a student's placement decision. Further, if preparing students for the real world is a paramount concern, then the sooner they learn to interact with others not their age the better because, as adults, individuals are not bound to interact with same-age peers.

Fourth, although research has identified benefits some students with disabilities realize from a general education versus pullout placement, it does not support the contention that every student benefits similarly.

Finally, school personnel must distinguish between plans that look good on paper but are ineffective because of poor execution and plans that only look good on paper because they really cannot be executed. An interesting point to ponder is why plans for the use of resource rooms were crafted at all. Could it have been because the plan for educating all students in a general education classroom was ineffective, and not really viable?

CONCLUSION

The law of the land with respect to the placement of special education students always has, and still does, allow for the use of various general and special education classes—and with good reason. Given the widely varying academic and nonacademic needs of numerous special education students, it is not reasonable to expect general education teachers, even with additional supports, to cover the core academic curriculum along with material these students need to master. Thus, although the universal inclusion movement is not a realistic practice, it has, conceptually, led to a refinement of the thinking behind decisions that are made regarding the placement of special education students. As a result, the education of all students will be enhanced.

COUNTERPOINT: Margie W. Crowe
University of Southern Mississippi

One of the considerations basic to educational decisions for students is where instruction is to be delivered. For students qualifying under the Individuals with Disabilities Education Act (IDEA) for special education services, this means that their services must be delivered in the least restrictive environment (LRE). The LRE is determined to be the placement most like the general education setting in which students can best be served. The placement decision process often fails to consider or gives only surface consideration to the supplemental aids and services that must be provided as supports for students with disabilities. These decisions are often made for students, arbitrarily based on their disabilities rather than on careful consideration of what supplemental aids and services can support them in less restrictive settings.

The lack of careful and creative consideration often unintentionally and unnecessarily segregates students with disabilities. The situation gets progressively more complicated as students age and the discrepancies in academic, social, and behavioral performance increase because they are segregated. This may be the easy way out for schools officials, but is not in the best interests of students or even within the scope of the intent of the IDEA. This counterpoint essay maintains that this debate is not as much about inclusion as it is about the degree and quality of inclusion. It also posits that there are reasons why students sometimes need to be removed from general education settings, but only when it is in their best interests.

PLACEMENT DECISIONS DEFINED BY LAW

Before the mid-1970s, the primary settings for serving students with disabilities were self-contained classrooms. These settings were usually segregated as unseen classrooms somewhere down halls or in portable units outside of main buildings. These self-contained educational placements for students with disabilities provided for little interaction with general education classrooms or programs. The influence of the civil rights movement, federal and state legislation, litigation, and advocacy created a change to mainstreaming in the mid-1970s. Students went from special education rooms to general education classes during the day, thus allowing them dual citizenship in special education classrooms while attending general education for a time. The educational placements and instructional goals of students with disabilities were generally vague and undefined. The segregation was on a more limited scale and under greater scrutiny but, nonetheless, still there.

The U.S. Supreme Court held in *Brown v. Board of Education* (1954) that students cannot be segregated solely based on characteristics such as race. *Brown* became the focus of parent and advocacy groups in the name of students with disabilities in an attempt to secure appropriate educational services for children. The resulting litigation became the precursor for important legislation, primarily the Education for All Handicapped Children Act (EAHCA) in 1975 with many revisions resulting in what is now known as the IDEA.

The basic foundation of the legislation since the 1970s has been to individualize programs to meet the unique needs of students who, for reasons of their disabilities, need specialized help and support. As noted, it is not a question of inclusion or no inclusion in general education but rather the level or quality of inclusion.

The precept that general education classrooms are the natural settings for students is foundational but must be tempered by the needs of specific students. Otherwise, such placements can result in reverse discrimination.

School boards must make every effort to provide the services and instructional attention to students in the natural settings of general education classrooms. However, when necessary, and in compliance with the IDEA's concept of the continuum of placements for the least restrictive environment, there are reasons for students to leave general education classrooms. This is an accepted conclusion to stay in compliance with IDEA. It is the responsibility of educators to consider carefully, on an individual basis, how and when this should be done. It often becomes, in the light of day, a question of whether the separation from general education settings is the best for individual students or for beleaguered school staff members. The complexity of the actual determination of the amount of time students are included in classes is often defined by school variables such as workforce or other resources as well as, secondarily, parent and professional opinions. As a major tenet of the IDEA, LRE requires that students with disabilities be removed from general education settings only when it can be documented that they cannot benefit from general education.

To answer the questions swirling around mainstreaming for LRE compliance, the IDEA created a more individualized approach. Although mainstreaming involves only participation in the general education setting, the practice of inclusion places students in general education classrooms with specific goals that can be best met in that setting. Inclusion to the maximum extent is not just a reaction to legislation but also to litigation.

In *Daniel R.R. v. State Board of Education* (1989), the Fifth Circuit set forth the criteria for making responsible inclusion decisions. According to the court, educators and parents must evaluate whether students will make adequate progress in general educational settings even with appropriate supplementary aids and services before they can be removed to more segregated settings.

The Third Circuit, in *Oberti v. Board of Education of the Borough of Clementon School District* (1993), further supported and clarified placement issues by finding that placements in general education settings with supplementary aids and services must be first offered to students with disabilities before more restrictive or segregated settings can be considered. The Ninth Circuit reached a similar outcome in *Sacramento City Unified School District Board of Education v. Rachel H.* (1994). Inclusion, then, is, theoretically, based on the careful evaluation of the skills needed for students with disabilities to work in settings with peers who are not disabled or where it is breaking down academically and socially for them and teaching them in those placements. In other words, removal from general education settings is a last resort for students with disabilities.

THE PULLOUT APPROACH

Critics formed on both sides of the argument for the settings in which services would be delivered. Should students be served in inclusive settings or self-contained locations? Some advocated that separate settings for serving students with disabilities were advantageous, providing the necessary venues for service delivery by well-trained special educators creating settings wherein a variety of instructional models, curricula, and motivational strategies could be used with specific monitoring for unique progress and student growth.

A compromise seemed to form in the introduction of resource rooms. Resource rooms allowed students to spend parts of their days in general education settings with specialized needs being met by being "pulled out" for special education services in separate rooms in schools and delivered by special education professionals. Supporters believed that the resource room model allowed students to be more involved in the activities of peers who were not disabled while having the opportunity to participate more fully in school activities. Further, resource rooms, supporters thought, allowed instruction from more than one person which in turn, required a cross pollination of expertise between special education and general education professionals. Critics questioned the advisability of creating situations in which students experiencing difficulty learning were being required to learn from several teachers, which could be confusing or create instructional gaps. Some critics feared that pullout programs, though well-intended, caused disruptions in the scheduling and flow of general education classrooms, calling attention to the students who were pulled out, and often causing them to miss favorite activities in general education classrooms, therefore creating barriers.

Pullout programs, perhaps theoretically, provide intensive support for students in specific areas of need. This is, perhaps, a case of the common phrase "It looks better on paper." The practicality of resource rooms is a different matter. Commonly, pullout programs require resource room teachers to travel from room to room collecting students, which, in reality, results in loss of instructional time while allowing transition time ripe for misbehavior. The alternative is to dismiss students to go independently to resource room locations. Either way requires students who are most likely to experience behavioral issues with transition, to experience multiple transitions during the day. Students are required often to leave abruptly because the clock says it is time to go to the resource room regardless of what is happening in the classroom, which may mean leaving an interesting activity or a job unfinished. The flow of continuity is at risk for students who need the security of continuity the most. This leaving or being pulled out also calls attention to the fact that these students are different or special. Often, several times a day, depending on the needs of specific students, there is a time when they are required to obviously come and go from classrooms when all of their peers are staying.

On arrival in resource rooms, students are often placed with peers from other grades depending on their skill levels and the schedule of the schools. Working in isolated settings with students who may not be age-appropriate or whose behavioral needs may be quite different creates less than ideal situations. This may follow the letter of the law as far as LRE placements are concerned under the IDEA, but clearly is not in the best interests of students. In the cases of special education teachers responsible for multiple classrooms and even multiple grades, such an approach may become just another homogenized way to meet needs but in isolated situations. If resource room teachers are responsible for 12 to 15 students at a time, their situations depend on school routines. Scheduling the instruction is, thus, no longer individualized except in theory. This lack of individualization creates situations not originally intended or as they "looked like on paper."

GOOD INSTRUCTIONAL DELIVERY ACCORDING TO RESEARCH

There is no perfect educational setting for all students. If this were the case, there would be no need for legislation or litigation. Students would go to school in Stepford-like fashion. There is no magic to special education instructional strategies. Good teaching is good teaching. Ongoing and authentic assessment is necessary in every setting. Matching the needs of learners to the strategies and materials needed is not unique to special education classrooms. This is what good teachers do in any setting. Research-based and supported instruction occurs in classrooms daily. There are specialized needs of a few students with severe or unique characteristic requirements of their disabilities. Leaving these general classroom settings on limited bases for specific therapies or health requirements may be necessary, but even when required, such arrangements create segregating situations for students who may be most in need of peer acceptance. This is counterproductive and in some cases sets the stage for life-long social segregation. General education classrooms are the natural setting or the real world that special education is focused on preparing students to function within.

The resulting benefits of well-designed and carefully monitored inclusive settings are supported by research. Students with disabilities are successful academically in inclusive settings at least to the same degree as in resource or self-contained classrooms. Students with disabilities in inclusive settings manifest improved work habits, higher self-esteem, risk-taking and on-task behaviors. Academically, students with disabilities educated in responsible and well-designed inclusion settings often achieve at a higher level. Students with disabilities given appropriate supports, supplementary aids, and services in inclusive settings improve their social skills while developing larger numbers of and more significant peer friendships.

CONCLUSION AND RESPONSE TO THE POINT ESSAY

Effective service plans are as good only as the individualized design and implementation. Legislative mandates and litigation define educational planning as dependent on the carefully assessed needs of a student. The proliferation of self-contained and pullout programs largely results from quickly made or incompletely informed decisions. Once made, these decisions often set the course for the remainder of the school careers of students with disabilities. Pullout programs, though well intended and good on a theoretical basis, most often do not translate to effective settings in the harsh reality of many school environments. Inclusive settings are ripe with experiences available only under artificial conditions in segregated settings.

To assume that the LREs for students with severe disabilities require pullouts or self-contained classrooms for them to receive appropriate services is counterproductive and not the intent of IDEA. Legislation and case law have repeatedly supported LRE decisions in the general education setting. To assume that the presence of severe disabilities requires segregated placements is as far into the discriminating edge of the continuum of placement options required by IDEA as is refusing to allow all students with milder disabilities to have pullout services. Either argument is not LRE.

Beginning in early intervention, the best practice for infants and children, including those with disabilities, is to receive services in the "natural setting." For young students, that means services that are delivered in their homes, preschools, or day care settings. This does not magically change the minute these students enter school rooms. The natural setting for students with disabilities is with peers in classrooms, assemblies, pep rallies, and cafeterias *with appropriate supports.* The "natural setting" is not in a segregated classroom with adults no matter how skilled or well meaning they are.

It is hard to dispute the need for specialized therapies and services dictated by severe disabilities. However, this is simply not the argument. The LRE is about just that—the environment in which educators deliver these specialized therapies and services. Considering the natural environment that students, regardless of their disabilities, must function in outside of the walls of their schools requires a paradigm shift in preparing them for these environments. Most therapies that are well thought out, planned, and supported can be integrated into natural settings with peers. This is limited only by lack of administrative support, resources, and creative planning by educators working in conjunction with parents on the individualized education program teams of their children.

The IDEA requires that a great deal of effort and resources be spent in developing transitional plans for students as they exit school settings. Preparing students to leave school settings clearly cannot happen in short lengths of time. This preparation must be systematically and creatively done from the earliest stages. Why is it considered good practice to take children from natural settings so important in early intervention, transition them to the artificial settings of segregated classrooms only to transition these same students back to a natural setting? Engineers tell us that dams, houses, structures once built require much more expense and energy to alter after the fact. Educators do this daily in the decision making for students by using a template stamped "Severe Disability = Pullout." Unfortunately, often LRE becomes LRR (least restrictive resources) or ECS (easiest, cheapest setting) to the detriment of untold numbers of students with disabilities.

FURTHER READINGS AND RESOURCES

Brown, L., Schwarz, P., Udvari Solner, A., Frattura Kampschroer, E., Johnson, F., Jorgensen, J., et al. (1991). How much time should students with severe intellectual disabilities spend in regular education classrooms and elsewhere? *Journal of the Association for Persons With Severe Handicaps, 16*(1), 39–47.

Deno, E. (1994). Special education as developmental capital revisited: A quarter century appraisal of means versus ends. *The Journal of Special Education, 27*(4), 375–392.

Downing, J. E., & Eichinger, J. (2002). Educating students with diverse strengths and needs together. In J. E. Downing, *Including students with severe and multiple disabilities in typical classrooms: Practical strategies for teachers* (2nd ed., pp. 1–16). Baltimore: Paul H. Brookes.

Gargiulo, R., & Metcalf, D. (2010). *Teaching in today's inclusive classrooms: A universal design for learning approach.* Belmont, CA: Wadsworth.

Hallahan, D. K. (2009). *Exceptional learners: An introduction to special education* (11th ed.). Boston: Allyn & Bacon.

Kauffman, J. M., & Hallahan, D. P. (1995). *The illusion of full inclusion: A comprehensive critique of a special education bandwagon.* Austin, TX: PRO-ED.

Kavale, K., & Forness, S. (2000). History, rhetoric, and reality: Analysis of the inclusion debate. *Remedial and Special Education, 21*, 279–296.

Osborne, A. G., & Russo, C. J. (2007). *Special education and the law: A guide for practitioners* (2nd rev. ed.). Thousand Oaks, CA: Corwin.

Russo, C. J., & Osborne, A. G., Jr. (2008). *Essential concepts and school-based cases in special education law.* Thousand Oaks, CA: Corwin.

Salend, S., & Garrick Duhaney, L. (2007). Research related to inclusion and program effectiveness. In J. McLeskey (Ed.), *Reflections on inclusion: Classic articles that shaped our thinking* (pp. 127–159). Arlington, VA: Council for Exceptional Children.

Smith, T. P., Pollway, E., Patton, J., & Dowdy, C. (2004). *Teaching students with special needs in inclusive settings.* Upper Saddle River, NJ: Pearson.

Yell, M., Rogers, D., & Rogers, E. (1998). The legal history of special education: What a long, strange trip it's been! *Remedial and Special Education, 19*, 219–228.

Zigmond, N. (2003). Where should students with disabilities receive special education services? Is one place better than another? *The Journal of Special Education, 37*(3), 193–199.

Court Cases and Statutes

Assistance to the States for the Education of Children with Disabilities, 34 C.F.R. §§ 300.1–300.818 (2006).

Board of Education of Hendrick Hudson Central School District v. Rowley, 458 U.S. 176 (1982).

Brown v. Board of Education, 347 U.S. 483 (1954).

Daniel R.R. v. State Board of Education, 874 F.2d 1036 (5th Cir. 1989).

Education for All Handicapped Children Act of 1975, 20 U.S.C. § 1401 *et seq.* (1976).

Individuals with Disabilities Education Act, 20 U.S.C. §§ 1400 *et seq.* (2006) (formerly the Education for All Handicapped Children Act).

Mills v. Board of Education of the District of Columbia, 348 F. Supp. 866 (D.D.C. 1972).

No Child Left Behind Act of 2001, 20 U.S.C. §§ 6301 *et seq.* (2006).

Oberti v. Board of Education of the Borough of Clementon School District, 995 F.2d 1204 (3d Cir. 1993).

Pennsylvania Association for Retarded Children v. Pennsylvania, 334 F. Supp. 1257 (E.D. Pa., 1971), 343 F. Supp. 279 (E.D. Pa. 1972).

Sacramento City Unified School District Board of Education v. Rachel H., 14 F.3d 1398 (9th Cir. 1994).

Do current laws adequately protect the educational rights of homeless children?

POINT: Emily Richardson, *Indiana University*
COUNTERPOINT: Allison S. Fetter-Harrott, *Franklin College*

OVERVIEW

The U.S. Department of Education estimates that more than 800,000 students in the United States experience homelessness. Congress passed the McKinney-Vento Homeless Assistance Act in 1987 to address problems associated with homelessness. The McKinney Act, the first significant federal legislation to address homelessness, provides federal funds for a wide range of services for homeless individuals, including homeless shelter programs. Recognizing that states and local communities are in the best position to deal with issues related to homelessness, the act provides funds to assist them in meeting the needs of this population. To ensure coordination of efforts, the McKinney Act also established the Interagency Council on Homelessness, an independent entity within the executive branch of the U.S. government consisting of the heads of 15 federal agencies. States accepting grants under this legislation must appoint a homelessness coordinator to ensure the act's proper implementation and to establish policies and procedures consistent with the statute. Many states have also passed homelessness legislation of their own.

The McKinney Act, which has been reauthorized and amended several times since 1987, is a conditional funding statute, meaning that the federal government provides funds to states that accept the terms of the law. States are not required to implement the McKinney Act, however, if they choose not to accept the federal grants. Although the original legislation did not specifically address the educational needs of homeless children, Title VII of the act now specifically provides protection for homeless children regarding education.

Specifically, the McKinney Act mandates that states and, by designation school districts, must provide free transportation to and from school for homeless students. Under provisions of the statute, students may continue to attend the school they were enrolled in at the time they became homeless, regardless of the school district in which the family resides. This ensures that children may remain in their school of origin even if the family is not living in that school district. Recognizing that homeless families may not have all necessary documentation, the act further stipulates that schools must enroll children even if they cannot produce required items such as immunization records, previous school records, or proof of residence. Each school district within a state receiving federal grants under the statute must appoint a liaison to facilitate services for homeless students and to make sure that all school staff are aware of the rights and needs of homeless children.

The authors in this chapter debate the issue of whether current federal and state homelessness legislation adequately meets the needs of homeless students. In the point essay, Emily Richardson, Indiana University, argues that the current provisions of the McKinney Act are adequate, that further protections are unnecessary, and that school districts cannot afford to do more. After thoroughly reviewing the extensive provisions of the statute, Richardson surmises that the law adequately addresses important educational issues associated with mobility, such as school attendance. Further, she feels that the law gives schools the flexibility they need to determine what is best for their own students. Richardson also points out that the act's requirements for notifying parents of its provisions provides additional protections. Noting that the costs of implementing the McKinney Act are already expensive, she expresses concern that providing additional protections could take funding away from other necessary programs.

Allison S. Fetter-Harrott, Franklin College (Indiana), conversely, argues that the McKinney Act has not done enough to protect the interests of homeless children. First, she argues that it has not been fully implemented as intended. She also stresses that its provisions are not sufficient to meet the needs of preschool homeless children. Further, Fetter-Harrott expresses concern that there are few reliable mechanisms to make sure that schools are following the act's mandates. Though acknowledging that the McKinney Act is a good start for providing students with services, she contends that it has not been effective in meeting its own goals. The result, according to Fetter-Harrott, is that many homeless children have been left unserved.

Both of the essayists in this chapter provide compelling arguments for their respective positions that the McKinney Act is either sufficient or insufficient for meeting the educational needs of homeless children and youth. If one accepts the rationale that we can always do more for children, readers should consider whether the problem of homelessness should be an even greater priority than it is now. As with many programs, the answers are not easy. In reading these essays, you may wish to think about the following questions: In our current economic climate, can we afford to spend more on programs and services for children from homeless families? Conversely, can we afford not to? Is the McKinney Act sufficient to meet those needs? If so, is there a problem with the law's implementation? If additional legislation is needed, what should be included?

Allan G. Osborne, Jr.
Principal (Retired), Snug Harbor Community School,
Quincy, Massachusetts

POINT: Emily Richardson
Indiana University

H omeless children are particularly susceptible to academic, health, and social stress. With the recent rise in homelessness because of the economic crisis, it continues to be vital that schools support homeless children. The McKinney-Vento Homeless Assistance Act, which was originally enacted in 1987 and has been amended several times since, provides extensive benefits to homeless children. This point essay argues that the McKinney-Vento Act currently provides adequate protections for homeless children and that further protections are unnecessary and would be too expensive and arduous for school districts to implement.

PROTECTIONS OFFERED BY THE MCKINNEY-VENTO ACT

The McKinney-Vento Act offers adequate protections for homeless children in several ways. First, it defines *homelessness* broadly, encompassing situations that may not have traditionally been viewed as homelessness. Second, it eliminates some of the traditional barriers homeless children faced in the past when trying to enroll in school. Third, it provides a mechanism for students to attend former schools, ensuring that the negative effects of school mobility are minimized. Finally, it provides requirements for notice of the act's protections and processes to appeal school district decisions about placement.

Under the McKinney-Vento Act, homeless children are defined as those "individuals who lack a fixed, regular, and adequate nighttime residence" (42 U.S.C. § 11302(a)(1)). The act further lists examples of what constitutes homelessness for children. These examples include some typical views of what the term *homelessness* encompasses, such as children who are living in cars, shelters, public spaces (e.g., train stations), and private spaces not appropriate for residence (e.g., warehouses), but it also offers a broader view of homelessness. For example, children are considered homeless if they are living with friends or family because of an economic situation. Children are also considered homeless if they are staying in a campground, hotel, or trailer park because an alternative placement is unavailable. Additionally, children waiting for foster care placements are considered homeless. The statute further specifies that the children of migrant workers are not exempt from these definitions.

This broad definition of homelessness ensures protection for a large number of at-risk children. It recognizes that the negative effects of homelessness are not limited simply to those children who live in shelters or on the street;

instead, students who are living with an aunt or a best friend because their parent(s) lost a job or some other circumstance are also at risk of experiencing the negative academic and social effects of homelessness.

Additionally, the McKinney-Vento Act removes some of the traditional barriers to attending school that homeless children have experienced in the past. Because of the transient nature of being homeless, children may have little access to medical and school records. They may have moved multiple times without the benefit of the space or the time to bring important possessions to new living arrangements. The McKinney-Vento Act requires that children should be immediately enrolled in school, even if they do not have immunization, residence, or academic records. Immediate enrollment means full participation in all aspects of the academic program, including academic support, such as testing for disabilities or gifted and talented programs, and other extracurricular activities. After initial enrollment, the school must immediately work to obtain the child's previous school academic records and must refer the child to a liaison who can help with getting immunization and other important records (e.g., birth certificate, social security card).

Access to transportation may be another barrier to homeless students' attendance at school. Homeless students are usually low-income and so may not be able to afford their own transportation. Under the act, schools must provide transportation for homeless students, even if they do not typically provide transportation to the student body at large. Ensuring transportation is important because it allows for consistent school attendance and allows students to remain in their home school with their friends and familiar teachers.

Another barrier to academic success in the past was the segregation of homeless students. Under the act, schools may not segregate homeless children, even if the segregation has the purpose of advancing educational goals. For example, schools cannot provide regular classes to homeless children at a shelter. Instead, a school must enroll the student to attend the actual school. Additionally, schools must provide "services comparable to services offered to other students in the school" (42 U.S.C. § 11432(g)(4)). Homeless children should be allowed to enroll in vocational education and should receive other educational assistance for which they are eligible (e.g., special education services, Title I services).

Enabling homeless children to attend their school of origin is a large part of the McKinney-Vento Act. To ensure consistency in education, the act prefers to maintain school attendance at the school of origin to ensure that the child continues to have a stable school environment. The school of origin is either the school attended when the child first became homeless or the school the child most recently attended.

The determination of school setting is made by assessing the best interests of the child, which should be a "student-centered, individualized determination" (U.S. Department of Education, 2004, p. 14). Factors considered in this determination include the age of the child; the distance of the commute and its effect on the child; the child's safety; the duration of the homelessness; the need for additional services; and the amount of time remaining in the school year. However, the school of origin is presumed to be the appropriate placement unless the parents disagree or the school of origin is not a feasible option.

Notice that the issue of cost is not included in the best interest of the child determination. Theoretically, although the law provides that transportation services must be comparable to those provided to other students, if it is in the best interest of the child, the school district might need to provide transportation for longer distances, which could be quite costly. This occurrence, however, is outside of the norm. Usually, a school of origin may be in the next town or even across town. Schools in large cities may only have to provide certain public transport passes. The school of origin should work together with the child's local school to arrange transportation; if the schools cannot agree, the cost of the transportation should be shared equally.

Placement in the school of origin continues until the child no longer is homeless, allowing students to finish the academic year if this event occurs within it. Again, this provision is designed to limit the negative effects of school mobility.

The McKinney-Vento Act also provides some processes for homeless children and parents. First, schools are required to provide written notice of the act and its provisions at enrollment and twice yearly. This notice must explain the act in clear and explicit terms and be signed by the parents. The act also recommends that school districts should publicize rights at places where homeless people traditionally congregate, such as soup kitchens, food pantries, and shelters. Second, if parents do not agree with the school's determination of the school to be attended, parents may appeal. If the school does not place the student in the school of origin or the school disregards the parents' wishes, the school must provide written notice of its decision and explain the right to appeal. If parents wish to appeal the determination, the school liaison will hold a dispute resolution session. During the appeal, the student should be placed at the school of origin.

The funding mechanism for McKinney-Vento is through federal allocation. A yearly allotment is provided, and in 2009, additional funds were distributed as part of the American Recovery and Reinvestment Act. Each year, individual states receive at least $250,000 to implement the statute. This allotment depends on the estimated number of homeless children in the state. The funds are distributed to state educational agencies, which may use as much as 25% of the funds to cover their administrative costs. The remaining funds are distributed to the school districts that apply for grant funding. The statute gives clear examples of what uses are appropriate for these funds; however, it also offers local educational agencies flexibility to choose which services for homeless children will be most effective to implement. Suggestions in the statute include

1. tutoring or other educational services,

2. accelerating assessment of student needs (e.g., students with disabilities),

3. implementing professional development for teachers and staff,

4. referring students for medical needs,

5. defraying otherwise uncovered transportation costs,

6. providing early childhood education,

7. recruiting for attendance,

8. providing summer school and other mentoring activities,

9. paying fees for records, and

10. educating parents of homeless children about available resources. (McKinney-Vento Act, 42 U.S.C. § 11433(d))

Though none of these services is required by the McKinney-Vento Act, some schools, especially those with large homeless populations, benefit from having these grant-funded activities.

PROVIDING ADDITIONAL ASSISTANCE IS COST- AND TIME-PROHIBITIVE

As can be seen, the McKinney-Vento Act provides many protections for homeless youth. The blueprint that it provides is more than adequate to fully meet the needs of homeless children, and further regulation would be unwieldy and at the expense of other services.

The McKinney-Vento Act's school of origin requirement already addresses many of the negative issues that affect students who experience school mobility. Scholars have identified three ways in which school mobility hurts academic achievement and social and emotional well-being (Julianelle & Foscarinis, 2003). First, schools may have difficulty in recognizing the educational needs of students who change schools often. Students who are somewhat transient are harder to assess, and communication with parents is often harder to accomplish. Second, even if schools recognize a student's educational needs, school mobility often interferes with the school's ability to meet those needs. For example, students may move again before a full assessment is completed, and teachers and other staff may be reluctant to fully access students who they fear will move soon. Also, assessments, like testing for disabilities, often have a waiting list, which may further impede a student's assessment. Third, students who move often do not have the benefit of stable social relationship, having to repeatedly adjust to new schools and make new friends. Indeed, school procedures and rules vary, so students who change schools often may spend much of their time trying to learn the requirements of each school. As illustrated, school mobility affects children's education, and the requirements of the McKinney-Vento Act already address this important issue of school mobility.

Some may argue that schools should do more for homeless children, and schools would agree that working with homeless children is important. Schools, however, have access to increasingly scarce resources. States across the country are cutting funding to social service organizations, including schools, in part because of decreased state revenues. Additionally, schools may have decreased attendance, which results in lower revenues, because of urban flight and the increase of charter schools. To mandate any additional prescriptions without fully funding them would necessarily take funding away from another vital service that schools provide. Indeed, the requirements of the McKinney-Vento Act are already costly for schools, and these costs are often not covered by the federal allotment. For example, providing for individual transportation to a school of origin may cost thousands of dollars per year, especially if transportation is not normally provided or if the school of origin is far away. Ensuring additional rights for homeless children may cause a fiscal drain on already limited resources.

In addition to the scarcity of resources, another argument against providing additional rights to homeless children is the variance of needs by localities. Schools have different populations, abilities, and needs. Some schools may have only one or two homeless children, but others may have dozens. If the McKinney-Vento Act mandated additional services, such as tutoring to all homeless children or weekly counseling sessions, these additional rights might be effective only in some localities. In other localities, these rights may be entirely inefficient and ineffective because of increasing administrative burdens. For example, a small rural school mandated to provide tutoring for the one child classified as homeless in its district may not be using its resources efficiently, and the amount of administrative time that is spent in achieving that tutoring program may be great. Also, schools may not have the proper infrastructure to provide additional services for homeless students. A school that has only 1 counselor and 20 homeless students may not be able to provide weekly counseling sessions. One of the benefits of the McKinney-Vento Act's comprehensive blueprint is that beneficial activities and programs are suggested, not mandated. Schools can choose to implement the programs that best fit their students.

One of the requirements of the McKinney-Vento Act is that schools should refer homeless children for local social services. Advocates of additional rights for homeless children in schools often point out that homelessness is a severe and comprehensive issue that schools are uniquely situated to address. However, local social services may be better situated for serving some of the needs of some homeless children. For example, schools may not know how to provide temporary housing, clothing, or food; a local social service agency could aid in these tasks. Further, local social service agencies may have more extensive knowledge of the medical and psychological services that are available at a low cost to low income people.

Though some may argue that required test data should be disaggregated for homeless status, this too would be too burdensome on schools. Under NCLB, schools must disaggregate data for certain groups of students; however, these groups are likely to have a stable membership. For example, race is an inherent characteristic, and participation in special education is unlikely to dramatically change from year to year, so disaggregating data using these criteria is less difficult than with homelessness, which is a more fluid status. A student may be homeless for a few months, and those months may not be when a standardized test is actually given. Further, homeless students are likely to already be included in at least one disaggregated test data category, that of low income students.

CONCLUSION

The McKinney-Vento Act effectively meets the needs of homeless students, while allowing for flexibility for schools. This act defines homelessness broadly and removes traditional barriers to attending school for homeless children. It also limits school mobility for homeless children by allowing attendance in most cases at the school of origin. Finally, it provides some processes to inform parents and children of their rights under the law and to appeal school decisions. Additional rights would only burden already taxed schools, both financially and logistically.

COUNTERPOINT: Allison S. Fetter-Harrott
Franklin College

Years ago, working in a recreation program for children living in homeless shelters and other transitional housing in an urban center, this writer learned firsthand how "school" can be different for homeless kids. Children who lived in a homeless shelter described being taught in one big multigrade class in the gymnasium of the local public school. At some point, someone had explained to the children why they were relegated to this status. Kids in the shelter, they come and go, the children relayed. In a regular class, they are more work for the teacher because they are new. Sometimes, they are behind, too. If teachers invest effort into them, it had essentially no payoff, the children explained, because they would soon move on to another school, given the nature of their temporary housing status. For this reason, children of the shelter were educated in a one-room schoolhouse for homeless kids.

THE EDUCATIONAL TOLL OF HOMELESSNESS

Homelessness can have a lasting detrimental effect on the education—and therefore the future—of children who experience its challenges. Some of these challenges result from the impact of homelessness on school attendance. For example, many homeless students experience more absences because of lack of transportation or other stressors relating to housing insecurity. Nearly one-quarter of homeless children do not regularly attend school, and less than one fifth of homeless children are enrolled in early childhood programs (U.S. Department of Education, 2002).

Additionally, homeless persons often are highly mobile, moving from a friend's couch to a family member's guest room and so on, shuffled through a sometimes unpredictable shelter system, or often forced to move when a family can no longer afford housing. This mobility has an impact on children's school success. Mobility can have a disastrous effect on school attendance, can affect a child's access to materials or information needed to complete school work, and can make after-school hours a challenging time to complete homework. Given the variance in local curricula, children who change schools may find themselves dropped in the middle of a foreign classroom or lesson, and if this occurs regularly, children may develop a sense of futility and sadness regarding going to school or completing work. Unsurprisingly, then, the U.S. Department of Education has observed, "Literature on highly mobile students indicates that it can take 4 to 6 months for a student to recover academically after changing schools" (U.S. Department of Education, 2004, p. 14). One can imagine how ongoing mobility, a challenge faced by many homeless children, can have a seriously detrimental impact on their school learning. Perhaps for this reason, a 2004 collection of data on the performance of homeless students being served under the McKinney-Vento Act showed that less than half of homeless elementary school students who took assessments met or exceeded proficiency standards in either reading or math (U.S. Department of Education, 2006, p. 12). At the high school level, only about a quarter of those who took the assessments were proficient. Sadly, these figures, which reflect assessments only of students present to take them and who were already identified, may even *overestimate* the proportion of homeless children meeting proficiency levels because absent, unenrolled, or unidentified students are not included in the data.

Additionally, homeless children experience a range of high stressors at a greater rate than their peers do. For example, frequent moving and poverty can lead to significant challenges in maintaining teacher-student relationships and friendships, can increase anxiety, and can cause or exacerbate other emotional challenges (Jozefowicz-Simbeni & Israel, 2006). All in all, U.S. homeless children are more likely to have low attendance, to have lower grades, to have higher rates of disciplinary challenges, to experience educational disability, and to drop out of school altogether. These outcomes are often related to the challenges of mobility and the stresses of homelessness. It cannot be doubted, therefore, that homeless children are at significant educational risk.

THE GROWING PHENOMENON OF HOMELESSNESS

Additionally, homelessness is a significant problem for children in the United States. Approximately one million children experience homelessness in the United States every year, with 1 in 214 children residing in a homeless shelter (U.S. Department of Housing, 2010). Recent statistics suggest that the economic downturn has led to an increase in homelessness among children. Homeless families increased by 10,000, or nearly 7%, between 2007 and 2009 alone, and the length of family stays in shelters and transitional housing expanded during that period as well. That trend appears to be continuing as a more recent report indicates that between September 2009 and December 2010 there was a 9% increase in the number of families experiencing homelessness in 27 major cities (U.S. Conference of Mayors, 2010). Accordingly, given the prevalence of children facing the challenges of homelessness and the impact that these stressors can have on children's development, homelessness is not just a poverty issue, a housing issue, or a general social services issue. Homelessness is a school issue as well.

THE MCKINNEY-VENTO HOMELESS ASSISTANCE ACT OF 1987

So what is being done to encourage and support schools in providing needed supports for children facing the challenges of homelessness? The McKinney-Vento Homeless Assistance Act, first enacted in 1987, is a federal funding statute aimed at requiring state education agencies and local schools to provide certain supports for homeless and unaccompanied youth. The McKinney-Vento Act prohibits schools from discriminating against homeless children by segregating them into certain schools or programs. Additionally, the McKinney-Vento Act affirmatively requires schools to provide a range of services aimed at meeting the unique education needs of children experiencing homelessness. For children who are mobile because of housing insecurity, schools must provide transportation permitting those children to consistently attend a school of origin if requested by a parent. Additionally, when enrollment disputes arise, schools must immediately enroll students pending resolution of the dispute. Schools must admit children who are homeless with relaxed requirements on parents or guardians providing documentation such as proof of residence or immunizations. All districts must also employ McKinney-Vento liaisons who are delegated many important tasks under the act, including the duty to ensure that school officials identify eligible children and families and that families are notified of transportation and other services available to them in the school and the community.

The McKinney-Vento Act defines *homelessness* more broadly than some might conceptualize it. In addition to covering children living in shelters, the McKinney-Vento Act recognizes that homeless children additionally live in hotels, motels, campers, and cars; in public or private spaces not meant to be residences; in temporary situations awaiting foster care; and "doubled up" with family or friends, sharing inadequate housing. Homeless children protected by McKinney-Vento also include both those living with homeless parents and "unaccompanied" youth who have no caregiver.

HOW MCKINNEY-VENTO FALLS SHORT
Enforcement of McKinney-Vento

Lawmakers, school professionals, and other service providers widely accept that homeless students are vulnerable to low attendance and educational interference caused by mobility and other stresses of homelessness. McKinney-Vento is aimed at prohibiting discrimination against these students and requiring the provision of needed services, yet there is reason to think that the act is unenforced or underenforced in many locales. Many school officials simply are not aware of the act and its protections, which quite obviously makes them prone to failures in informing homeless youth and their families of their rights and to omissions in providing services. While there appear to have been some improvements in raising awareness about the McKinney-Vento Act in recent years largely because of the work of local liaisons, many school districts either do not have a local liaison, experience high turnover among liaisons, appoint liaisons who are already overburdened with other duties, or have liaisons who themselves are not aware of their duties under the act (Jozefowicz-Simbeni & Israel, 2006). Uninformed school personnel may unknowingly deny enrollment inappropriately, refuse to maintain a child's enrollment in a school of origin, or fail to offer transportation or other services that might have kept a child's school attendance more stable. As is evidenced by the earlier discussion regarding the effects of mobility on children's school progress, even one such omission may have a serious impact on a child's education.

There are relatively few reliable mechanisms for ensuring that schools meet the McKinney-Vento Act's directives. Although the act requires state coordinators to oversee implementation and provide technical assistance, which includes resolving disputes generally, it does not provide a clear framework giving parents and children recourse when a school fails to meet its duties under McKinney-Vento. Additionally, at least one court has recognized that the chief remedy for violation of the McKinney-Vento Act can be obtained not through an administrative hearing but instead through a lawsuit in federal court under Section 1983 of the Civil Rights Act of 1871 (*Holmes-Ramsey v. District of Columbia*, 2010). But given the effort, expense, and sophistication it can take to bring a suit to obtain such basics as stable school enrollment, transportation to school of origin, and the right to be free from segregation based on homeless status, it is perhaps unsurprising that many eligible parents cannot or do not make a federal case out of failures to live up to McKinney-Vento's promise. Of course, for many homeless parents, the school is a chief source of information about their children's rights under the McKinney-Vento Act. Where homeless parents are unaware as to these rights or are disempowered from pursuing them, such as by lacking access to counsel, lacking a phone or reliable mail receipt address, or by limited time for advocacy caused by busy work schedules, they may be in need of other methods for ensuring that schools comply with the McKinney-Vento Act. And for unaccompanied youth who have no parents or guardians to advocate for them, the challenges are perhaps even greater.

Identification of Homeless Students

Given ongoing challenges in training school officials on the features of the McKinney-Vento Act, the U.S. Department of Education has observed that challenges in identification of homeless students eligible for services under the act is a "persistent barrier" to its effective implementation (U.S. Department of Education, 2006). In addition to challenges presented by lack of information by school officials, many parents—who often look to the school for information on their children's rights—are uninformed or under-informed about the act and the potential benefits it can offer homeless students. Additionally, the stigma that often attaches to homelessness creates an additional barrier that McKinney-Vento has yet to overcome. Parents or children may be afraid or embarrassed to report their needs to the school. They may worry that reaching out for services under McKinney-Vento might lead to unwanted social service intervention into their private lives or fear that children will be removed from the family. If McKinney-Vento is ever to be effective in truly serving the highly needy homeless children it aims to protect, the statute must account for these inherent challenges in identification.

Services for Preschool Children

Perhaps McKinney-Vento's biggest failure, however, is how little it does to support the educational progress of preschool children. As the U.S. Department of Education has observed, "Over 40 percent of children living in homeless shelters are under the age of five, yet homeless preschool-aged children are greatly underrepresented in preschool programs" (U.S. Department of Education, 2006, p. 17). Although the act prohibits discrimination against preschool age children because of homelessness, it does not require that public agencies provide parents of early childhood students the same kind of stability and transportation services that K–12 students enjoy. Little progress has been observed in recent years in efforts to help young children facing homelessness gain stable access to early childhood education programs. Expansion of the act to provide such services to prekindergarten homeless children might well lead to better outcomes for them and their families.

In the areas of identification and provision of services to prekindergarten children, the McKinney-Vento Act might be best expanded in a manner modeled after the Individuals with Disabilities Education Act, which provides for early childhood services to eligible children and imposes on schools an affirmative duty to identify students who are entitled to a free appropriate public education under the provisions of the statute.

Test Scores

Schools are not currently required to focus on the test scores of homeless students as they must with other groups of at-risk students. One way of encouraging schools to better attend to the needs of educationally vulnerable homeless youth would be to require schools to disaggregate the test scores of such students in evaluating whether the school has made adequate yearly progress (AYP), an accountability measure required under the No Child Left Behind Act of 2001 (NCLB). At present, NCLB requires schools to calculate benchmark testing passage rates for all students and to disaggregate the scores of certain groups of students, such as students of color, students receiving special education services, and low income students generally, but it does not require disaggregation of the scores of homeless students. One aim of the disaggregation requirement of NCLB is to encourage schools to focus on the success of all children, including those who belong to groups that have historically been denied access to education or otherwise been academically vulnerable. Given that homeless students are at the low end of the poverty continuum and face unique challenges relating to discrimination and mobility, a true commitment to positive education outcomes for these youth would include disaggregation of their test scores, providing greater incentive for schools to focus on their achievement on equal footing with their peers. Disaggregation would provide data on the number of students and their achievement, revealing failures, if any, in both identification of homeless students and in educating them toward measurable progress.

CONCLUSION

Opponents of these additional mandates might argue that already burdened schools should not further be tasked with providing additional supports for homeless children. Of course, all recognize the ever-increasing fiscal pressures faced by public schools today. But the choice we face is not simply whether to fund services for homeless children at all. Rather, the choice we face is whether to support these children proactively in school or encounter even greater economic and human costs in failing to support them. If more than half of the nation's homeless students fail to meet benchmark proficiency in math and reading today, if they are at far greater risk of dropping out today, if they feel alienated from school and their peers because of the stresses of homelessness today, then what kind of future do we envision for our nation's homeless youth? Do we indeed wish to live in a society where childhood poverty is so strong an indicator of educational promise? Can we put a price tag on supports that might make the difference between dean's list and dropping out for students with the greatest need? Although the McKinney-Vento Act is a good start at providing our nation's homeless children and youth with necessary supports and services, it is not appropriately effective in accomplishing its goals. The act continues to be misunderstood or unknown to many school professionals, and the dearth of awareness has made the challenge of identification increasingly difficult to overcome. Even once identified, there is little clarity as to how to ensure that schools are indeed meeting their obligations to homeless students and their families. Without further action to encourage actual enforcement and broadening of McKinney-Vento's protections, many of our nation's homeless children will remain unseen and unserved.

FURTHER READINGS AND RESOURCES

Dworak-Fisher, S. (2009). Educational stability for students without homes: Realizing the promise of McKinney-Vento. *Clearinghouse Review, 42*, 542–550.

Indiana Department of Education. (2004, August). *Education for homeless children and youth program, Title VII-B of the McKinney-Vento Homeless Assistance Act, non-regulatory guidance.* Retrieved September 8, 2011, from http://www.doe.in.gov/alted/pdf/mckinney_nonreg_guidance.pdf

Jozefowicz-Simbeni, D. M. H., & Israel, N. (2006). Services to homeless students and families: The McKinney-Vento Act and its implications for school social work practice. *Children & Schools, 28*(1), 37–45.

Julianelle, P. F., & Foscarinis, M. (2003). Responding to the school mobility of children and youth experiencing homelessness: The McKinney-Vento Act and beyond. *Journal of Negro Education, 72*(1), 39–54.

U.S. Conference of Mayors. (2010). *Hunger and homelessness survey: A status report on hunger and homelessness in America's cities, a 27-city survey.* Retrieved from http://www.usmayors.org/pressreleases/uploads/2010_Hunger-Homelessness_Report-final%20Dec%2021%202010.pdf

U.S. Department of Education. (2004). *Education for homeless children and youth program.* Washington, DC: Author.

U.S. Department of Education. (2006). *Report to the President and Congress on the implementation of the education for homeless children and youth program under the McKinney-Vento Homeless Assistance Act.* Retrieved September 8, 2011, from http://www2.ed.gov/programs/homeless/rpt2006.doc

U.S. Department of Education. (n.d.). *Education for homeless children and youths grants for state and local activities.* Retrieved from http://www2.ed.gov/programs/homeless/index.html

U.S. Department of Education, Planning and Evaluation Service, Elementary and Secondary Education Division. (2002). *The education for homeless children and youth program: Learning to succeed* (Executive Summary, Doc. No. 2001-032). Washington, DC: Author.

U.S. Department of Housing and Urban Development, Office of Community Planning and Development. (2010). *The 2009 annual homeless assessment report to Congress.* Retrieved September 8, 2011, from http://www.hudhre.info/documents/5thHomele ssAssessmentReport.pdf

Wong, J. H., Thistle Elliott, L., Reed, S., Ross, W., McGuirk, P., Tallarita, L., et al. (2009). McKinney-Vento Homeless Assistance Act Subtitle B—Education for Homeless Children and Youths Program: Turning good law into effective education, 2008 update. *Georgetown Journal of Poverty Law and Policy, 16,* 53–113.

COURT CASES AND STATUTES

American Recovery and Reinvestment Act (ARRA) of 2009, Pub. L. 111-5, 123 Stat. 115.

Civil Rights Act of 1871, Section 1983, 42 U.S.C. § 1983 (2006).

Holmes-Ramsey v. District of Columbia, 747 F. Supp. 2d 32 (D.D.C. 2010).

Individuals with Disabilities Education Act, 20 U.S.C. §§ 1400 *et seq.*

McKinney-Vento Homeless Assistance Act, 42 U.S.C. § 11431 *et seq.*

No Child Left Behind Act of 2001, 20 U.S.C. §§ 6301 *et seq.*

Are the tests that the Supreme Court provided in dealing with peer-to-peer and teacher-on-student sexual harassment workable?

POINT: Stacey L. Edmonson, *Sam Houston State University*
COUNTERPOINT: Mark Littleton, *Tarleton State University*

OVERVIEW

For many years, when female students were harassed by their male peers or teachers in schools, the unacceptable behavior was often dismissed or ignored as the actions of "boys were just being boys." Faced with growing frustration over the sad state of affairs in schools, the Supreme Court finally entered the fray by expanding the reach of Title IX of the Education Amendments of 1972 in an attempt to put an end to sexual harassment in schools.

Initially enacted in 1972, Title IX was designed to ensure gender equity in intercollegiate sports. In its most relevant part, the law reads, "No person in the United States shall, on the basis of sex, be excluded from participation in, be denied the benefits of, or be subjected to discrimination under any education program or activity receiving Federal financial assistance."

A major impetus in the battle to eliminate sexual harassment in schools was a case from higher education, *Cannon v. University of Chicago* (1979). In

Cannon, the Supreme Court addressed whether a female who unsuccessfully applied to two private medical schools could challenge their actions under Title IX. The Court ruled that insofar as the medical schools were subject to Title IX because they received federal financial aid, they were liable for discrimination because the woman was denied admission because of her gender. The Court explained that the woman's suit could proceed because she was a member of the class that Title IX was designed to protect and the legislative history of the law evidenced the intent to permit a private cause of action, meaning that she could file suit in her own name rather than rely on a governmental agency to intervene on her behalf. The Court added that allowing the woman to file suit in her own name was consistent with the intent of Title IX because the federal government had a legitimate concern to eliminate discrimination based on gender. Even so, more than 10 years passed before the federal courts allowed students in K–12 settings to use Title IX in the fight to end sexual harassment in schools.

Beginning in 1992, the Supreme Court resolved three cases dealing with sexual harassment in school settings, the first two of which involved disputes wherein teachers engaged in inappropriate sexual misconduct with students. In *Franklin v. Gwinnett County Public Schools* (1992), the Court essentially extended *Cannon* in allowing a high school student in Georgia to file suit in her own name under Title IX against a school board after she was subjected to coercive sexual intercourse by a male teacher.

Six years later, in *Gebser v. Lago Vista Independent School District* (1998), the Justices clarified the conditions under which school boards could be liable for teacher-on-student sexual harassment. In *Gebser*, the Court declined to impose liability in a case where a male teacher engaged in sexual relations with a female student in Texas because no official with the authority to institute corrective measures received actual notice of the sexual misconduct and was not deliberately indifferent to it.

A year later, in *Davis v. Monroe County Board of Education* (1999), another case from Georgia, the Supreme Court devised standards to combat peer-to-peer sexual harassment in schools. In remanding the case for further consideration, the Court noted that boards that are recipients of federal aid cannot be liable for damages unless, at the outset, officials exercise substantial control over both harassers and the context in which the known harassment occurs. The Court added that boards "are properly held liable in damages only when they are deliberately indifferent to sexual harassment, of which they have actual knowledge, that is so severe, pervasive, and objectively offensive that it can be said to deprive the victims of access to the educational opportunities or benefits provided by the school" (p. 650).

Not surprisingly, the standard that emerged in these three cases has since been used in seemingly countless numbers of federal and state cases involving sexual harassment of students, no longer limited to females, by peers and teachers. Yet, litigation over sexual harassment in school continues at a brisk pace.

The essays in this chapter both rely largely on the same Supreme Court cases. Yet, the authors reach different outcomes on whether the judicial tests are adequate to eliminate sexual harassment in schools. If anything, the debates highlight, albeit indirectly, that although the Court has attempted to craft tests to be used in the different circumstances of teacher-on-student and peer-to-peer harassment, the Court has not been as helpful as it could have been during the past decade in helping define evolving standards of harassment.

In her point essay, Stacey L. Edmonson, Sam Houston State University, is convinced that the tests that the Court enunciated work effectively. She maintains that the tests work because they provide clear guidance that balances the need to protect boards from unnecessary liability with the need to protect students from harassment by peers or teachers when they are in school settings. Conversely, in the counterpoint essay, Mark Littleton, Tarleton State University, posits that the tests leave something to be desired. He argues that insofar as electronic media such as cell phones, texting, Facebook, MySpace, and YouTube that have been involved in many sexual harassment suits were either in their infancies or nonexistent when the Court ruled, educators need more guidance in dealing with the difficult issues that electronic media present.

As you read the two following essays, ask yourself the following questions: First, do you think that the tests that the Supreme Court has devised provide adequate guidance for school boards and officials in the fight to end sexual harassment in educational contexts, regardless of whether it is committed by peers or teachers? Second, given how prevalent electronic and social media are in schools, if you could modify the guidelines that the Court has offered, what would you add?

Charles J. Russo
University of Dayton

POINT: Stacey L. Edmonson
Sam Houston State University

Congress enacted two federal statutes to deter sexual harassment in educational settings: Title IX of the Education Amendments of 1972 and Title VII of the Civil Rights Act of 1964. Title VII claims generally involve employee-to-employee harassment in the workplace, while Title IX claims also include student-to-student and employee-to-student harassment issues. Title IX specifically protects students in K–12 settings from sexual harassment by their peers or by school board employees such as teachers and other educational personnel.

The Supreme Court defined statutory and judicial remedies in three major cases dealing with sexual harassment of students in school settings. But are the guidelines that the Supreme Court provides for dealing with peer-to-peer and teacher-on-student sexual harassment workable? In a word, yes. This point essay maintains that the tests work effectively even though the Court has placed responsibility for reporting harassment on students. The Court has provided guidance that protects school boards from frivolous or unsubstantiated harassment claims while protecting students by establishing standards under which school boards may be rendered liable when students are harassed at school by peers or educational employees.

SUPREME COURT PRECEDENT ON HARASSMENT

In dealing with litigation involving sexual harassment of students, the Supreme Court has handed down three relevant decisions relating to sexual harassment of students. The first two cases, *Franklin v. Gwinnett County Public Schools* (1992) and *Gebser v. Lago Vista Independent School District* (1998), dealt with sexual harassment of students by teachers. The third case, *Davis v. Monroe County Board of Education* (1999), concerned peer-to-peer sexual harassment.

In *Franklin*, the Supreme Court allowed a student in Georgia who was subjected to coercive sexual relations at the hands of a male teacher to proceed with a private right of action to recover damages for sexual harassment under Title IX. For the first time, the Court allowed a high school student to initiate litigation in her own name under Title IX rather than relying on a governmental agency to act on her behalf. Reversing earlier judgments in favor of the school board, the Court ruled that plaintiffs may seek damages that include both compensatory as well as punitive awards. However, in its analysis, the

Court did not address standards for liability for sexual harassment, a topic it would address in later litigation. Instead, the Court essentially adopted the position that because a statute without a remedy would have been ineffective, the claim could proceed.

In *Gebser* and *Davis*, the Supreme Court laid out specific tests by which school boards and educators can be liable for peer-to-peer and teacher-on-student sexual harassment. *Gebser* involved a male teacher who maintained a sexual relationship with a minor female student for about a year and a half. When the relationship was discovered, the teacher was arrested, and the board terminated his employment. The student and her mother unsuccessfully sued the school board. The Supreme Court affirmed the denial of the student's claim for damages in establishing the guideline of deliberate indifference, whereby school officials must have actual awareness of specific incidents of sexual harassment and choose not to take action or respond.

The *Gebser* Court firmly placed the burden on students to come forward with complaints of harassing conduct while ensuring that appropriate school officials have full, actual knowledge of the inappropriate conduct. Under this standard, schools do not necessarily have to monitor behavior or assume that harassing conduct may be taking place (Grube & Lens, 2003); nor may boards incur more or greater responsibility simply because of the "notorious and flagrant nature of the conduct" (p. 180). Indeed, this means that the obligation of boards to respond to sexual harassment is not defined by whether the inappropriate behavior stops but, rather, whether officials took some sort of reasonable action on learning of the harassment.

Davis involved student-on-student harassment, the first time that this issue reached the Supreme Court. In this case, a fifth-grade female was harassed repeatedly by a male in her class, and after repeated complaints from the parents, the school took only minimal action. In its analysis, the Supreme Court again established specific criteria for how a district can be held responsible for student-on-student behavior. Specifically, the Court noted that, to avoid liability, the district must have "responded to known peer harassment in a manner that is clearly not unreasonable" (p. 867). Additionally, the school must have "exercise[d] substantial control over both the harasser and the context in which the known harassment occurs" (p. 855). In other words, incidents that take place on school grounds within the school day are the school's responsibility, but harassment that happens at the mall on the weekend is beyond the reasonable expectation of what schools should handle. A third prong of the precedent set by *Davis* requires that the harassing conduct be "severe, pervasive, and objectively offensive that it can be said to deprive the victims of access to the educational opportunities or benefits provided by the school" (p. 858).

This verbiage indicates that not all behavior is harassment, given the sometimes immature teasing or conduct in which students may engage. In fact, the Court specifically acknowledged that "schools are unlike the adult workplace" and "children may regularly interact in a manner that would be unacceptable among adults" (p. 859). Thus, the behavior must be judged, and responded to, according to subjective criteria that could include both students' ages, the frequency of the behavior, and the degree of interruption it causes the other student(s). Even so, rather than render a final judgment on liability, the Supreme Court remanded the dispute to the Eleventh Circuit for further consideration.

ENFORCEMENT OF SEXUAL HARASSMENT POLICIES

Enforced by the Office for Civil Rights (OCR) of the U.S. Department of Education, Title IX protects individuals from sexual harassment in school settings. The OCR requires school boards to establish sexual harassment policies. Unfortunately, compliance with the requirements of Title IX is not as well monitored as some would like. Lauren Lichty, Jennifer Torres, Maria Valenti, and NiCole Buchanan (2008) recommended 10 components that should be included in school board sexual harassment policies to comply with federal OCR guidelines, including definitions of harassment, grievance procedures, timelines, consequences, and contact information. At the same time, these authors found that most policies addressed only 5 of the 10 needed components, and a mere 14% of sexual harassment policies were available to the public on the Internet. Thus, these authors reported that students and their parents may not be aware of the policy in their districts regarding sexual harassment and, as a result, may not understand what behaviors do or do not constitute forbidden sexual harassment. In addition, parents and students may not recognize their own level of responsibility in reporting this harassment to school officials. Accordingly, the authors suggest that educational officials must work diligently in line with Supreme Court precedent to ensure that parents and students are aware of policies regarding appropriate behavior and requirements for reporting inappropriate sexual behavior.

School boards can perform the important job of making parents and students aware of their rights by enacting clear definitions of sexual harassment. Generally, sexual harassment in schools can be defined as any unwanted behavior of a sexual nature that negatively affects a student's life (Lichty et al., 2008). More specifically, the OCR defines sexual harassment, specifically a hostile environment, as any unwelcome sexual advances, requests for sexual favors, and other verbal, nonverbal, or physical conduct of a sexual nature by an employee, or another student, or by a third party, that is sufficiently severe, persistent, or pervasive that it limits a student's ability to participate in or benefit from an educational program or activity, or to create a hostile or abusive educational environment (U.S. Department of Education, 1997, p. 12038).

IMPACT OF SEXUAL HARASSMENT

Unfortunately, sexual harassment of students is a current and real problem in today's schools. As many as 80% or more of students report being sexually harassed at some point in their educational career (Lichty et al., 2008). Further, between 15% and 57% were both harassed within the past two weeks and upset by the experience (Duffy, Wareham, & Walsh, 2004; Walsh, Duffy, & Gallagher-Duffy, 2007). Still, accurately measuring the prevalence or degree of student sexual harassment in schools is inherently difficult.

Two foundational studies by the American Association of University Women (1993, 2001) increased awareness of the great extent to which sexual harassment of students was taking place in school settings. Also contributing to this inability to gauge the status of sexual harassment in schools adequately are the ambiguous definitions of behaviors that constitute sexual harassment (Terrance, Logan, & Peters, 2004). Based on the level of intrusiveness of the behavior, some behaviors that could, by definition, be classified as sexual harassment are actually overlooked. The lines are likewise blurred regarding what behaviors constitute sexual harassment based on gender—particularly same-sex actions. In other words, courts need to clarify the extent to which verbal behavior and physical contact or lack thereof can be treated as harassment (Terrance et al., 2004).

As noted, sexual harassment of students negatively affects children in a variety of serious ways. Students' grades may suffer as a result of harassment, and students may experience appetite loss, nightmares, social isolation, anxiety, or depression. Likewise, students may experience physiological symptoms such as weight loss or gain, headaches, ulcers, and insomnia (Klusas, 2003). Psychological consequences for students who are sexually harassed may include fear, low or reduced self-esteem, embarrassment, and problems with engaging in healthy relationships (Duffy, Wareham, & Walsh, 2004). The types and severity of the negative consequences vary according to the harassment as well as by the age or grade level of the students, with high school girls experiencing more harassment but with somewhat less impact than middle school girls (Gruber & Fineran, 2007). Additionally, the age and gender of students may influence teachers' recognition or responses to peer sexual harassment in schools, which can further complicate the effect this behavior has on students (Stone & Couch, 2004).

THE CURRENT SUPREME COURT STANDARDS WORK

Given the prevalence of sexual harassment in school settings and the psychological or physiological damage that it can have on students, the question remains: Are the protections against student sexual harassment workable? The Supreme Court, through its interpretations of Title IX rendered in the *Gebser, Franklin*, and most significantly *Davis* cases, has established strict and specific guidelines under which students may recover monetary damages from school boards and their employees for teacher-on-student and student-on-student sexual harassment. Even though the cases do not, as the counterpoint author argues, address social networking and electronic media that were minimal to nonexistent a decade ago, the three Supreme Court rulings have established clear guidelines that boards ought to be able to adapt to their own unique situations.

The standard of proof, coupled with the burden of evidence needed to establish liability that the Supreme Court enunciated in *Gebser* and *Davis*, in particular, after opening the door in *Franklin*, are as high as they should be when dealing with sexual harassment in schools. Although being mindful of the need to protect students in light of the trauma that sexual harassment can impose, the standards that the Court created in these cases protect school boards from frivolous litigation that could arise from disgruntled parents or students. In fact, in *Davis* the Court rejected the arguments of the dissent in intending this high level of protection for boards. In its rationale, the Court specifically rejected the idea that boards can be liable for employee or student behavior of which it was unaware, including the notion that officials somehow should have known something inappropriate was taking place between students and peers or teachers.

In this regard, the Supreme Court offered guidance and protection to school officials in both *Davis* and *Gebser* to prevent opening floodgates to litigation that would render boards liable for the acts of employees or students of which they were unaware and could not control. As the Court indicated in these cases, its failure to protect school boards in this way could have resulted in the loss of large amounts of public funds, essentially requiring taxpayers to expend additional resources for defending themselves for failing to intervene to prevent the behavior of employees or even students.

In sum, perhaps most importantly, the Supreme Court's analysis in establishing the twin standards of actual knowledge and deliberate indifference by school board employees who have the authority to redress wrongs provides students who are subjected to harassment by peers or teachers with appropriate, adequate remedies. Pursuant to the tests set forth in *Davis* and *Gebser*, the Court has maintained a kind of equilibrium by protecting students from sexual harassment in school by establishing fair, reasonable, and enforceable standards that boards can rely on in protecting themselves from potentially frivolous and expensive litigation in the fight to eliminate sexual harassment in schools.

COUNTERPOINT: Mark Littleton
Tarleton State University

The question posed in this debate—whether the tests that the Supreme Court has provided in dealing with peer-to-peer and teacher-on-student sexual harassment are workable—is difficult to answer. The Court has offered some guidance on how educators or school boards can be rendered liable for sexual harassment of students by peers and teachers. However, school officials still have limited legal options in dealing with the constantly changing milieu of sexual harassment. This counterpoint essay maintains that the tests that the Court has devised are not fully adequate to address the serious issue of sexual harassment in schools.

TEACHER-ON-STUDENT SEXUAL HARASSMENT

The two landmark Supreme Court cases pertaining to teacher-on-student sexual harassment are *Franklin v. Gwinnett County Public Schools* (1992), and *Gebser v. Lago Vista Independent School District* (1998). In *Franklin*, a female high school student was continually sexually harassed and abused by a teacher. The student filed a complaint with the federal Office of Civil Rights (OCR) alleging that school board officials violated her rights by allowing her to be subjected to sexual harassment and abuse at the hands of a male teacher. The OCR ultimately concluded that officials violated the student's rights but that because the teacher resigned and the board implemented a grievance procedure, the latter had come into compliance with Title IX. Subsequently, the student filed suit under Title IX of the Education Amendments of 1972 in a federal trial court in Georgia alleging that school officials were aware of the harassment, failed to take action to stop it, and attempted to dissuade her from pressing charges against the teacher. When the student filed her complaint, the teacher resigned, and the board ceased its investigation into the matter.

The federal trial court determined, and the Eleventh Circuit affirmed, that the student's complaint should be dismissed because Title IX did not authorize an award of damages. Yet, on further review in *Franklin*, the Supreme Court reversed in favor of the student. In a unanimous judgment, the Justices held that the student could seek an award of damages under Title IX. Without question, the Court's opinion caught the attention of educators and school board attorneys. Even so, the Court failed to provide educators with any direction on how to address teacher-on-student sexual harassment claims.

Later, in *Gebser*, the Supreme Court considered a case where a female student was engaged in a sexual relationship with a teacher. Unlike in *Franklin*, the student in *Gebser* did not inform school officials about the relationship. The relationship came to the attention of school officials only after a police officer discovered the student and teacher engaged in sexual intercourse off school grounds. On being informed of the teacher–student relationship, the school board terminated the teacher's employment. The student and her mother then filed suit in a federal trial court in Texas, claiming that the board's lack of a grievance policy and failure to distribute an official procedure for filing a sexual harassment complaint, as directed by U.S. Department of Education regulations, violated Title IX. The trial court granted the board's motion for summary judgment, essentially dismissing the claim, and the Fifth Circuit affirmed in its favor.

The Supreme Court then affirmed in favor of the board in *Gebser* on the basis that school officials could not have known about the relationship between the student and teacher. The Court explained that a school board can be rendered liable only when a student provides actual notice of a Title IX violation to an appropriate educational official, meaning one who has the authority to end the discrimination, and that official acts with "deliberate indifference" by doing nothing to end the harassment.

In light of *Franklin* and *Gebser*, school boards were quick to draft grievance policies and publish procedures for reporting sexual harassment. Wise educational leaders also trained employees on how to avoid inappropriate relationships and identify clues of sexual misconduct by fellow employees. Even so, these tend to be "common-sense" responses to the ongoing problem of sexual harassment in schools rather than adherence to clear guidance provided by the Supreme Court.

Following *Franklin* and *Gebser*, the U.S. Department of Education's OCR drafted the revised *Sexual Harassment Guidance: Harassment of Students by School Employees, Other Students, or Third Parties* (1997). Although intended to provide "guidance," this document further complicated the matter by providing examples that were better illustrations of academic injustice than of sexual aggression. The document notes, for example, "The repeated sabotaging of female graduate students' laboratory experiments by male students in the class could be the basis of a violation of Title IX" (¶ 10). In the highly competitive academic environment often found in public secondary schools, students seek to create a competitive advantage in ways that have little to do with sexually aggressive behavior. Although the example is of undesirable behavior, such behavior hardly carries with it the connotation of bullying or harassment predicated on sexual desires as addressed by *Franklin* and *Gebser*.

Similarly, the document states,

> Although a comprehensive discussion of gender-based harassment is beyond the scope of this Guidance, in assessing all related circumstances to determine whether a hostile environment exists, incidents of gender-based harassment combined with incidents of sexual harassment could create a hostile environment, even if neither the gender-based harassment alone nor the sexual harassment alone would be sufficient to do so. (¶ 10)

Guidance of this nature, although often relied on by school boards and their attorneys, is overbroad and, at best, unfocused. Operating in an educational environment that is fast-paced and pressure-packed, educators find these guidelines ineffective. This lack of effective guidance is likely demonstrated by the comment in the point essay that compliance with the OCR document is not monitored well.

PEER-TO-PEER SEXUAL HARASSMENT

The landmark Supreme Court case involving peer-to-peer sexual harassment is *Davis v. Monroe County Board of Education* (1999). In *Davis*, a fifth-grade female student complained to her mother and classroom teacher about sexually harassing behavior from a fellow male student that continued for months. The victim's grades dropped, she became unable to concentrate on her studies, and she allegedly entertained suicidal thoughts that her father discovered in a note. During the extended period of harassment, the victim and her parents filed complaints with the school principal, who took little or no action. Eventually, the victim was allowed to change seats in her classroom so that she was not seated next to the harasser. The harassing behavior finally ended when the harasser pled guilty to sexual battery. Still, school officials did not take formal actions against the harasser.

The student and her parents unsuccessfully filed suit in a federal trial court in Georgia, which observed that Title IX did not create a cause of action for peer-to-peer sexual harassment. Applying a different rationale, the Eleventh Circuit affirmed in favor of the school board.

On further review, the Supreme Court reversed and remanded the dispute for further consideration. More specifically, the Court decided that school boards receiving federal funds can be liable for peer-to-peer sexual harassment under Title IX. Providing a modicum of direction to boards, the Court declared,

> We thus conclude that funding recipients are properly held liable in damages only where they are deliberately indifferent to sexual harassment, of which they have actual knowledge, that is so severe, pervasive, and objectively offensive that it can be said to deprive the victims of access to the educational opportunities or benefits provided by the school. (p. 650)

In essence, this means that school boards have a three-pronged standard for Title IX liability for peer-to-peer harassment. First, the conduct must be "severe, pervasive, and objectively offensive." Given the rapidly changing dynamics of social interactions among children, school officials face the awesome tasks of determining what behavior is sexual harassment and if it is sexual in nature, it is uncertain at what point it becomes "severe, pervasive, and objectively offensive." Interestingly, the Supreme Court itself is unclear on what sexual harassment is. As a sign of how the Court grapples with these difficult issues, in a later decision involving same-sex adults in a nonschool setting involving workers on an oil rig in the Gulf of Mexico, the Justices muddled the issue by writing that "The real social impact of workplace behavior often depends on a constellation of surrounding circumstances, expectations, and relationships which are not fully captured by a simple recitation of the words used or the physical acts performed" (*Oncale v. Sundowner Offshore Services*, 1998, p. 82).

In *Oncale*, the Supreme Court added, without a great deal of clarity, that sexually harassing behavior "requires neither asexuality nor androgyny in the workplace [school]; it forbids only behavior that is so objectively offensive as to alter the "conditions" of the victim's employment [education]" (p. 81). There is little guidance from the Court here. "Objectively offensive" is generation-dependent, contextually driven, and predicated on the still wildly varying values of the school officials. Uncertainty brought about by social relationships is illustrated by these examples. Although often sexually suggestive, music of the 1950s bears little resemblance to the overt vulgarities often used in the lyrics of current musical recordings. Additionally, an astute observer of televised media will readily note that much of the behavior and language allowed on television programs today would have been "objectively offensive," and consequently censored, fewer than 20 years ago. Kathleen Conn (2004), for example, notes that the "courts, on more than one occasion, have admonished plaintiffs that 'simple teasing' and name-calling are not illegal and may even be protected by the First Amendment" (p. 5).

Second, under this standard, school officials must have actual knowledge of the sexual harassment. Actual knowledge occurs when a student reports the harassing actions to an individual who possesses the authority to end the behavior. That individual is ordinarily an administrator. In a 1995 Fifth Circuit case, the court found that a teacher who knew of an affair between a teacher and a student for 5 months before reporting it to an administrator was not liable because the teacher possessed no administrative authority (*Doe v. Rains*, 1995).

Third, the guidelines dictate that school officials must be deliberately indifferent to the plight of the victim. *Deliberate indifference* means having knowledge that the harassing behavior is occurring, but failing to take action to stop it from continuing. A plethora of cases reveal that school officials were not liable for deliberate indifference when they acted, even if their responses were arguably less than appropriate, perhaps consisting of verbal reprimands and no more.

THE STANDARDS ARE NOT WORKABLE

If the Supreme Court tests were workable, then school officials could act aggressively, and proactively, to prohibit inappropriate student and teacher sexual relationships. In addition, school officials could act aggressively to teach students appropriate behaviors and language. However, the data do not seem to support the notion that officials possess the tools, legal or otherwise, to address sexual harassment in schools.

Teacher-on-Student Harassment

The American Association of University Women (2001) reported that in 2001, 38% of students reported being harassed by school employees. Further, a large portion of the educator certificate-related sanctions by state agencies or professional practices boards is related to inappropriate sexual conduct with students. For instance, the Texas Education Agency (2009) reported the percentage of investigations opened on sexual misconduct, violence, sexual harassment, and inappropriate relationships with a student or minor accounted for 59.7% of the investigations opened during the 2008–2009 fiscal year. Undoubtedly, teacher-on-student sexual contact is far too common.

Peer-to-Peer Harassment

Of the cases cited in this counterpoint essay, all were decided before 2000. Yet, in 2001, the American Association of University Women released the results of a survey concluding that sexual harassment is widespread in schools. The report highlighted that 83% of the girls and 79% of the boys experienced sexual harassment. Additionally, in 2001, the electronic social networks such as texting, instant messaging, Facebook, MySpace, and YouTube that were so prevalent by 2011 were nonexistent or in their infancy, at best. Today, sexting (sending sexually explicit text messages or photos) is common, and social media facilitate cyberbullying (online bullying) that can be sexual in nature (Chaffin, 2008).

Sexting and its electronic communication contemporaries such as cyber-bullying fall outside of the guidelines as provided by the Supreme Court. When, then, does electronic banter such as this become okay? become severe or pervasive? Do the courts weigh the actions of harassers against the possible reactions of the victims? Historically, bullies confronted their victims in locations where the victim had limited options for egress—at hall lockers, in gymnasiums, or on school playgrounds. With electronic media, particularly cellular telephones, options for egress increase. Victims can, of course, refuse to give their e-mail addresses and cellular phone numbers to others besides friends, change their telephone numbers, or delete offending messages. Regardless, the available options do not minimize the seriousness of the harassing behavior, nor do the options indicate that the behavior should not be addressed. Yet, the options are available.

Does "actual knowledge" occur when victims inform school officials of sexting incidents or must they have actual, firsthand knowledge that it occurred by seeing pictures? Granted, capturing electronic content should provide verification that the harassing behavior occurred while minimizing the chances that harassers can lie about their behavior. Yet, actual knowledge, much like face-to-face harassment, depends on the victims who must make the harassing behavior known. Possibly the most distressing concern is determining what constitutes deliberate indifference to acts of sexting. Must the official take possession of offending phones or computers? How do officials separate students in cyberspace? The Supreme Court's previous holdings simply do not supply enough guidance in the cyber age.

Unfortunately, it appears that the Supreme Court has provided little direction or assistance to school officials. Teacher-on-student and peer-to-peer sexual harassment have not abated since the court decisions of the late 20th century.

CONCLUSION

Instead of establishing guidelines to defend charges of liability for sexual harassment, the Supreme Court should send a clear message that school officials can terminate the employment of any school employee who engages in even one instance of inappropriate conversation or behavior with students. The Court should also clarify the extent to which school boards and their employees can be liable for sexually oriented misbehavior by students. The sooner that the Justices revisit these issues, the better the lives of students will be.

FURTHER READINGS AND RESOURCES

American Association of University Women Educational Foundation. (1993). *Hostile hallways: The AAUW survey on sexual harassment in America's schools.* Washington, DC: Author.

American Association of University Women Educational Foundation. (2001). *Hostile hallways: The AAUW survey on sexual harassment in America's schools.* Washington, DC: Author. Retrieved from http://www.aauw.org/learn/research/upload/hostile hallways.pdf

Chaffin, S. M. (2008). The new playground bullies of cyberspace: Online peer sexual harassment. *Howard Law Journal, 51,* 773–818.

Conn, K. (2004). *Bullying and harassment: A legal guide for educators.* Alexandria, VA: Association for Supervision and Curriculum Development.

Duffy, J., Wareham, S., & Walsh, M. (2004). Psychological consequences for high school students of having been sexually harassed. *Sex Roles, 50,* 811–821.

Grube, B., & Lens, V. (2003). Student-to-student harassment: The impact of *Davis vs. Monroe. Children and Schools, 25*(3), 173–185.

Gruber, J. E., & Fineran, S. (2007). The impact of bullying and sexual harassment on middle and high school girls. *Violence Against Women, 13*(6), 627–643. Retrieved September 8, 2011, from http://vaw.sagepub.com/content/13/6/627.abstract [doi:10.1177/1077801207301557]

Klusas, J. A. (2003). Providing students with the protection they deserve: Amending the Office of Civil Rights' guidance or Title IX to protect students from peer sexual harassment in schools. *Texas Forum on Civil Liberties and Civil Rights, 8*(1), 91–116.

Lichty, L. F., Torres, J. M. C., Valenti, M. T., & Buchanan, N. T. (2008). Sexual harassment policies in K–12 schools: Examining accessibility to students and content. *Journal of School Health, 78*(11), 607–614.

Ormerod, A. J., & Collinsworth, L. L. (2008). Critical climate: Relations among sexual harassment, climate, and outcomes for high school girls and boys. *Psychology of Women Quarterly, 32*, 113–125.

Russo, C. J., & Ford, H. H. (1999). Peer-to-peer sexual harassment: The Supreme Court speaks. *School Business Affairs, 65*(9), 10–16.

Russo, C. J., Nordin, V. D., & Leas, T. (1992). Sexual harassment and student rights: The Supreme Court expands Title IX remedies. *Education Law Reporter, 75*, 733–744.

Stone, M., & Couch, S. (2004). Peer sexual harassment among high school students: Teachers' attitudes, perceptions, and responses. *High School Journal, 88*(1), 1–13.

Terrance, C., Logan, A., & Peters, D. (2004). Perceptions of peer sexual harassment among high school students. *Sex Roles, 51*, 479–490.

Texas Education Agency, State Board for Educator Certification. (2009). *Investigations and fingerprinting update 080709.* Retrieved from http://www.tea.state.tx.us/index2 .aspx?id=5828&menu_id=846&menu_id2=794

U.S. Department of Education, Office for Civil Rights. (1997). *Sexual harassment guidance: Harassment of students by school employees, other students, or third parties* (*Federal Register, 62*, 12034–12051). Retrieved September 8, 2011, from http://www2 .ed.gov/about/offices/list/ocr/docs/sexhar00.html

Walsh, M., Duffy, J., & Gallagher-Duffy, J. (2007). A more accurate approach to measuring the prevalence of sexual harassment among high school students. *Canadian Journal of Behavioral Sciences, 39*(2), 110–118.

Court Cases and Statutes

Cannon v. University of Chicago, 441 U.S. 677 (1979).

Davis v. Monroe County Board of Education, 526 U.S. 629 (1999), *on remand*, 206 F.3d 1377 (11th Cir. 2000).

Doe v. Rains, 66 F. 3d 1402 (5th Cir. 1995).

Franklin v. Gwinnett County Public Schools, 503 U.S. 60 (1992), *on remand*, 969 F.2d 1022 (11th Cir. 1992).

Gebser v. Lago Vista Independent School District, 524 U.S. 274 (1998).

Oncale v. Sundowner Offshore Services, 523 U.S. 75 (1998).

Title VII of the Civil Rights Act of 1964, 42 U.S.C. §§ 2000d *et seq.*

Title IX of the Education Amendments of 1972, 20 U.S.C.A. § 1681.

10

Should charges of sexual misconduct against teachers be public records?

POINT: Ralph D. Mawdsley, *Cleveland State University*

COUNTERPOINT: James L. Mawdsley, *Stark State College*

OVERVIEW

The U.S. Constitution does not explicitly spell out privacy rights. Nevertheless, several privacy rights are implied in other constitutional provisions. For example, the basic rights to marry, raise a family, enter into personal relationships with others, and form friendships can be inferred from the Ninth and Fourteenth Amendments (Osborne & Russo, 2011). In accepting public employment, teachers and other school employees do not automatically lose their constitutional rights; however, some limitations can be placed on teachers' privacy, and, as public employees, teachers have a diminished expectation of privacy. As the discussion in this chapter clearly shows, a particularly controversial privacy issue concerns what aspects of teachers' personal information can be released to the public, particularly when teachers have been charged with sexual misconduct.

Sexual misconduct can range from sexual harassment to actually engaging in sexual relations with students. As one would expect, teachers can be, and usually are, dismissed for engaging in inappropriate sexual activities with students. Students are minors, so criminal charges can also be brought against teachers for engaging in sexual relations with students even when the activity is consensual. The concern here is that teachers who may have been wrongly accused of sexual misconduct can have their personal and professional reputations permanently damaged by such false allegations even when they are later completely exonerated of the charges. A case from Washington shows that teachers do have some rights to privacy in this situation. A dispute began when 37 teachers filed an invasion of privacy suit objecting to their school districts' release to newspapers of records identifying teachers accused of, investigated, or disciplined for sexual misconduct within the previous 10 years. A state appellate court held that the names of teachers who were falsely accused of sexual misconduct and were subjects of unsubstantiated but not necessarily false accusations were not subject to disclosure (*Bellevue John Does v. Bellevue School District # 405*, 2008). On appeal, the Supreme Court of Washington stated that when there is an allegation of sexual misconduct against a public school teacher, the identity of the teacher may be disclosed to the public only if the misconduct is substantiated or the teacher's conduct results in some form of discipline.

Courts have consistently supported school boards' efforts to dismiss teachers who have engaged in sexual relations with students. Any kind of sexual contact with a minor that results in a criminal conviction clearly is grounds for termination, but teachers may be dismissed even when their transgressions do not result in criminal convictions. Courts are also likely to sustain the dismissal of teachers who engage in consensual relationships with students even when the students are over the age of consent. In one high-profile case, an appellate court in Oklahoma affirmed the dismissal of a female teacher who had a romantic relationship with a 17-year-old male student (*Andrews v. Independent School District*, 2000). Courts are even prone to uphold the termination of teachers who engage in relationships with former students, particularly those who have only recently graduated. In such a case, the Sixth Circuit upheld the denial of tenure to a teacher in Michigan who had a romantic relationship with a former student. Teachers can be disciplined for inappropriate sexual relations with students even when the charges stem from incidents that occurred many years in the past.

School systems operate in an environment where their business is open to public scrutiny. Thus, under the umbrella of the public's right to know, and as provided by states' public records statutes, school officials routinely release information about many aspects of the school district operations. Even so, public employees still have a right to expect some degree of confidentiality regarding their personal information. To illustrate, although parents may have the right to know the qualifications of their child's teacher, they do not necessarily have the right to know all of the intimate details of teachers' lives, such as why teachers may have taken medical leaves of absence (Osborne & Russo, 2011).

Though information concerning disciplinary actions against teachers is often part of the public record, it is questionable whether those who face disciplinary actions or dismissal have a right to privacy before formal action has been taken. This issue is critical because charges brought against a teacher may be unfounded, and their mere existence will often damage a teacher's professional reputation even when those charges are unsubstantiated. In one such case, Minnesota's state supreme court ruled that the release of personnel information is not authorized by state statute even when disciplinary action is being taken against the teacher (*Navarre v. South Washington County Schools*, 2002). The court ruled that the only information that could be disclosed before the final disposition of the disciplinary action was the existence and status of complaints lodged against the teacher. Disciplinary action may be disclosed, however, once proceedings have been finalized (*Wiese v. Freedom of Information Commission*, 2004).

Unfortunately, teachers are sometimes accused of sexual misconduct. When the alleged misconduct involves students or minors, it has implications regarding the safety of the students in the teacher's charge. However, such charges likely will destroy a teacher's reputation and ability to continue in the classroom even when they are completely unfounded and the teacher is later exonerated. Regrettably, under such circumstances, doubts may always remain. Thus, as the discussion in this chapter clearly indicates, a balance must be struck between teachers' privacy rights and the rights of parents and students to know when a teacher has been accused of sexual misconduct.

In the point essay, Ralph D. Mawdsley, Cleveland State University, advocates for making charges of sexual misconduct against teachers part of the public record. He acknowledges that teachers can be wrongly accused, and that such false charges can damage their professional standing, but states that they have recourse by way of name-clearing hearings and even taking legal actions against their accusers. Mawdsley recognizes that the issue of disclosure of teachers' identities in such situations is a difficult public policy question, but he believes that it should be decided on the side of protecting children. He suggests that one solution may be to remove investigations of sexual misconduct from local school boards and place them in the hands of state education agencies. That way, he contends, licensure sanctions against teachers would become part of the public record. In sum, Mawdsley contends that teachers' privacy interests should not take precedence over parents' rights to know the identities of teachers who have been charged with sexual misconduct. Such a position assumes that parents, not school boards, have the primary responsibility for protecting their children. Concealing such information, he claims, will only erode public confidence in all teachers.

In the counterpoint essay, James L. Mawdsley, Stark State College, argues that making sexual misconduct allegations public runs the risk of doing irreparable harm to the reputations of teachers who have been unjustly accused. Noting that the mere mention of sexual impropriety can destroy a teacher's career, Mawdsley disagrees with the point essayist that investigations should be turned over to state educational agencies who may have greater expertise in such matters. Although he acknowledges that there are many benefits in doing so, he contends that those benefits may be illusory, especially because state boards may be no better equipped to handle investigations than are local boards and parents are likely to have no greater confidence in a state agency. Further, observing that teachers' reputations are more fragile than those of other professionals, Mawdsley contends that the remedies available to falsely charged teachers are inadequate to mend reputations that are likely to be permanently damaged even when the teachers have been cleared of all accusations.

The essays in this debate highlight several important, but difficult, public policy questions. In reading the chapter you may want to think about these issues. To what degree should teachers give up certain privacy rights when they accept public employment? Should the public's right to know trump teachers' privacy concerns when complaints of sexual misconduct have been leveled? Do adequate protections exist to protect teachers' reputations against false accusations?

Allan G. Osborne, Jr.
Principal (Retired), Snug Harbor Community School,
Quincy, Massachusetts

POINT: Ralph D. Mawdsley
Cleveland State University

In assessing whether allegations of teacher sexual misconduct involving students should be public records, the responses to three critical policy issues argue in favor of public records: (1) whether school officials or board members are the appropriate persons to investigate allegations of teacher sexual misconduct and to make decisions regarding the substantiated or unsubstantiated results of such investigations, (2) whether sexual misconduct charges related to teacher performance of their public educational duties is (or, should be) protected by privacy, and (3) whether the quality of K–12 education is best served by teacher responsiveness to public resolution of student or parent charges of teacher sexual misconduct.

Although issues concerning teacher privacy and disclosure of information are state specific, the overarching issue, regardless of current state law, is whether teachers should have a protectable privacy interest at all in complaints about their performance as public employees. Whether information requested for disclosure should be denied as an invasion of privacy is the threshold issue in all jurisdictions, although courts do not reach the same conclusions. Generally, courts have held that information regarding teacher sexual misconduct can be revealed as long as the teacher's name is removed. Claims against guilty teachers cannot always be substantiated, so removing information about teacher identities whenever a student claim cannot be substantiated may only send the message to the public that children may still be vulnerable. As the dissent in one court opinion stated,

> Under the majority's holding, the public in Washington will not have access to information necessary for determining whether the State's school districts satisfactorily address allegations of teacher sexual misconduct. As a consequence, predatory teachers may go undetected and unpunished. But the most unfortunate consequence, and one that is completely unacceptable, is that if predatory teachers are undetected, children will continue to suffer at their hands. (*Bellevue John Does v. Bellevue School District # 405*, 2008, p. 154)

ROLE OF SCHOOL OFFICIALS

Allowing school officials "to control the scope and depth of its investigation" (*Bellevue*, p. 158) amounts to adopting a "foxes guarding the henhouse" position, one that erodes public trust and leaves the public with the perception that "the school board is not responsive to the taxpayers, and the school board is hiding something" (Stuart, 2008, p. 1331). Media reports suggest that far too many cases involving sexual abuse of students are unfolding publicly at any given time, reinforcing the notion that school officials have not been successful in their responsibility to keep students safe and resulting in multimillion-dollar jury verdicts for victims or in costly out-of-court settlements. Indeed, case law indicates examples where school boards have agreed with dismissed teachers to withhold information about their misconduct to avoid litigation. This often allows teachers who are guilty of misconduct to obtain positions in other school districts (Sorenson, 1997). In addition, school districts can have practices of issuing oral reprimands or warnings reflecting the pressures on them to not document misconduct even though certain safety measures may not be in place to guarantee that successive administrators would have information concerning the oral discipline. Where the purported motives for school district nondisclosure of complaints of sexual misconduct are to keep the incident secret so as not to alarm the public, embarrass the alleged victims of abuse, or even not disclosing the charges against the teacher because his or her career may be irreparably harmed, one can question whether the willingness of school boards to give such breadth of discretion qualifies them to even conduct investigations at all.

Some courts have questioned the adequacy of internal investigations of teacher sexual misconduct, particularly where those investigations substitute for reporting the alleged misconduct to social services. However, even if school districts forgo investigation of sexual misconduct complaints by referring all complaints to social welfare agencies as required under state child abuse statutes, such referrals do not necessarily require disclosure of the teacher's identity (including teacher name, certificate/license number, and schools taught at) if the investigation does not substantiate that sexual misconduct occurred, or if the result generates a "letter of direction" that allegedly is not based on a finding of sexual misconduct. In other words, if a social service agency investigation does not produce a substantiated finding of child abuse, the public is likely to discover the names of teachers against whom complaints of sexual misconduct have been made only if a student is willing to pursue a lengthy, costly, and cumbersome lawsuit for negligent hiring, supervision, or retention. More troublesome, though, is that even if parents can pursue these negligence claims, actions against state officials for inadequate investigations may be blocked by state immunity statutes.

TEACHER RIGHT TO PRIVACY

Privacy in its broadest meaning is the protection of an individual's interest in making decisions free of government interference. The U.S. Supreme Court has recognized that the Liberty Clause of the Fourteenth Amendment protects "a right of personal privacy" that includes "the interest in independence in making certain kinds of important decisions" (*Whalen v. Roe*, 1977, pp. 599–600). However, the right to make decisions without government interference is not without limits. For public school teachers, their expectation of privacy, one can argue, is diminished by the reality that they have been employed to instruct students, most of whom are minors required under state compulsory attendance laws to attend school.

Certainly, one can argue that insomuch as teachers are viewed as student role models, the threshold for determining when a teacher acts immorally should be fairly low and acts of moral turpitude, criminal convictions, and sexual misconduct with students should constitute the typical grounds for disciplinary action on the grounds of immorality. In a recent survey by the U.S. Department of Education, "9.6 percent of all students in grades 8 to 11 reported contact and/or noncontact educator sexual misconduct that was *unwanted*" (U.S. Department of Education, 2004, p. 17), and "6.7 percent reported physical sexual abuse" (p. 18). The range of teacher sexual misconduct ran the gamut from making sexual comments, jokes, gestures, or looks to touching, grabbing, pinching, or pulling at or removing clothing and forcing students to perform sexual acts. Students who disclose inappropriate faculty member conduct can find little vindication when a teacher is still permitted to continue teaching. Students who have been victimized by a teacher may understandingly be confused when the teacher, following a conviction for criminal conduct with a student where the conviction was subsequently dismissed after the teacher had completed a rehabilitation program, was recertified, and later permitted to return to the classroom (*Garcia v. State Board of Education*, 1984). Though a teacher who has been convicted of criminal misconduct toward a student and later returns to the classroom may not be claiming privacy protection, the message to students of the ineffectiveness of reporting sexual misconduct is compounded when teachers alleged by students to be involved in sexual misconduct, in the absence of criminal charges being filed against the teachers, remain unidentified and protected by privacy.

When students do make complaints, disclosure of information related to administrative investigations by school officials or social service agencies becomes mired in judicial interpretations of statutory privacy exemptions. Just how broadly a state chooses to draw the circle of privacy protection can affect both individual teachers and the school district as a whole. Recognizing that school boards have responsibilities to protect the interests of both teachers and students, the quality of education will be defined in significant part by an emphasis on whatever protection state law provides to each group—in this case, the best interest of teachers. However, the quality of a school district's education can also encompass less readily definable components such as public confidence in its school officials acting appropriately to protect the safety of their children.

QUALITY OF EDUCATION

The administration of school districts relies on a structure whereby elected school boards are responsible for selecting administrators who evaluate and provide direction for their staffs. However, even though the electorate can replace board members, one wonders how well-informed the electorate can be if, administrators can make teacher evaluations inaccessible merely by not including references to teacher misconduct, or the board can make information about teacher misconduct inaccessible through negotiated settlement agreements with confidentiality provisions. Even without the formal settlement agreement, permitting teachers to quietly resign without having to face dismissal proceedings accomplishes the same result. One can at least query whether education is best served by an administrator or school board attitude that treats student safety and well-being simply as removal of the cause of sexual misconduct. Without schools furnishing specific, identifiable information about teachers who have been charged with sexual misconduct, one wonders how the well-being of victims of sexual misconduct who have reported abuse but have seen no results, or the well-being of victims of abuse who are afraid to report it, or the well-being of parents who are completely unaware of abuse, has been served.

By declaring that teachers have a personal identity privacy right in not having sexual misconduct charges revealed, parents are left only with reports about the number of sexual misconduct reports that provide no information as to school officials' or the school board's resolution of those complaints. Although in loco parentis can often be considered to be a legal fiction, it nonetheless still has mirrored the reality that schools' work with students requires a collaborative effort among teachers, school officials, and parents. Arguably, permitting school officials and school boards to conceal information from parents when such withholding affects the safety and physical well-being of their children significantly marginalizes this collaboration with parents.

Admittedly, balancing professional harm to teachers where their identities are disclosed for unsubstantiated or false complaints and harm to students where complaints of sexual misconduct are either discouraged or ineffectively investigated presents difficult public policy choices. Unquestionably, teacher reputations will be harmed, perhaps irreparably, where their names are associated with even false claims of sexual misconduct. However, teachers would have a post hoc due process entitlement to a name-clearing hearing, a due process right to defend themselves against discharge, or the opportunity to pursue state law tort or statutory claims against the student complainant or his or her parents. No legal process, though, can be invoked to compel students to make complaints about teacher sexual misconduct when, as suggested by the *Bellevue* dissent, students refuse to report sexual misconduct either because they are afraid to do so or because past complaints by their friends have effected no changes.

   The prevailing view that teachers' privacy interests take precedence over parents' and the public's entitlement to knowledge of the identity of teachers against whom sexual misconduct complaints have been made is based on the assumption that school boards and school officials, not parents, are responsible for protecting the safety of students. Although this approach has appeal from a school management perspective, one may question whether concealing information from parents about some teachers against whom sexual misconduct complaints have been made may in the long run only erode trust and confidence in all teachers.

CONCLUSION

Resolving the conflict between teacher privacy and the reporting of charges of teacher sexual misconduct is difficult. One obvious solution would be to simply eliminate the statutory privacy protection that exists in most states. However, as reflected in this essay, public policy has favored protecting teachers from the harm to their reputations of unsubstantiated allegations of sexual misconduct, even at the risk of inadequate investigation of the allegations by school officials. Another possible resolution of this dilemma concerning the adequacy of school officials' investigation of sexual misconduct allegations might be to remove this function totally from the local level and transfer it to the state department of education. All investigations would then become matters of professional responsibility with licensure sanctions being imposed for findings of misconduct. Although parents may not necessarily have access to the names of all teachers charged with sexual misconduct, the identities of sanctioned teachers, including those who receive "letters of admonishment" or who enter into consent agreements, would be public knowledge. Arguably, this is a better midpoint in balancing the professional interests of teachers and the interests of parents in their children's safety because it removes the decision-making authority from local school boards and places the authority with a body that can impose licensure sanctions. At the very least, it removes the wall of silence that *Bellevue* sanctions under its state privacy act for all but the relatively few allegations of sexual misconduct where a finding of abuse has been made.

Clearly, the disclosure of teacher identities when a complaint of sexual misconduct has been made by students presents difficult public policy questions. Unquestionably, teachers have a great deal at stake when they are alleged to have been involved in sexual misconduct, especially considering that such charges can be filed anonymously and maliciously. However, one can question whether public school teachers should be permitted to hide behind state privacy statutes to prevent disclosure of their names. To suggest, as the *Bellevue* majority does, that parents should be satisfied with deleted information revealing the existence of sexual misconduct charges but not the names of those charged nor the resolution of those charges, takes a diminutive, if not demeaning, view of the role of parents in protecting their children. If the record of responsible investigation by school officials were more convincing, perhaps judicial deference to such investigations would be more compelling. One wonders, though, how the best interests of parents and the public are served when school officials are permitted to negotiate resolution of sexual misconduct complaints without having to account to the public for those resolutions. Where parents and the public receive only information regarding the reported number of incidents of teacher sexual misconduct, the effect, arguably, is to make all teachers suspect.

COUNTERPOINT: James L. Mawdsley
Stark State College

Making charges of sexual misconduct a matter of public record even when the charges have not been substantiated runs the risk of doing irreparable and ongoing harm to the reputations of the accused teachers. This essay addresses three reasons why such allegations should be kept from the eyes of the public in general and parents in particular. First, investigations are often conducted by school officials, who may not have any particular expertise in conducting such inquiries. Second, teachers retain a right to privacy, even if their job places them in the public eye. And third, the quality of education will diminish if teachers are forced to plead their innocence, over and over throughout the rest of their careers, to parents and students who have just recently uncovered a long-ago allegation. It is simply unrealistic to expect parents to take a rational view of unsubstantiated charges. One can hardly imagine parents declaring, on seeing the name of their daughter's basketball coach or science teacher on a list of those against whom allegations have been made, that because it was only one allegation, was made years ago, and was never substantiated, their daughter is at little or no risk. Parents would be much more likely to take a cautious approach. Indeed, they might even warn their children to stay away from the coach or teacher. However understandable this reaction might be, it would be impossible to expect a teacher to do his or her job in such an atmosphere of suspicion.

Yet there are several reasons why one might argue in favor of allowing the community to hear the allegations. First, an allegation might be unproven, but that does not make it untrue. Second, and deriving from the first, a series of allegations against a single teacher, even if unproven, might give parents and students some warning of the possibility that the teacher is a sexual predator. Third, and perhaps most importantly, is the question of why teachers should be treated differently from any other adult who has been accused of a crime. Nevertheless, advocates of making all allegations a matter of public record fail to take into account the harmful consequences not to the teacher but to the educational process more generally. This counterpoint essay considers a number of problems with the policy advocated in the point essay.

RESPONSIBILITY FOR CONDUCTING INVESTIGATIONS

As discussed later, the mere mention of an allegation of sexual impropriety can destroy a teacher's career. It is perfectly true that such an investigation will lead the public to believe that "the school board is not responsive to the taxpayers, and the school board is hiding something" (Stuart, 2008, p. 1331). But this presumes bad faith by administrators. If one begins by assuming that school officials are blithely unconcerned for the safety of their students, and that they can view with perfect equanimity the prospect of working alongside sexual predators, then handing over all investigations to an impartial, outside state agency would be appropriate.

Giving responsibility for investigating allegations of misconduct to state departments of education, with licensure sanctions being imposed for any findings of misconduct, would seem to solve several problems. First, there would be a perception of impartiality, which would give parents some assurance that children's accusations would be taken seriously. Second, it would relieve the burden upon local administrators, who, as we have noted, are not necessarily trained to handle such investigations. Third, it would give force to any finding of misconduct, by ensuring that the guilty teacher's license was suspended or revoked. This would prevent repetition of those inexcusable and unfortunate cases, which my colleague mentions, in which sexual predators with teacher's licenses move from school to school without ever being fired.

On closer examination, however, these benefits may prove illusory. First, there is no reason at all to think that a frantic parent, whose child has accused his or her teacher of the most disgusting crimes, would be any more likely to see the state board of education than local school officials as an impartial arbiter. If the state body determines that the allegations are unfounded and recommends no discipline for the teacher, and yet the child continues to maintain that the misconduct occurred, then the parent will still view this as a case of the "foxes guarding the henhouse." Indeed, if one is willing to assume bad faith of local officials, why should one believe that state officials will be any better? Parents would most likely ask for outside, truly impartial investigators because no matter how far removed the state department of education may be from the day-to-day running of local schools, the perception will remain that a state bureaucracy is being called on to investigate itself.

This brings us to a second problem with my colleague's proposed solution. There is no guarantee that state departments of education are any better equipped to handle such investigations than local school officials. Therefore, if they wish to complete their inquiries in a timely, professional, and evenhanded manner, they will need to hire people who are qualified, or at least identify those persons within their ranks who are qualified, and appoint them to a special panel or committee (although, for the reasons stated in the previous paragraph, pressure from the community will be for outside investigators). In either case, whether the investigators come from within the department or are hired from outside, the result will be considerable expense to the department, either in new salaries, or in labor lost when an employee is transferred from some other position. At a time when most state governments are struggling to balance their budgets in the face of declining tax revenues, it seems far-fetched to imagine that state legislatures would willingly accept this added expense.

The third problem with giving state departments of education the responsibility to investigate allegations is that there is no guarantee that making teacher sexual misconduct a matter of teacher licensure would be any more effective than the current system. State officials would not be immune from the kind of pressures (from teacher unions, for example) that make it so difficult to fire a teacher. Indeed, because they are somewhat closer to the center of power in the state capital, where political influences are strongest, state departments of education might be more susceptible to these pressures than local officials. The board or committee charged with investigating the allegations would find itself besieged by union officials, demanding, both in individual cases and in general, that the committee treat teachers fairly and adhere to the collective bargaining agreement.

SUBSTANTIATED VERSUS UNSUBSTANTIATED ALLEGATIONS

Teachers should not have their careers and professional reputations put in jeopardy over unsubstantiated or false allegations of sexual misconduct. For that reason, and in view of the fact that local school officials may not be properly equipped to conduct a fair investigation into the allegations, the Washington Supreme Court in *Bellevue John Does v. Bellevue School District # 405* (2008), was correct to draw a line between, on the one hand, substantiated allegations resulting in discipline and, on the other hand, unsubstantiated allegations, which necessarily include those allegations that were patently false. Where an accusation has not been proven, further publicizing it would seem to serve no useful purpose. As the court in *Bellevue* pointed out, the very fact of a teacher being accused of sexual misconduct toward a minor may hold the teacher up to hatred and ridicule in the community, even without any evidence that the alleged misconduct ever occurred.

An administrative inquiry into a student's allegations of teacher sexual misconduct is not a criminal investigation (though a criminal investigation may result). An administrative hearing is not a criminal trial, with all the rights for the accused that a trial entails. Thus, the fact that the names of criminal defendants are made public is not a reason to release the names of teachers who are under investigation. Note that this logic applies whether the investigators are local school officials or state department of education employees.

In the point essay, my colleague suggests that rather than focusing exclusively on the privacy rights of teachers, states should broaden their focus to consider the value of protecting students. But this would mean sacrificing a real and tangible right (the teacher's privacy) for a mostly illusory benefit. If unsubstantiated allegations are made public, along with substantiated ones, then there can be no guarantee that any given teacher on the list of those against whom allegations have been made has actually committed any act of sexual impropriety. Parents who read the list could have no confidence that the teachers listed were actually dangerous.

The student-teacher relationship is one of the most important ingredients of student learning, so care must be taken that these relationships are not needlessly harmed. When parents caution their children against a certain teacher, the danger they apprehend might be entirely imaginary. Warning one's children against imaginary dangers does precisely nothing to increase the children's safety. However, the student–teacher relationship will have been needlessly poisoned, and the teacher's right to privacy will have been wantonly trampled for no appreciable benefit at all.

THE INADEQUACY OF LEGAL REMEDIES FOR FALSE ACCUSATIONS

It is inadequate to suggest that a teacher has legal remedies in response to false accusations of sexual misconduct against students. The obvious remedy would be a civil defamation suit against the accuser, but this requires that the teacher further publicize the false accusation. One might respond that the same is true of any defamation suit, but teachers, who hold a special trust from the community in relation to children, have good reason not to want the allegations to be widely known. Once the teacher's name is associated with such misconduct, many in the community will believe that the allegations are true, no matter that the administrative investigation has ruled the allegation unfounded and the teacher has filed a lawsuit against the accuser. Although a teacher may be absolved of all wrongdoing in a court of law, the same may not hold true in the court of public opinion.

Considering the glacial pace of the legal system, a teacher might find that he or she must pursue the case over several years, all the time keeping the original false allegation before the public eye. In essence, the point essay suggests that we make allegations of sexual misconduct public, but that teachers should not worry, because if they are falsely accused, they can give the accusations even more publicity. Further, even if a teacher is successful in bringing a defamation lawsuit, is there an adequate remedy for having one's professional stature destroyed?

Most teachers will understandably be reluctant to pursue a remedy that involves suing one of their students. No matter how justified an innocent teacher may be, the fact remains that an adult suing a child looks something like a bully. A child who had made a false accusation will have benefited initially from the sympathy and indignation of the community, and that child will benefit again in a defamation suit from the perception that he or she is being attacked (in court) by an adult. Beyond this, however, most teachers enter the profession out of a sincere desire to help their students, and hauling a student into court is antithetical to this desire. Some teachers, as victims of false accusations, might well decide to forego legal retribution, on the grounds that losing a lawsuit would damage a child's future prospects. The teacher might well hope that the accuser has learned his or her lesson.

In the end, even if a teacher succeeds in his or her defamation suit, most likely years after the allegation is made, the damage to the teacher's reputation will have been done. As previously noted, parents are under no obligation to be scrupulously fair when assessing threats to their children's safety. There will be an inevitable tendency by some parents to blame the victim and to wonder what the teacher might have done to encourage an "innocent" child to make such an accusation in the first place. Parents, unless they are teachers themselves, will naturally see the situation from the point of view of the accuser, imagining what might have happened if their children had been in that situation. The innocent teacher will spend the remainder of his or her career under the dark shadow of heightened parental and student scrutiny, with every word and action examined for evidence of immoral intent.

Teachers' reputations are inherently more fragile than are those of the members of other professions, because the nature of a school is that new students (and parents) are brought into the school community every fall, where they learn the traditions and lore of the school from the upperclassmen. A doctor's new patients will not necessarily be in contact with his old patients, and an attorney's new clients will not necessarily speak with her former clients. But as long as a teacher remains at the same school, it is an absolute certainty that the class he or she teaches this year will meet and talk in the halls with students who took the same class the year before. There is no remedy for this kind of damage to a teacher's reputation; a court cannot realistically hope to enjoin students from spreading rumors in the halls of a school. The least that state legislatures can do is not compound the problem by making records of unsubstantiated allegations public.

CONCLUSION

My colleague rightly points out that teacher sexual misconduct is a serious problem. But it is precisely because it is so serious and so widespread that teacher privacy must be protected, for the sake of innocent teachers who are maliciously slandered by false accusations. Because the media have widely broadcast stories of teachers who are found guilty in criminal trials, the tendency of parents and fellow students will be to believe the accuser, even when evidence is lacking. The only reason why records of unfounded allegations should be made public is if one believes that they have some kind of probative value. In other words, the records might indicate to parents and students that a certain teacher could be more likely than other teachers to engage in future misconduct. But if the allegations are untrue, then the records prove nothing at all. The only result of making them publicly available would be to further damage the reputations of innocent teachers.

FURTHER READINGS AND RESOURCES

DeMitchell, T. A. (2002). The duty to protect: Blackstone's doctrine of in loco parentis: A lens for viewing the sexual abuse of students. *Brigham Young University Education and Law Journal, 2002*(1), 17–52.

Mawdsley, R., & Mawdsley, J. (2009). Balancing teacher privacy with the public's right to know: *Bellevue John Does v. Bellevue School District No. 405* and public access to reports of teacher sexual misconduct. *Education Law Reporter, 242,* 1–19.

Meruelo, N. C. (2008). The need to understand why patients sue and a proposal for a specific model of mediation. *Journal of Legal Medicine, 29*(3), 285–306.

Osborne, A. G., & Russo, C. J. (2011). *The legal rights and responsibilities of teachers: Issues of employment and instruction.* Thousand Oaks, CA: Corwin.

Sorenson, G. (1997). *Randi W.:* When half the truth in a letter of recommendation amounts to a lie. *Education Law Reporter, 119,* 331–334.

Stuart, S. P. (2008). Citizen teacher: Damned if you do, damned if you don't. *University of Cincinnati Law Review, 76,* 1281–1342.

U.S. Department of Education, Office of the Under Secretary, Policy and Program Studies Service. (2004). *Educator sexual misconduct: A synthesis of existing literature* (Doc #2004-09). Washington, DC: Author.

COURT CASES AND STATUTES

Andrews v. Independent School District, 12 P.3d 491 (Okla. Civ. App. 2000).

Bellevue John Does v. Bellevue School District # 405, 189 P.3d 139 (Wash. 2008).

Garcia v. State Board of Education, 694 P.2d 1371 (N.M. 1984).

Navarre v. South Washington County Schools, 652 N.W.2d 9 (Minn. 2002).

U.S. Constitution Amendment XIV, § 1.

Whalen v. Roe, 429 U.S. 589 (1977).

Wiese v. Freedom of Information Commission, 847 A.2d 1004 (Conn. Ct. App. 2004).

Should there be limits on student free speech?

POINT: Richard Fossey, *University of North Texas*
COUNTERPOINT: Jeffrey C. Sun, *University of North Dakota*

OVERVIEW

Perhaps the most cherished of all U.S. rights is the First Amendment right to freedom of speech. Yet, as central to democracy as the right to free speech is, it has led to no end of conflict, particularly when students seek to express themselves in public schools. Whether dealing with school policies delineating what students can wear to school, what they can say in school-sponsored assemblies, or what they may write in school-sponsored newspapers or on their own banners at school events, controversies have abounded. Moreover, the emergence of new technologies such as cell phones and communications via social networking sites has exacerbated disagreements as the law struggles to keep pace with technological advancements that affect the daily lives of schools and their students.

As detailed in greater depth in the following point and counterpoint essays, the legal principles governing the parameters of acceptable student free speech evolved out of four Supreme Court rulings. After initially finding that the students had a protected right to free speech, the three subsequent cases successively narrowed its scope. In these later cases, the Court granted school officials greater discretion in limiting the range of student expressive activities.

Tinker v. Des Moines Independent Community School District (1969), the Supreme Court's first case on the topic, represents the high-water mark of student free speech rights. In *Tinker*, the Court upheld the rights of students in Iowa to wear black armbands protesting U.S. military involvement in Vietnam. In its analysis, the Court created the often-cited standard that absent a reasonable forecast of material disruption, school officials could not limit student speech.

In *Bethel School District No. 403 v. Fraser* (1986), the Supreme Court held that a school in Washington State could discipline a student who delivered a nominating speech at a school assembly before elections for the student council. School officials characterized the speech as lewd because of its containing elaborate, graphic, and explicit sexual metaphors that caused a substantial disruption. At the heart of its rationale, the Court distinguished the nominating speech at issue from the passive political expression in *Tinker*. The Justices thus concluded that officials could exercise control over the student's expressive speech because it occurred in a school-sponsored forum and was inconsistent with the board's educational mission.

Two years later, in a dispute from Missouri, *Hazelwood School District v. Kuhlmeier* (1988), the Supreme Court further expanded the authority of educational officials. The Court ruled, "Educators do not offend the First Amendment by exercising editorial control over the style and content of student speech in school-sponsored expressive activities so long as their actions are reasonably related to legitimate pedagogical concerns" (p. 273).

Most recently, in *Morse v. Frederick* (2007), the Supreme Court clarified the free speech rights of students at school-supervised events. The dispute arose after the principal at a high school in Juneau, Alaska, had allowed students and staff, who supervised the event, to leave class to watch the Olympic Torch relay as an approved social event on the school calendar. The dispute arose when the principal suspended a student who displayed a banner at the event bearing what the principal interpreted as supporting illegal drug use. The Court decided that the principal could discipline the student for displaying the banner based on her reasonable fear that it promoted the use of illegal drugs at a school-supervised event.

The point and counterpoint essays both review these four same Supreme Court cases in defense of their positions. However, the essays go on to rely on an array of other cases discussing different aspects of student free speech to buttress their divergent perspectives on whether officials in public schools should have the authority to limit the First Amendment rights of students.

In the point essay, Richard Fossey, University of North Texas, questions the wisdom of cases that have given school officials the authority to regulate student speech only when it occurs in schools and causes or is likely to cause material and substantial disruptions. He argues that the cases involving the use of electronic communications demonstrate that *Tinker's* substantial disruption standard needs to be expanded to include speech and expressive activities that may have originated outside of schools but that affect activities within schools themselves. Fossey adds that educational officials should have the ability to discipline students for speech and expressive activities that are hurtful, bullying, or defamatory toward their peers or school employees, and thus are substantially disruptive by their very nature regardless of where they originated.

Conversely, the counterpoint essay by Jeffrey C. Sun, University of North Dakota, maintains that the courts have too often permitted educational officials to limit student speech unfairly. His essay posits that the judiciary needs to be more vigilant in protecting the free speech rights of students, regardless of form whether involving the spoken word, signs, dress, or the Internet. Only in adopting such an approach, Sun maintains, can school officials avoid interfering with parental rights and focus on implementing the educational missions of their schools as they inculcate societal values.

As you read these essays, ask yourself the following questions. First, should the post-*Tinker* Supreme Court cases be interpreted as primarily limiting the First Amendment speech rights of students or in enhancing the authority of educational officials to maintain safe and orderly learning environments? Second, should the Supreme Court reexamine the *Tinker* substantial disruption standard in light of the controversies that electronic communications devices can create? Put another way, should school officials be able to punish students who, for example, create parody websites of educators in their homes that eventually make their way into schools, regardless of whether their creators intended these materials to enter schools?

Charles J. Russo
University of Dayton

POINT: Richard Fossey
University of North Texas

This point essay argues that the courts should grant school officials greater authority to limit the free speech rights of students. In particular, in distinction to the counterpoint essay, this essay stands for the proposition that educational officials should be able to discipline students for offensive speech, including that which is delivered electronically from off-campus locations but that targets vulnerable peers or school employees.

The essay takes this position for three reasons. First, in the years since the Supreme Court's landmark decision in *Tinker v. Des Moines Independent Community School District* (1969), in which the Justices affirmed the free speech rights of students in the public schools, much of the litigation over the First Amendment rights of students has involved petty issues. Thus, student free speech litigation has often trivialized the First Amendment while affording some students, and their parents, the false impression that the First Amendment protects speech that is scurrilous, insulting, and even defamatory and involves absolutely no matter of public concern. Second, the easy access that students now have to electronic communications such as personal websites, blogs, e-mail, and social networking websites has given them enormous power to communicate to people all across the planet. Moreover, recent litigation has made it increasingly clear that some of students' cyberspeech is hurtful and wounding to peers, teachers, and school administrators, and that many children have not acquired the judgment or the moral sensitivity to refrain from using cyberspace in ways that are destructive to others. Third, courts have not rendered consistent judgments in student free-speech cases, leaving school administrators with no good guidance about what types of student speech can be regulated and what types are constitutionally protected.

At the same time, by arguing for a restriction of students' free speech rights, this essay is not endorsing Justice Clarence Thomas's views on the First Amendment rights of students in the schools, which in essence is that they should have no constitutional right of expression in school environments. In the 2007 case of *Morse v. Frederick*, Justice Thomas filed a concurring opinion in which he was of the view that the Supreme Court's holding in *Tinker* "is without basis in the Constitution" and should be overruled (p. 410). In this way, Justice Thomas argued that the notion that public school students have a First Amendment right of expression in the public schools has no foundation in our nation's history. To the contrary, the nation recognized the principle of in loco parentis until well into the 20th century while affording educational authorities broad discretion to act in a parental role over students while they are in school. In Justice Thomas's view,

> *Tinker* has undermined the traditional authority of teachers and educational officials to maintain order in public schools. "Once a society that generally respected the authority of teachers, deferred to their judgment, and trusted them to act in the best interest of school children, we now accept defiance, disrespect, and disorder as daily occurrences in many of our public schools." (Thomas, J., concurring, p. 421, quoting Dupre, 1996, p. 50)

This essay does not go as far as Justice Thomas. Nevertheless, it is clear that *Tinker* has spawned a subgenre of constitutional litigation in which students and their parents are claiming a right to speak in the schools over matters that are embarrassingly petty. It is also clear that the courts need to expand the authority of educational officials to regulate student speech outside of the school environment when it is delivered electronically and contains hurtful and even defamatory attacks on classmates or school authorities. After all, as Judge Richard Posner wrote in a 2008 Seventh Circuit opinion, "the contribution that kids can make to the marketplace in ideas and opinions is modest and a school's countervailing interest in protecting its students from offensive speech by their classmates is undeniable" (*Nuxoll v. Indian Prairie School District*, 2008, p. 671).

Most courts have limited the authority of educational officials to regulate student speech to that which occurs in the physical environment of their schools and causes or is likely to cause a "substantial disruption" in learning environments. This essay argues that recent cases show that the "substantial disruption" test as articulated in *Tinker* needs to be expanded to include student speech that is hurtful, wounding, bullying, or defamatory toward peers or school employees, because such speech is substantially disruptive by its very nature. Further, in recognition of the power of electronic media to communicate students' hurtful expressions and the disruptive impact that these communications can have in school settings, the essay takes the position that educational officials should have the authority to discipline students for inappropriate communications that target peers or school employees, even when those communications take place off-campus in the form of e-mail messages, blogs, personal websites, or social networking websites.

FREE SPEECH LITIGATION HAS ADDRESSED TRIVIAL ISSUES

More than 40 years ago, in *Tinker*, the U.S. Supreme Court affirmed the principle that students have a constitutional right under the First Amendment to express themselves in the public school environment. In *Tinker*, the Court made clear that students do not shed their constitutional rights at the schoolhouse gate. Unless student speech causes or is likely to cause substantial disruptions in school environments or interfere with the rights of others, the Court explained that they have the constitutional right to speak while on school grounds.

In the years since *Tinker* was decided, in three separate cases, the Supreme Court has qualified its broad holding in *Tinker*. In *Bethel School District No. 403 v. Fraser* (1986), the Court ruled that educational officials have a responsibility to inculcate civic values in their students; thus, school officials have the authority to censor student speech that is profane, lewd, or indecent. In *Hazelwood School District v. Kuhlmeier* (1988), the Court upheld the right of school authorities to regulate student speech in the context of school-sponsored student-expressive activities so long as officials have a legitimate pedagogical reason for doing so. Most recently, in *Morse*, the Court, in a narrow ruling, stated emphatically that school officials can prohibit student speech that promotes the use of illegal drugs. Nevertheless, *Hazelwood, Bethel School District*, and *Morse* together have not undermined the Supreme Court's core holding in *Tinker* that students have First Amendment speech rights while in school environments.

In *Tinker*, students in a district in Iowa wore black armbands to school to symbolize their opposition to the ongoing Vietnam War. After educational officials enacted a special rule prohibiting the students from wearing the armbands, the students were suspended from school when they refused to take the armbands off. Thus, *Tinker* involved political speech about an important and controversial public issue—the war in Vietnam.

Unfortunately, in the years since *Tinker*, litigation involving the First Amendment rights of students has rarely involved serious social or political issues. For example, in a 1995 case, the federal trial court in New Mexico rejected a student argument that he had a First Amendment right to wear sagging pants to school since doing so symbolized his affirmation of African American culture (*Bivens v. Albuquerque Public Schools*). In another case from 2005, a student's father, who was an attorney, sued a school board in Tennessee arguing that its uniform policy violated his daughter's constitutional rights under the First Amendment. The daughter apparently was arguing that she had a constitutional right to wear clothes she "feels good in" (*Blau v. Fort Thomas Public School District*, 2005, p. 389). The Sixth Circuit rejected these constitutional arguments, noting that her claim "amounts to nothing more than a generalized and vague desire to express her middle-class individuality" (p. 389). Other students have sued to assert a constitutional right to wear messages on their T-shirts; indeed, law review articles have been written about the constitutional litigation over students' T-shirt messages (Dupre, 1996; Fossey, Eckes, & DeMitchell, 2010).

Perhaps nothing illustrates the depth of pettiness to which litigation over students' free speech rights has sunk better than the Supreme Court's 2007 judgment in *Morse* where a principal of a high school in Juneau, Alaska, punished a student for displaying a banner that proclaimed "BONG HiTS 4 JESUS" at a school-sponsored event. The Ninth Circuit ruled that the principal violated the student's well-established First Amendment rights and could be sued personally for monetary damages.

On appeal to the Supreme Court, school officials argued that the phrase "BONG HiTS 4 JESUS" could be construed by other students as advocating or promoting illegal drug use. In fact, the student himself admitted that "the words were just nonsense meant to attract television cameras" (p. 401). Despite his contention that the phrase was basically meaningless, the student responded that he had a constitutional right to proclaim "BONG HiTS 4 JESUS" all the way to the Supreme Court.

Fortunately for school authorities all over the United States, the Supreme Court rejected the student's constitutional arguments. The Court ruled that educational officials can restrict student speech "that they reasonably regard as promoting illegal drug use" (p. 408), adding that they need not tolerate student speech at school events when such speech contributes to the dangers of illegal drug use and violates established school policy. Of course, the Court refused to impose financial liability on the principal.

WRONGFUL CONSTITUTIONAL PROTECTION OF HURTFUL SPEECH

A recent controversial decision of the Third Circuit illustrates the enormous potential harm that student speech can have when it gratuitously demeans school administrators and is delivered electronically on a social networking website. In *Layshock v. Hermitage School District* (2010), a high school student in Pennsylvania created a fake MySpace profile of his principal, implying that the educator used steroids and smoked marijuana. In the parody profile's "Interests" section, the student inserted the words "Transgender, Appreciators of Alcoholic Beverages" (p. 253), and he posted a photo of the principal on the MySpace profile that had been taken from the school's website. Even though the principal considered the parody profile to be demeaning and degrading, the court found that school officials had violated the student's First Amendment rights when it punished him for the MySpace escapade. In the court's view, educational officials had been unable to show that the student's parody MySpace profile, which he had created while off the school campus, created a substantial disruption at the school.

It is impossible to quantify the damage done when a student demeans a school principal in the manner described in *Layshock*. Certainly, for a school principal to see a web posting that intimates he uses marijuana and misrepresents his sexual identify goes beyond mere discomfort. Such a characterization of the principal must be deeply demoralizing to the principal himself and likely undermines his moral authority as the school's instructional leader. Moreover, persons who view the fake profile may very well conclude that the representations about the principal are true, which would cause some people to lose respect for the principal. When this type of demeaning speech expresses no important social or political message and is merely hurtful, it does not seem reasonable to give speech the protection of the First Amendment.

A 2010 case out of California also illustrates the inappropriateness of giving constitutional protection to adolescent prattle. In *J.C. v. Beverly Hills Unified School District*, a student posted a video on YouTube that showed a classmate calling another classmate a "slut" and expressing the opinion that she was ugly. After school officials punished the student who posted the YouTube video, she filed suit. A federal trial court determined that because the video had not created a substantial disruption in the school environment, educational officials exceeded their constitutional authority when they disciplined the student for expression that took place off-campus.

As with the *Layshock* case, the harm caused by the YouTube posting in *J.C. v. Beverly Hills Unified School District* seems obvious. Surely, school authorities should have the authority to discipline a student who uses electronic media to transmit a verbal attack on an eighth-grade girl, an action with no social or political significance.

INCONSISTENCY OF JURISPRUDENCE ON STUDENTS' FREE SPEECH RIGHTS

Finally, this essay argues that since federal jurisprudence on the contours of students' free speech rights has been inconsistent, it has afforded educational authorities little guidance about what kinds of student speech can be regulated, particularly electronically delivered speech. This inconsistency is dramatically illustrated by two recent Third Circuit opinions (McCarthy, 2010). In *Layshock* (discussed earlier), the Third Circuit ruled that a student's fake MySpace profile, which had demeaned a school principal, had not created a substantial disruption in the school environment. The court thus asserted that school officials could not punish the student who posted the profile on MySpace (Fossey & Dryden, 2010).

On the same day the *Layshock* opinion was released, the same Third Circuit panel, addressing facts similar to those in *Layshock*, reasoned that since a student's parody MySpace profile of a school principal had a clear potential for disrupting the school environment, educational officials could discipline him without violating the First Amendment (*J.S. v. Blue Mountain School District*, 2010). The court pointed out that although the MySpace profile in *Blue Mountain* did not identify the principal by name, it did feature his photograph. In addition, the parody profile described the principal as a "married bisexual forty-year-old man" and listed his interests as "f—ing in my office" and "hitting on students and their parents" (p. 291).

Not long after the initial opinions in *Layshock* and *Blue Mountain* were released, the Third Circuit accepted both decisions for en banc review. Affirming the earlier judgment in *Layshock* and partially reversing in *Blue Mountain*, the court agreed that educational officials could not discipline either of the students because they created their parodies off-campus and their actions were unlikely to disrupt school activities. Clearly, both of these rulings complicate the lives of school officials.

CONCLUSION

In the years since the Supreme Court decided *Tinker*, litigation over the First Amendment rights of students has frequently involved petty issues involving no political or social issue that concerns the public. However, in recent years, students have used MySpace, YouTube, personal websites, blogs, and e-mail to demean other students or school authorities with electronically delivered communications that are insulting, degrading, and sometimes defamatory. Courts have ruled inconsistently regarding the authority of school officials to discipline students who engage in these episodes of "cybertrashing."

Courts need to give school administrators the clear authority to discipline students who use the Internet to gratuitously insult school officials or their classmates. These cyberattacks, which demoralize the victims and undermine their self-esteem, are disruptive by their very nature and should be punished under the *Tinker* decision's "substantial disruption" test. Courts perform a grave disservice with regard to public education when they give constitutional protection to student speech that wounds others and has absolutely no social or political importance.

COUNTERPOINT: Jeffrey C. Sun
University of North Dakota

In *Tinker v. Des Moines Independent Community School District* (1969), the U.S. Supreme Court aptly noted that students do not "shed their constitutional rights to freedom of speech or expression at the schoolhouse gate" (p. 506). Nonetheless, there is evidence from case patterns and news reports that school administrators have attempted to place restrictions on student speech or acted in ways unduly limiting students' free speech rights within and beyond the schoolhouse gates. This essay argues that courts should provide students with greater free speech rights so that school officials can properly focus on their educational mission of inculcating societal values rather than placing their efforts on disciplining students and missing educational opportunities.

Although this essay argues that students need greater opportunities for free speech, it is not claiming that they need absolute freedom or that administrators should be stripped of all authority pertaining to the regulation and control of student behaviors and speech. Instead, the essay suggests that courts and school officials have, at times, gone too far in limiting student speech.

NARROWING THE SCOPE OF STUDENT FREE SPEECH RIGHTS

Between 1969 and 2007, the Supreme Court rendered four decisions addressing student free speech. Although the initial case, *Tinker*, recognized the free speech rights of public school students, the three subsequent opinions significantly curbed those rights by focusing on and delineating administrators' authority over student speech. The cases following *Tinker* appear to be outcomes that align with societal values; nevertheless, the rulings presented a symbolic shift away from student free speech rights with each increasingly granting administrators greater authority to limit student speech while imposing disciplinary sanctions.

Tinker v. Des Moines

In *Tinker*, the Supreme Court declared that public school students have a right to express themselves when the questioned speech cannot reasonably lead officials to forecast substantial disruption of or material interference with school activities or when they cannot demonstrate actual material or substantial disruption of school operations. In *Tinker*, administrators suspended students for wearing black armbands that symbolized their objections to the Vietnam War. Anticipating this silent protest, school principals adopted a policy that prohibited students from wearing armbands at school. On the next school day, five students who wore the armbands were suspended. Three of the students sued the board for violating their free speech rights. Ruling in favor of the students, the Court warned that public "schools may not be enclaves of totalitarianism. School officials do not possess absolute authority over their students" (p. 511). The Court set out an understanding that public school students have rights, and the administrators' "undifferentiated fear or apprehension of disturbance [was] not enough to overcome [the students'] right to freedom of expression" (p. 508).

Bethel v. Fraser

In 1986, the Supreme Court began carving out exceptions significantly limiting student free speech. In *Bethel School District No. 403 v. Fraser* (1986), the Court declared that school officials have permissible authority to discipline students who convey offensively lewd and indecent messages. According to the Court, those expressions did not constitute student free speech. The contested speech took place in a school assembly to nominate candidates for student government when a student delivered a speech that contained sexual metaphors. Reacting to his speech, students in the audience hooted, yelled, and made sexual gestures. The following day, the school suspended the speaker and removed him from the list of qualified candidates to deliver the graduation speech. Before delivering the speech, the student was aware of the potential consequences because teachers warned him that his messages might warrant disciplinary action. Even so, the student delivered the speech. In its analysis, the Court relied on a foundational case about the school environment, which established a lower standard for administrators to search and seize a student's belongings. The *Fraser* Court reiterated that as a general rule, "the constitutional rights of students in public school are not automatically coextensive with the rights of adults in other settings" (p. 682). Rationalizing the need for greater authority to restrict student speech, the Court repeatedly emphasized that schools have an educational mission of inculcating societal values that includes officials' capacity to regulate and control offensively lewd and indecent speech.

Hazelwood v. Kuhlmeier

Two years later, the Supreme Court again limited the capacity for students to speak in school. In *Hazelwood School District v. Kuhlmeier* (1988), the Court declared that educators can exercise editorial control over the style and content of student speech when it involves school-sponsored expressive activities and the controls are reasonably related to legitimate pedagogical concerns. Here, a principal exercised editorial control over two student articles—one on student pregnancy and the other about a student's experience with the divorce of her parents. The Court characterized the newspaper as school sponsored and having the school's imprimatur. Given these conditions and the school's role in advancing societal values, the Court indicated that educators may exercise editorial control when a school's name and resources make it possible for students to disseminate their speech.

Morse v. Frederick

In 2007, the Supreme Court again limited student free speech. The Court held that school administrators may prohibit speech when they reasonably believe that it promotes illegal drug use. More specifically, in *Morse v. Frederick*, the Court determined that a principal had the authority to suspend a student for 10 days when he did not comply with her order to remove a sign that read "BONG HiTS 4 JESUS," as students watched the Olympic Torch relay pass by the school. Although the event was off-campus, it was part of a school activity. Given the connection to a school activity, the Court recognized the principal's authority, declaring that officials "may take steps to safeguard those entrusted to their care from speech that can reasonably be regarded as encouraging illegal drug use" (p. 397). In other words, the Court recognized that because schools are institutions charged with the responsibility of advancing social values, officials must have authority, particularly for discipline, to limit student speech.

EXPANDING SCHOOL AUTHORITY BEYOND SUPREME COURT DECISIONS

Many other courts have narrowed student free speech beyond Supreme Court precedent. More specifically, in a variety of instances, lower courts have fashioned their opinions using more liberal readings of Supreme Court cases to justify giving school officials greater authority over student speech, thereby limiting students' rights.

Examples of cases narrowing students' speech rights even exist over matters of political speech. The courts have long recognized that political speech deserves a high level of protection from government interference. Quoting an earlier Supreme Court case, *Morse*, the latest of the highest court's opinions on student free speech, emphasized, "Political speech, of course, is 'at the core of what the First Amendment is designed to protect'" (*Morse*, 2007, p. 403). In accordance with that general proposition, the *Tinker* Court, which protected students' political speech conveyed in a symbolic manner, established a rule of substantial disruption or material interference as narrowed circumstances in which educators may regulate or control student speech. Although that rule is intended to apply only to significant disruption, not to mere inconveniences or annoyances for school administrators, courts have liberally applied the disruption standard to meet the state's compelling interest of limiting student free speech—even in matters involving political speech.

In *Doninger v. Niehoff* (2008), the Second Circuit upheld discipline of a student for her public statements on a blog. The student, who also served on the student council, voiced her objections about the administrators' policies to change the venue of the annual battle of the bands concert several days before the event. The blog comments also encouraged readers to voice their opinions to try to convince the principal and superintendent to change their decision. On the following day, both the principal and superintendent received a flood of calls and e-mails expressing concerns about the venue choice. Later that day, the school administrators and student council agreed to reschedule the event in the new auditorium. The principal later learned about the blog posting and disciplined the student by disqualifying her from running for student council. When the student won through write-in votes, school officials disallowed her candidacy.

The Second Circuit agreed with school officials that *Tinker*'s disruption standard justified their actions. Indeed, *Tinker* permits officials to curb political speech as long as they can at least demonstrate a reasonable forecast of a substantial disruption or a material interference with school operations. To protect political speech, the court noted that this standard cannot rest on a mere desire to avoid the discomfort and unpleasantness resulting from students' expressions of unpopular views. Thus, some courts have examined similar incidents, including gang violence, outbursts from racial tension, psychological intimidation affecting academic performance, and students' perceived capacity to inflict harm onto another or school property, as barometers of forecasted problems. Yet, *Doninger* reflected student political speech to petition the administration to change a policy about an event. In short, *Doninger*, and other cases, extended *Tinker* to grant school administrators' greater authority over student speech.

Prior Supreme Court rulings narrowing student free speech have been extended to grant school officials the authority to discipline students for their off-campus speech. Most often, this line of cases has asserted *Tinker* as precedent. For instance, although the student's political speech in *Doninger* occurred off-campus, the Second Circuit held that under *Tinker*, administrators could discipline her because it was reasonably foreseeable that the blog message would reach school property and create a disruption. According to the court, the disruption was manifested in verbal protests of the administrators' decision by students and parents and in the principal's having to call student council members out of classes to discuss rescheduling the event. Although the actions may seem to amount to nothing more than mere inconveniences, *Doninger* illustrates how courts have given officials greater leeway in limiting student free speech—even to a point of departing from Supreme Court precedent.

EXPANDING SCHOOL AUTHORITY INTO THE PARENTAL DOMAIN

Limits on student free speech can conflict with parental rights and interests. The Supreme Court has made clear that parents have the right to direct the upbringing of their children free of government intervention. In *Troxel v. Granville* (2000), the Court declared that the Due Process Clause of the Fourteenth Amendment gives parents the fundamental right to make child-rearing decisions. Generally speaking, the Constitution does not permit the government, via public schools, to develop policies that interfere with parental decisions about the care, custody, and control of their children.

The cases discussed in this essay demonstrate that parents and guardians object to regulations on school speech. Generally speaking, minors cannot file suit, but their parents or guardians can act on their behalf. In these student free speech challenges, the parents' involvement essentially conveys their disagreement with the actions of officials who seek to censor students or discipline them for their speech. Although some of the disputes about dress codes appear as insignificant and petty legal questions, to some students and their parents, they represent cases in which the parties oppose specific regulations and object to the reach of school officials whom they claim meddled into matters best left for parents.

For instance, in *Palmer v. Waxahachie Independent School District* (2009), school officials adopted a dress code policy banning T-shirts with printed messages unless they were connected to clubs, sports teams, universities, or "school spirit." When a high school student wore a T-shirt stating "San Diego," an administrator informed him of his violation. The student called his parents, who brought him another T-shirt, which this time displayed a political message: "John Edwards for President '08." An administrator informed the student that he could not wear that T-shirt either. The student, through his parents, unsuccessfully sought a preliminary injunction that would have allowed him to wear the shirt.

On appeal, the Fifth Circuit affirmed in favor of the board. The court reasoned that the policy was simple; it generally barred all T-shirts with only a few exceptions. The policy was also arguably content-neutral because it did not bar messages of which school officials disapproved.

The significance of *Palmer* and other cases addressing student dress code challenges is that they announced a broad legal policy. Specifically, these cases grant officials the authority to impinge on students' expression on clothing at school, even when the clothing addresses important social and political matters. Certainly, some T-shirts may display such obscene and offensive images and words that they add little or no social or political value. Under the law, these shirts warrant low levels of constitutional protections, if any at all. Nonetheless, as *Palmer* illustrates, some student clothing contains expressions that qualify as pure speech, which is more explicit than the symbolic speech in *Tinker* involving social or political matters worthy of debate and discourse. Despite the social or political messages, which often present age-appropriate educational opportunities, many courts have contended that no First Amendment issues arise in student challenges of dress code policies. In *Palmer*, the circuit court acknowledged that clothing could convey pure speech protected under the First Amendment and that the dress code policy would cause irreparable harm to the student by violating his right to free speech. Still, the court was satisfied that given the important governmental interest of maintaining a safe and orderly learning environment, the content-neutral policy did not violate the student's First Amendment right to free speech.

The rationalization of the court in *Palmer* and cases like it is less comforting to parents. In these cases, some parents feel that by affirming school policies, the courts have granted officials authority over areas within parents' domain. Further, parents interpret the rulings as validating the school's use of discipline rather than providing educational opportunities. Together, these concerns draw attention to claims about the actions of school officials unduly limiting student free speech.

CONCLUSION

Supreme Court cases establishing rules for student free speech aside, an ongoing tug of war remains between parents and their children on the one hand and educational officials on the other, over who should control the content of student speech in schools. Although these cases may appear petty, they raise an important question: How far can administrators go in determining acceptable content of student speech and how and when can students express themselves? In various instances, courts have allowed school administrators to go too far with their limits on student free speech.

Further Readings and Resources

Backus, M. S. (2009). OMG!: Missing the teachable moment and undermining the future of the First Amendment—TISNF! *Case Western Reserve Law Review, 60*(1), 153–204.

Dupre, A. P. (1996). Should students have constitutional rights? Keeping order in the public schools. *George Washington Law Review, 65*, 49–105.

Dupre, A. P. (2009). *Speaking up: The unintended costs of free speech in public schools.* Cambridge, MA: Harvard University Press.

Fossey, R., & Dryden, J. (2010, July 22). Do students have a constitutional right to humiliate school principals on MySpace? Maybe yes, maybe no. *Teachers College Record.* Available from http://www.tcrecord.org (ID Number: 16080)

Fossey, R., Eckes, S., & DeMitchell, T. A. (2010). Anti-gay T-shirt litigation in the Seventh and Ninth Circuits: Conflicting outcomes but shared values. *Education Law Reporter, 255*, 1–16.

Ianelli, J. F. (2010). Punishment and student speech: Straining the reach of the First Amendment. *Harvard Journal of Law & Public Policy, 33*(2), 885–906.

McCarthy, M. (2010). Cyberspeech controversies in the Third Circuit. *Education Law Reporter, 258*, 1–14.

Waldman, E. G. (2010). Regulating student speech: Suppression versus punishment. *Indiana Law Journal, 85*(3), 1113–1147.

Warnick, B. R. (2009). Student speech rights and the special characteristics of the school environment. *Educational Researcher, 38*(3), 200–215.

Court Cases and Statutes

Bethel School District No. 403 v. Fraser, 478 U.S. 675 (1986).

Bivens v. Albuquerque Public Schools, 899 F. Supp. 556 (D.N.M. 1995).

Blau v. Fort Thomas Public School District, 401 F.3d 381 (6th Cir. 2005).

Doninger v. Niehoff, 527 F.3d 41 (2d Cir. 2008).

Hazelwood School District v. Kuhlmeier, 484 U.S. 260 (1988).

J.C. v. Beverly Hills Unified School District, 711 F.Supp. 2d 1094 (C.D. Cal. 2010).

J.S. v. Blue Mountain School District, 593 F.3d 286, *reh'g en banc granted, opinion vacated* (3rd Cir. 2010), *affirmed in part, reversed in part*, —F.3d——, 2011 WL 2305973 C.A.3 (Pa.), 2011.

Layshock v. Hermitage School District, 593 F.3d 249, *reh'g en banc granted, opinion vacated* (3rd Cir. 2010), *affirmed*, —F.3d——, 2011 WL 2305970 (3d Cir. 2011).

Morse v. Frederick, 551 U.S. 393 (2007).

Nuxoll v. Indian Prairie School District, 523 F.3d 668 (7th Cir. 2008).

Palmer v. Waxahachie Independent School District, 579 F.3d 502 (5th Cir. 2009).

Tinker v. Des Moines Independent Community School District, 393 U.S. 503 (1969).

Troxel v. Granville, 530 U.S. 57 (2000).

12

Should there be limits on teacher free speech rights?

POINT: Robert C. Cloud, *Baylor University*

COUNTERPOINT: Jeffrey C. Sun, *University of North Dakota*

OVERVIEW

The First Amendment of the U.S. Constitution states that Congress, and by extension state governments and local school boards, cannot pass laws or resolutions abridging the freedoms of speech or press. Although it is fairly well settled that teachers do not forfeit the basic right of all citizens to speak out on matters of public concern, as the essays in this chapter show, controversy still exists about whether certain expressions constitute matters of public concern and to what extent school boards can control the speech of teachers in their classrooms. For the most part, a matter of public concern is one that is of interest to a community for social, political, or other reasons (*Dill v. City of Edmond*, 1998). Thus, teachers may voice criticisms of school board policies or speak out on school matters as long as they are issues of public concern, but teachers cannot air private grievances under the guise of free speech. In the same way that freedom of speech does not give one the right to yell "fire" in a crowded theater, expressions that disrupt the educational environment can be curtailed. Further, to the extent that school boards can control curricula, teachers lack the freedom of speech in their classrooms that they have in public meetings.

As detailed in both the point and counterpoint essays in this chapter, a line of Supreme Court cases, beginning with *Pickering v. Board of Education of Township High School District 205* (1968), recognizes that the rights of teachers to speak on matters of public concern cannot be curtailed unless there is a compelling state interest in curbing such speech. In another case, *Connick v. Myers* (1983), the Court added that the First Amendment does not extend to the expressions of public employees about their personal interests and that even when individuals speak out on matters of public concern, they are not protected when the government's interest in efficiency outweighs the value of their statements to the public.

More recently, in *Garcetti v. Ceballos* (2006), the Supreme Court held that statements made as part of the official duties of public employees do not enjoy First Amendment protection because employees in such situations are not speaking as private citizens. The Court reasoned that public employers need some control over the words and actions of their employees to preserve the efficient delivery of public services. The task for courts and other adjudicators is to determine whether the challenged expressive activities of employees dealt with public matters, and if so, whether those making the expressions did so as private citizens or as part of their official responsibilities.

Teachers have limited free expression rights in their classrooms. School boards have the authority to establish and control curricula, and teachers at the elementary and secondary levels have little academic freedom, so their speech within their classrooms can be restricted. In this respect, teachers particularly need to guard against expressing political and religious views in their classrooms. Courts recognize that school boards may regulate teacher speech for pedagogical reasons. For example, the Tenth Circuit explained that insofar as classrooms are not public fora, the speech of teachers in classes can be treated as school sponsored for First Amendment purposes. Moreover, since students are captive audiences within public school classrooms, the court noted that the right of teachers to express or advocate viewpoints departing from official curricula can be restricted (*Mayer v. Monroe County Community School Corporation*, 2007).

In the point essay, Robert C. Cloud, Baylor University, maintains that the free speech rights of public school teachers have always been limited so that prudent educators have had to take care in what they said and did. He agrees that teachers should be able to speak out on school-related issues without fear of dismissal but argues that there are good reasons why public policy and the courts have limited teachers' free speech rights. Specifically, Cloud postulates that some expressions can damage the working relationships between and among teachers with their colleagues and supervisors or violate the privacy rights of students. He also argues that provocative speech that may create distractions, demoralize staff, or reduce the efficiency and effectiveness of schools can be controlled. Cloud believes that insofar as courts have balanced the rights of teachers with those of school boards and the general public, the current limitations are likely to remain in place.

Jeffrey C. Sun, University of North Dakota, takes a different view in the counterpoint essay, responding that the law should not place any limits on the speech of teachers other than those reasonably necessary to advance the educational missions of schools. He observes that courts have recognized that schools have unique organizational contexts and have thus acknowledged that teachers require a slightly different legal framework than other public employees require. Even so, Sun posits that the courts have gone too far in limiting the speech rights of teachers and that, as professionals, they should be given the freedom to practice their profession. Unnecessary limits on teacher speech, he states, unduly restrict their professional practice, which can inadvertently make schools inefficient and obstruct the achievement of educational goals.

As this discussion, coupled with the point and counterpoint essays in this chapter, demonstrates, the issue of the extent to which the free speech rights of teachers should be limited remains controversial. In reading these essays, reflect on the following questions: As public employees, should teachers have the same rights as private citizens have to criticize or question the actions of their employers without restriction? Should schools provide their employees with a forum for expressing their views on important topics without fear of reprisal? In accepting public employment, should teachers expect to give up some of their constitutional rights? Do the free expression rights of teachers allow them to air their personal views in the classroom when those views are contrary to the approved curriculum? Should teachers be allowed to use their classroom as a soapbox or a forum for proselytizing? How should teachers respond when students ask them about their personal beliefs on topics being studied in class?

Allan G. Osborne, Jr.
Principal (Retired), Snug Harbor Community School,
Quincy, Massachusetts

POINT: Robert C. Cloud
Baylor University

S hould there be limits on the free speech rights of public school teachers? Perhaps the better question might be, will the existing limitations on teacher free speech rights be continued? The free speech rights of public school teachers have always been limited, whether they speak inside or outside of their classrooms. In the first place, because public employment has long been considered a privilege rather than a right, teachers were expected to restrain their speech in exchange for the security of a public job.

Teachers who did speak out on controversial issues or questioned the actions of school officials were often dismissed or otherwise disciplined, regardless of the circumstances. School boards and the general public have expected teachers to serve in loco parentis and as role models for their students. Consequently, prudent teachers have been careful about what they said and did. Ironically, membership in the education profession itself has influenced the speech and actions of public school teachers for a long time. The general public tends to judge schools by the speech and personal conduct of educational leaders, so teachers are obligated to speak accurately and exercise appropriate restraint in interpersonal relations; each of these obligations tends to temper, if not limit, free speech (American Association of University Professors, 2001, p. 2).

During the first half of the 20th century, the First Amendment was seldom cited when teachers were disciplined for challenging school board actions. Courts applied the common law reasonableness test in assessing speech-related issues. If there was a reasonable relationship between a board's action and a legitimate educational purpose, courts typically sustained their actions even if they infringed on the free speech rights of teachers. When teachers did succeed in First Amendment claims, courts based their rulings on the reasonableness test rather than alleged violations of constitutional rights. Given this reality, generations of public school teachers limited their comments on school-related or other public matters whether they were speaking to students, parents, or the general public.

LITIGATION ON TEACHERS' FREE SPEECH RIGHTS: BALANCED AND LIMITED

In a series of cases beginning with *Pickering v. Board of Education* in 1968, the U.S. Supreme Court articulated standards by which to evaluate the extent of free speech protection for teachers and other public employees. In subsequent decisions, the Court added further guidance in terms of when teachers may exercise their free speech rights on matters of public concern.

Pickering v. Board of Education

First Amendment protection for teachers increased dramatically in 1968 when the Supreme Court ruled in *Pickering v. Board of Education* that teachers have a right to speak as citizens on matters of public concern without fear of retribution. Indeed, the Court emphasized the importance of allowing public school teachers to speak out on school matters.

> Teachers are, as a class, the members of a community most likely to have informed and definite opinions as to how funds allocated to the operations of the schools should be spent. Accordingly, it is essential that they be able to speak out freely on such matters without fear of retaliatory dismissal. (*Pickering*, p. 572)

After *Pickering*, public school boards were required to show a compelling state interest to overcome the First Amendment rights of teachers to comment on matters of public concern.

Marvin Pickering was fired from his teaching position after his letter criticizing the local school board's fiscal policies was published in the local newspaper. In reinstating Pickering, the Supreme Court acknowledged the judiciary's challenge in adjudicating free speech claims of schoolteachers and other public employees.

> It cannot be gainsaid that the State has interests as an employer in regulating the speech of its employees that differ significantly from those it possesses in connection with regulation of the speech of the citizenry in general. The problem is to arrive at a balance between the interests of the teacher, as a citizen, in commenting on matters of public concern and the interest of the State, as an employer, in promoting the efficiency of the public services it performs through its employees. (*Pickering*, p. 568)

Under the now famous *Pickering* balancing test, a court's initial analysis focuses on whether a teacher spoke as a citizen on a matter of public concern. If the answer is no, the teacher lacks First Amendment protection from an adverse employment action. If the speech does involve a matter of public concern, the balancing test is triggered and the court must consider whether the teacher's right to speak as a citizen trumps the interest of the board in providing efficient public services. Even if a teacher's speech addresses a public concern, it may be so disruptive to the work environment or may so impede the individual's effectiveness and relationships with supervisors that a board is justified legally in disciplining the speaker. Clearly, the speech rights of public school teachers are restricted even under *Pickering*, which is widely recognized as the landmark decision ensuring First Amendment protection for public employees. Subsequently, the Supreme Court refined the legal framework for public employee speech analysis in a series of cases.

Mt. Healthy v. Doyle

In 1977, the Supreme Court dealt with another teacher free speech case in *Mt. Healthy City School District v. Doyle.* Doyle, a probationary teacher, was not rehired after his involvement in several incidents that embarrassed the school board. He was involved in altercations with another teacher and school cafeteria workers. On two other separate occasions, the teacher swore at students and made obscene gestures to two female students who failed to comply with his directives as a cafeteria supervisor. Subsequently, Doyle telephoned a radio program and released information from an internal administrative memorandum regarding a teacher dress code. The board cited the obscene gestures and radio station incidents when it notified Doyle of the nonrenewal of his contract. Doyle filed suit alleging violation of his First Amendment rights, and the two lower courts ruled in his favor.

The primary issue in *Mt. Healthy* was whether the school board could dismiss the teacher who engaged in protected speech when there was justification for the nonrenewal separate and apart from the speech issue. Stated another way, will a school board's dismissal decision be upheld when it can show that it would have dismissed the employee even in the absence of the employee's constitutionally protected expression? The Supreme Court's answer was yes. Often employees are dismissed for more than one reason. If the employee can successfully make the claim that one of the reasons for his dismissal was for conduct that was constitutionally protected, the employer must then show that even absent that reason, it would have reached the same result because of the other stated reasons for dismissal. If it can do that, its decision will be upheld. The moral of *Mt. Healthy* is that public employers do not have to retain disruptive or incompetent employees who file free speech claims to obfuscate legitimate employment concerns.

Givhan v. Western Line

Two years after *Mt. Healthy*, the Supreme Court dealt with another teacher free speech case in *Givhan v. Western Line Consolidated School District* (1979). In *Givhan*, a public school teacher was fired for complaining directly and privately to her principal about district employment policies and practices that she believed were discriminatory. When the teacher sought reinstatement, a federal appeals court upheld the school board's dismissal decision because she had expressed her complaints and opinions privately to the principal. On appeal, the Supreme Court reversed, finding that a teacher's private speech to the employer enjoys the same constitutional protection as speech that is expressed publicly (*Givhan*, pp. 415–416). To the Court, Bessie Givhan's allegation that the board violated federal equal employment statutes was a matter of public concern. Consequently, the Court concluded that the speech was protected by the First Amendment regardless of whether it was expressed privately or publicly.

Connick v. Myers

In *Connick v. Myers* (1983), an assistant district attorney was fired after circulating a questionnaire among colleagues concerning office transfer policies, employee morale, and the political climate in the office. Sheila Myers sued her employer, alleging violation of her First Amendment right to speak. Both lower courts ruled in Myers's favor, agreeing that distributing the questionnaire, not her refusal to accept a transfer, was the real reason for her dismissal. Agreeing that the questionnaire contained matters of public concern, the lower courts held that the state had not clearly demonstrated that the questionnaire interfered with the operation of the district attorney's (DA's) office.

The Supreme Court reversed in favor of the employer, ruling that Myers's questionnaire focused more on her personal interests in the workplace than on legitimate matters of public concern. The Court held that "whether an employee's speech addresses a matter of public concern must be determined by the content, form, and context of a given statement, as revealed by the whole record" (*Connick*, pp. 147–148). Noting that "the manner, time, and place of contested speech" is germane in determining whether it reflects a matter of public concern (*Connick*, p. 152), the Court ruled that Myers's questionnaire touched on matters of public concern only in a limited sense and her survey focused primarily on a personal grievance regarding an office transfer policy rather than a matter of public concern.

After balancing Myers's personal rights against Harry Connick, Sr.'s interest in maintaining order and efficiency in the DA's office, the Court thought it unnecessary for an employer to wait until working relationships were damaged or office operations disrupted before taking action. In *Connick v. Myers*, the Court refined its free speech jurisprudence to clarify that a public employee's speech must pertain to matters of genuine public concern if it is to merit constitutional protection. According to the Court, speech on personal interests in the workplace is not protected and is not an appropriate matter for adjudication in the courts.

> When a public employee speaks not as a citizen upon matters of public concern, but instead as an employee upon matters only of personal interest, absent the most unusual circumstances, a federal court is not the appropriate forum in which to review the wisdom of a personnel decision taken by a public agency allegedly in reaction to the employee's behavior. (*Connick*, p. 147)

Based on the Supreme Court's instructions in *Pickering, Connick*, and their progeny, federal courts used a two-pronged inquiry to determine free speech protection for public employees. Under *Pickering*, courts first evaluate whether an employee spoke as a citizen on a public issue. If not, and the speech was on a personal matter, then the employee's speech was unprotected. Next, if the speech was a matter of public concern, courts determine whether the public employer's interest in efficiency outweighed the public value of the employee's expression. If it did, then its action is upheld in the face of the First Amendment challenge. Consequently, under this analysis, employees such as Myers who speak on matters of personal interest lack causes of action. The *Pickering-Connick* analysis was used as a standard in free-speech jurisprudence for more than 20 years.

Garcetti v. Ceballos

In *Garcetti v. Ceballos* (2006), the Supreme Court altered the *Pickering-Connick* analysis standard, considering whether the First Amendment protects a government employee from discipline based on speech made pursuant to the employee's official duties. Richard Ceballos, a deputy district attorney, claimed that supervisors retaliated against him for expressing concern that a search warrant was flawed and then testifying in court for the defense about the issue. The district attorney argued that since Ceballos spoke on matters directly related to his assigned duties as a public prosecutor and not as a citizen on a matter of public concern, the office could exercise reasonable control over what the employer commissioned or created.

Ultimately, the Supreme Court ruled against Ceballos. In a 5–4 decision, the Court found that when public employees make statements pursuant to their official duties, they are not speaking as citizens for First Amendment purposes, and the Constitution does not protect their communications from employer discipline (*Garcetti*, p. 410). The Court noted that when citizens enter government service, they by necessity must accept certain limitations on their freedom and that the government, like private employers, needs a significant degree of control over the words and actions of its employees. Otherwise, the Court indicated, there would be little chance for the efficient provision of public services. Reflecting on *Connick*, the Court concluded that governmental offices could not function if every employment decision became a constitutional matter. The Court's message in *Garcetti* is clear when applied to public school teachers and the schools: Schools cannot operate efficiently without reasonable administrative control over the speech and actions of the instructional staff.

Four Justices dissented in *Garcetti*, expressing concern that the judgment could have a negative effect on the general public's trust in government. Critics predicted that public employees would become increasingly reluctant to report wrongdoing or inefficiency in the workplace if doing so could result in retaliation by vindictive supervisors. Insofar as exposing corruption and waste is a high priority for the general public, Justice David Souter emphasized that public employees should be protected when they report on official dishonesty, deliberately unconstitutional action, other serious wrongdoing, and threats to health and safety in their organizations even when they are speaking pursuant to their official duties. Justice Souter also expressed concern about the potential impact of *Garcetti* on academic freedom in public colleges and universities where teachers necessarily speak and write pursuant to their official duties. Yet, the majority countered that they had not considered whether *Garcetti* would apply in the same manner to free speech cases related to scholarship and teaching. Justice John Paul Stevens described *Garcetti* as "misguided" and likely to discourage all public employees from reporting wrongdoing and other organizational issues to their supervisors (*Garcetti*, p. 427).

Clearly, *Garcetti* limited the free speech rights of public employees by introducing a new employer-friendly dimension into free speech jurisprudence. Before *Garcetti*, courts used the *Pickering-Connick* analysis standard to evaluate free speech rights. After *Garcetti*, courts first must consider whether a public employee spoke pursuant to official duties or as a citizen. If the employee speaks pursuant to official duties, then it makes no difference whether the speech involved is a matter of public concern; the speech is unprotected, and the case is dismissed.

DISCUSSION

Based on current case law, it is now a settled matter of law that states cannot condition public employment on bases that infringe the constitutionally protected interests of employees in freedom of expression. Through *Pickering* (1968), *Mt. Healthy* (1977), *Givhan* (1979), *Connick* (1983), and *Garcetti* (2006), the Supreme Court has made it equally clear that the free speech rights of public employees must be balanced with the interests of their employers and that employers can limit those rights when necessary to promote efficient public services.

Like all citizens, public school teachers have First Amendment rights that the Supreme Court has verified on numerous occasions. Under *Pickering*, for example, teachers were assured the right to speak as citizens on matters of public concern as long as their speech did not disrupt the school district's interest in providing efficient services. In summarizing *Pickering*, the Court encouraged teachers to express their views on school operations because teachers are the members of the community most likely to have informed opinions regarding how funds allotted to the schools can be spent most wisely. Consequently, teachers should be able to speak out on all school-related issues without fear of retaliatory dismissal.

Since *Pickering*, public employees have been authorized to speak on public issues because the interest at stake is as much the public's interest in receiving informed opinion as it is the employee's right to disseminate it. Indeed, the Court ruled in *Waters v. Churchill* (1994) that government employees are often in the best position to know what ails the agencies for which they work and that public dialogue may gain much from their informed opinion. To this end, federal courts have recognized the right and responsibility of governmental employees to comment on issues of public concern.

Conversely, teacher free speech rights have been limited by public policy and the courts for good reasons. Teachers are often privy to confidential information that is necessary to carry out assigned duties. Breaching a confidence can damage working relationships with colleagues and supervisors while violating the privacy rights of students. Faculty members who speak incorrectly or inappropriately can contravene public policy and damage the school's reputation. Provocative speech can cause distractions, demoralize staff, and reduce efficiency and effectiveness. In extreme cases, irresponsible speech can endanger lives and property. For these and other reasons, the Supreme Court has balanced the First Amendment rights of teachers with those of their school board employers and the general public. Rights that are balanced are limited by definition. Without doubt, those limitations will remain as the Court continues efforts to balance the rights of teachers and schools alike.

In fairness, the counterpoint essay argues persuasively that current legal constraints on teacher speech are counterproductive and that they interfere with achievement of the public school mission. Without question, current case law gives school boards and administrators significant authority to control teacher speech on and off the school premises. *Garcetti v. Ceballos*, in particular, has introduced a new employer-friendly dimension into public employee free-speech jurisprudence. Teachers who now speak "pursuant to official duties" can be terminated or otherwise disciplined if school officials decide that there is a legitimate reason to limit their speech.

It seems clear that existing case law has reduced the professional discretion and freedom of teachers to comment on school-related issues. If true, the situation prompts at least three concerns about working conditions in the public schools. First, prudent teachers who like (and need) their jobs will be reluctant to speak openly on issues important to their students, the schools, and society in general. The resulting conspiracy of silence could reduce the quality of a public school education and preclude the school's successful attainment of stated goals. Second, classroom teachers should be equal partners with administrators and trustees in the development of school policies and procedures and delivery of the curriculum. Faculty members cannot fulfill that role if they are not free to speak openly and honestly on the issues. Third, outstanding individuals will not be attracted to a profession if they are not free to articulate their concerns on issues germane to the practice.

Although this point essay respects the aforementioned and other legitimate points made in the counterpoint essay, it has argued that trustees and administrators have the final responsibility for the efficient and effective operation of the schools. Certainly, school officials have much to learn from teachers, and in truly outstanding schools, they do exactly that. No one, including this author and the courts, believes that administrators and board members have all the answers about the schools, or anything else for that matter. Yet, in the end, and for good or bad, because administrators and boards are legally responsible for what happens in the schools, they must have the right to limit the speech of teachers.

COUNTERPOINT: Jeffrey C. Sun
University of North Dakota

In crafting judicially created policies, the law historically has recognized education as a social institution with a special status. In particular, the U.S. Supreme Court has articulated this special institutional context through a specific framework that is slightly different from other governmentally operated institutional contexts such as state and local human services agencies. Case law frequently relies on a conceptual framework that emphasizes the role of teachers as public employees whose speech often takes place in school-sponsored contexts. This approach attempts to balance the free speech interests of teachers as citizens with the need to control teacher speech for the sake of efficiency in school operation. However, although this framework appears to consider issues of fairness, it does not reflect an appreciation of the unique educational mission of schools and the role of teachers in fulfilling this mission. Alternative legal frameworks are needed to ensure that the free speech rights of teachers are acknowledged and that they have the professional discretion they need to carry out these responsibilities. Such alternative frameworks, which have been most evidently applied in equal protection cases such as challenges against the government over fair and equitable treatment of individuals, often include examinations of educational missions as a core element driving the rationale behind decisions and affording professional discretion to educators.

Recognizing that educational institutions present a unique organizational context, courts have acknowledged that analyzing the rights and responsibilities of teachers as professionals requires a slightly different legal framework from that used with other public employees such as police officers and government-employed nurses. In fact, the Supreme Court has articulated the importance of protecting academic freedom. Thus, the Court has interpreted the First Amendment to give teachers the freedom to conduct their work without unjustified governmental interference through actions of the school board. Most notably, in *Keyishian v. Board of Regents* (1967), the Court stated,

> Our Nation is deeply committed to safeguarding academic freedom, which is of transcendent value to all of us and not merely to the teachers concerned. That freedom is therefore a special concern of the First Amendment, which does not tolerate laws that cast a pall of orthodoxy over the classroom. "The vigilant protection of constitutional freedoms is nowhere more vital than in the community of American schools." (p. 603, quoting *Shelton v. Tucker*, 1960, at 487)

However, despite the *Keyishian* Court's declaration that society values teacher academic freedom as a special concern of the First Amendment, case law largely overlooks this constitutional authority as a source of teachers' rights to free speech in the workplace.

THE FRAMEWORKS

Cases in which teachers claim that their free speech rights have been violated generally follow one of two legal frameworks, the general public employee speech or the school-sponsored speech framework. A review of these frameworks helps illustrate some of the barriers to the ability of teachers to speak freely in their attempts to advance the educational mission.

Public Employee Speech Framework

The Supreme Court has formulated the principles of public employee speech. This section reviews three key cases describing the legal considerations pertaining to treating public school teachers like all other public employees.

In *Pickering v. Board of Education* (1968), a school board dismissed a teacher because his editorial in a local newspaper criticized its handling of bond proposals and its allocation of resources. To consider each party's interest, the Supreme Court established a balancing test between the rights of teachers as citizens to speak on matters of public concern and the ability of boards to promote efficiency of public services. The Court observed that the teacher did speak about a matter of public concern: how school funds were allocated. In addition, the Court observed that the speech did not implicate anyone with whom the teacher was in regular work contact. Ruling in favor of the teacher, the Court concluded that his speech did not present problems for school administrators to supervise him and that his comments did not create a disharmonious setting with his coworkers.

Connick v. Meyers (1983) clarified the two-part *Pickering* balancing test even more significantly. Here, a district attorney dismissed a staff attorney who opposed her scheduled transfer and distributed a survey to office colleagues that a supervisor perceived as her attempt to create a "mini-insurrection." The survey posed questions about office climate including concerns about the office transfer policy, staff confidence in supervisors, and pressures to work on political campaigns. The Court found that some of the survey questions represented protected speech while others represented private speech. Differentiating between the two, the Court explained that matters of public concern involve social, political, or similar community concerns. Thus, questions asking about employees feeling pressured to work on political campaigns qualified as a matter of public concern, whereas questions about the transfer policies and other employee policies, which were intended to redress a personal grievance, reflected private concerns and thus constituted unprotected speech. To evaluate the public/private concerns, the Justices directed courts to examine whole records and consider the context, form, and content of speech to determine whether it rises to a matter of public concern.

The most noteworthy post-*Connick* case is *Garcetti v. Ceballos* (2006). In *Garcetti*, after a county deputy prosecutor decided that an affidavit used to obtain a search warrant contained serious misrepresentations, he sent a memorandum to his supervisor recommending dismissal of the case. The supervisor nevertheless chose to move forward with the case. The deputy prosecutor spoke publicly about the discrepancy, and opposing counsel even called on him to testify about his findings regarding the discrepancy.

Subsequently, the deputy prosecutor claimed that he faced retaliatory employment actions such as reassignment and being passed over for a promotion as a result of his expressions about the case. According to the Supreme Court, because the deputy prosecutor's speech was based on his employer's commissioned memo, he was not speaking as a private citizen but in his capacity as an employee. In *Garcetti*, the Court declared that when the speech of public employees is made in furtherance of their job responsibilities, such speech is unprotected and no further inquiry such as the *Pickering-Connick* balancing test is needed. Thus, *Garcetti* significantly altered the framework by introducing an initial inquiry that may make further analysis of a public employee's speech more complicated.

School-Sponsored Speech Framework

The courts have also used a framework based on *Hazelwood School District v. Kuhlmeier* (1988), which enunciates an education-specific rule. Unlike the cases presented in the previous section, *Hazelwood* employs what is referred to as a forum analysis. Some governmentally owned spaces are public forums ripe for open debate and dialogue and require a compelling state interest for the government to restrict speech. For instance, public parks and sidewalks generally qualify as traditional public forums, but schools do not.

In *Hazelwood*, former students who worked on a newspaper that was published as part of a journalism class for academic credit sued their board and various officials for deleting stories about their experiences with pregnancy and family divorce. The students contested the administration's involvement as encroaching on their First Amendment rights. Using "forum" analysis, the

Supreme Court first differentiated between cases dealing with educators' ability to silence students' expressions that happen to take place on school premises and officials' authority over school-sponsored activities, which the public might reasonably perceive as school-sponsored speech. The Court determined that the latter issue applied in *Hazelwood* because the students worked on the newspaper as part of a class that took place under direct supervision of its instructor. Given this oversight of the newspaper's publication, the Court refused to treat it as a public forum that would have afforded the students additional legal rights. The Court established a two-part test to evaluate whether officials had authority to exercise over the school paper without violating the students' free speech concerns. The inquiry examines whether the speech is school sponsored and reasonably perceived as bearing the imprimatur of the school and whether faculty members supervise the speech and activities that are designed to impart knowledge to students. The Justices observed that if a court finds both parts of the test met, then officials have authority over the speech.

Federal trial and appellate courts have adopted this rationale in resolving cases in which public school teachers allege protected speech rights against board policies or adverse employment actions arising from their speech on school premises. Adapting the *Hazelwood* rule, courts have asked whether officials' authority is reasonably related to legitimate pedagogical concerns pursuant to institutional missions.

ARGUMENTS FOR TEACHER FREE SPEECH

The legal frameworks described in the preceding section do not fully account for the critical nature of public school teachers' roles in the educational mission. As a result, they do not offer sufficient protection for public school teachers as they pursue educational goals that society is likely to value. Given this unintended consequence, this counterpoint essay's overall argument is that there should be no limits on teacher free speech other than those reasonably necessary to advance the educational missions of schools.

Pedagogical Contribution

U.S. society expects school officials to inculcate values of a democratic society, with teachers being principally responsible for executing this critical social expectation. Courts and educational research report the value of classrooms as venues, specifically as government forums, for exchange in the marketplace of ideas. Nevertheless, courts often treat classrooms as closed environments for purposes of free speech activities, even when they involve teacher speech. For example, in *Mayer v. Monroe County Community School Corporation* (2007), the Seventh Circuit ruled that a probationary teacher's in-class speech regarding her participation in an antiwar demonstration did not constitute protected speech under the First Amendment even though she was responding to a student's question.

The speech in *Mayer* took place during the probationary teacher's lesson on current events to a multilevel class of fourth through sixth graders. As part of the school's approved curriculum, the students read a newsletter that discussed peace marches in Washington, D.C. A student asked the teacher if she had ever participated in a peace march. The teacher initially responded that peace marches take place across the nation including in the city where the school is located. The teacher mentioned that she witnessed a peaceful protest by the city's courthouse square. She stated that when driving by the courthouse, she saw the participants' signs to honk if you also oppose the U.S. military operations in Iraq, and honked as her expression of a peaceful protest. Parents complained about the teacher's response, and she was later dismissed. Citing *Garcetti*, the Seventh Circuit noted that because the teacher's speech fell within her official duties, thus, it was unprotected.

Though *Garcetti* presents a seemingly easy clear-cut rule, it fails to address underlying concerns about educational missions. In such situations, *Garcetti* summarily dismisses classroom expressions as unprotected speech. Such an oversimplified analysis unduly constrains student learning and the opportunities of teachers to present topics worthy of dialogue and debate in classrooms with sufficiently mature students who would benefit from the discussion. Such a rule reflects an outcome antithetical to the recognition in *Keyishian* that academic freedom is a special interest within the First Amendment. In *Pickering*, the Court, citing *Keyishian*, explicitly rejected the proposition that public employees may be subjected to any conditions, regardless of how unreasonable.

Many courts, though, do not agree that broad conditions controlling the classroom speech of teachers reflect unreasonable constraints. For example, in *Mayer*, the court asserted that school boards hire teachers to speak about academic matters. When boards hire teachers to speak, they commission their speech, but do not regulate it. Thus, limitations of teacher speech can be seen as part of this commissioning rather than regulation. Also, boards have the authority to disallow the use of classrooms as platforms for teachers' perspectives, even about matters related to lessons. Consequently, even though the teacher in *Mayer* conveyed a lesson germane to the issue about peaceful expressions, her comments did not fall within the realm of protected speech under *Garcetti* or *Hazelwood*. However, this reasoning counters educational interests.

Put simply, *Mayer* and other cases illustrate constraints placed on academically relevant teacher speech, which academic freedom intended to protect. Instead, these judicial rules make it more difficult to achieve the educational goals of illustrating and exercising democratic ideals such as dialogue and debate that reflect critical dimensions of a democratic society.

Educational Practices Reexamined

Under both the public employee speech and the school-sponsored speech frameworks, teachers' expressions about administrative decisions or other educational practices that affect their jobs typically fall outside the category of protected speech. The courts rationalize that these expressions are made in furtherance of one's official duties, do not qualify as matters of public concern, or represent legitimate pedagogical issues in which boards may exercise their authority. Still, these cases detrimentally limit government employees from speaking about questionable activities worthy of investigation such as allegations of fraud, corruption, harm to student well-being, or continued disruptions in educational settings.

A recent case that best illustrates this limitation is *Weintraub v. Board of Education* (2010), which uses *Garcetti* as precedent for not recognizing the teacher's speech as protected. In *Weintraub*, after a student threw books at the teacher on two occasions, the teacher sent the offender to the assistant principal, who simply returned him to the classroom without any discipline. The teacher complained to the assistant principal about the student's disruption and the potential harm that he posed to others. After the teacher learned that the student had injured a classmate who required medical attention, he filed a union grievance based on the assistant principal's failure to act. Once the teacher filed the grievance, officials allegedly retaliated against him. The case ultimately hinged on whether the teacher's formal grievance qualified as protected speech. In a broad reading of *Garcetti*, the court treated the grievance as speech pursuant to the teacher's official duties because he ultimately sought to use this mechanism to help him maintain classroom discipline.

Weintraub and other cases like it fail to protect the expression of public school teachers who speak about matters affecting the educational environment, including the interests of other students in the class. *Weintraub* also poses an interesting contrast to *Pickering* wherein the Supreme Court observed that teachers represent a group likely in the best position to comment about how school funds should be spent. In *Weintraub*, one might argue that analogous to *Pickering*, teachers are likely in the best position to comment about social concerns in correcting disruptive student classroom behaviors. This issue raises a community interest about educational environments, particularly as they pertain to student discipline while affecting social order. This being the case, teacher speech might likely meet the balancing interests of a public concern that is not outweighed by the government's interest in efficient operations. Indeed, one might argue that the speech creates awareness of concerns that might lead to more efficient mechanisms to handling future situations. Yet, *Garcetti* does not permit the analysis to proceed once speech is classified as pursuant to one's official duties.

IMPLICATIONS FOR THE EDUCATIONAL ENTERPRISE

Free speech has never been truly "free" from any constraints. This is undisputed. The issue at hand is whether governmentally imposed constraints in the context of public school boards reach too far and unduly limit teacher free speech. This counterpoint essay argued that the courts have granted public school employers overly expansive authority that serves as a barrier to their educational missions.

The point argument presents a nearly compelling case that public school boards should, and legally do, control the speech of teachers because of its potential implications on school images, working relationships among coworkers, and other related operations within districts. Although this essay respects such a stance, it argues that these constraints on teacher speech are not reasonably necessary to advance the educational missions of schools. In particular, the constraints overlook the true basis of the educational mission for the sake of organizational and personnel controls that tend to stifle rather than advance educational goals.

Current case law permits public school policies and practices that prescribe and monitor teacher speech. When teachers speak "pursuant to official duties" or school boards assert some legitimate pedagogical concern to restrain speech the courts generally agree that boards have the legal authority to deem what is educationally acceptable. The cases have firmly afforded administrators great authority to direct what teachers can say, how they say it, and when they say it. In essence, the case law permits policies and practices in which public school teachers essentially surrender their professional discretion under the guise of the boards' controls to advance the learning mission.

Under these constraints, professional environments for teachers have been substantially circumscribed. What happened to the teachable moment? The case law does not necessarily support the concept of teachable moments if public school boards do not recognize them. What happened to the opportunity for debate, posing a constructive argument, and presenting an alternative yet well-reasoned educational technique? Under the current case law, school boards can prevent, quash, and perhaps penalize such attempts. In other words, boards can assert that any deviations or considerations that they do not approve lead to disruption in school environments and compromise administrative controls, which, in turn, render educational environments arguably inefficient and ineffective. These administrative assertions may tip the balancing test in favor of boards.

Beyond the boundaries of what school administrators script, censor, or approve, teachers have a great deal to offer. Students and administrators can learn from teachers. Nonetheless, as this essay demonstrates, the case law too quickly dismisses the educational value of public school teachers. Thus, to reverse this trend, there should be no limits on teacher free speech other than those reasonably necessary to advance the educational mission of U.S. schools. The courts have gone too far in limiting speech rights of teachers. Teachers are professionals who should be given freedom to practice their profession as other professions do. Unnecessary limits on teacher speech unduly restrict their professional practice, which at times inadvertently makes the educational enterprise inefficient and obstructs the achievement of educational goals.

FURTHER READINGS AND RESOURCES

American Association of University Professors (AAUP). (2001). *Policy documents and reports* (9th ed.). Washington, DC: Author.

Bauries, S. R., & Schach, P. (2011). Coloring outside the lines: *Garcetti v. Ceballos* in the federal appellate courts. *Education Law Reporter, 262*, 357–397.

Cloud, R. C. (2009). Silence is golden when public employees consider speaking on matters pursuant to official duties. *Education Law Reporter, 245*, 1–11.

Giesel, R. T., & Kallio, B. R. (2010). Employee speech in K–12 settings: The impact of *Garcetti* on First Amendment retaliation claims. *Education Law Reporter, 251*, 19–35.

Mawdsley, R. D., & Osborne, A. G. (2007). The Supreme Court provides new direction for employee free speech in *Garcetti v. Ceballos. Education Law Reporter, 214*, 457–465.

Sharp, R. (2008). Academic freedom and censorship. In K. E. Lane, M. Gooden, J. Mead, P. Pauken, & S. Eckes (Eds.), *The principal's legal handbook* (4th ed., chap. 20). Dayton, OH: Education Law Association.

COURT CASES AND STATUTES

Connick v. Myers, 461 U.S. 138 (1983).

Dill v. City of Edmond, 155 F.3d 1193 (10th Cir. 1998).

Garcetti v. Ceballos, 547 U.S. 410 (2006).

Givhan v. Western Line Consolidated School District, 439 U.S. 410 (1979).

Hazelwood School District v. Kuhlmeier, 484 U.S. 260 (1988).

Keyishian v. Board of Regents, 385 U.S. 589 (1967).

Mayer v. Monroe County Community School Corporation, 474 F.3d 477 (7th Cir. 2007), *reh'g and reh'g en banc denied* (7th Cir. 2007), *cert. denied,* 552 U.S.823 (2007).

Mt. Healthy City School District v. Doyle, 429 U.S. 274 (1977).

Panse v. Eastwood, 303 Fed. Appx. 933 (2d Cir. 2008).

Pickering v. Board of Education of Township High School District 205, 391 U.S. 563 (1968).

Shelton v. Tucker, 364 U.S. 479 (1960).

Waters v. Churchill, 511 U.S. 661 (1994).

Weintraub v. Board of Education, 593 F.3d 196 (2d Cir. 2010).

13

Should educational malpractice be actionable?

POINT: Ralph D. Mawdsley, *Cleveland State University*
COUNTERPOINT: James L. Mawdsley, *Stark State College*

OVERVIEW

About 15 years after Rudolf Flesch published his widely known 1955 book, *Why Johnny Can't Read*, parents whose children were not doing well academically in regular educational settings attempted to sue their school boards under the then-novel legal theory of educational malpractice. In effect, the parents claimed that because school board officials hired teachers who were unable to provide their children with appropriate instruction to help them advance academically, the boards should have been liable for malpractice, a term of art that defies a precise definition for negligence ordinarily reserved for use in claims against professionals such as doctors or lawyers, who work closely with individual patients or clients.

The best efforts of parents to render school boards liable for the failings of their children in regular education notwithstanding, they have been unsuccessful. In fact, a federal trial judge in Illinois has since noted that educational malpractice is "a tort theory beloved of commentators, but not of courts" (*Ross v. Creighton University*, 1990, p. 1327).

In the leading case on educational malpractice, parents in California failed in their attempt to render school officials liable for improperly allowing their son, who could read only at the fifth-grade level, to graduate from high school (*Peter W. v. San Francisco Unified School District*, 1976). The record revealed that even though the student completed 12 years of schooling, his academic skills were so poor that he was qualified only for jobs requiring little or no ability to read or write. An appellate court, in rejecting the suit, discussed the concept of duty of care in the law of negligence. The court reasoned that the claim was without merit insofar as there was no workable rule of care against which to measure the alleged (mis)conduct of educators, the student did not suffer an injury within the established meaning of the law of negligence, and there was no clear connection between the actions of school personnel and the injury that the student claimed to have incurred. Put another way, the court explained that the student's claims were too open-ended to allow a negligence claim to proceed. In rejecting similar claims, other courts did not want to be placed in the position of second-guessing the performance of educational officials when children did poorly in school (*Donohue v. Copiague Union Free School District*, 1979).

Although courts are unwilling to allow educational malpractice claims to proceed in regular education, such charges may have a chance of success under the Individuals with Disabilities Education Act (IDEA) because of the statutory nature of student rights. Even so, cases in special education generally fail because the IDEA provides remedies such as tuition reimbursement when school officials do not provide students with the free appropriate public education (FAPE) called for in its provisions (*Suriano v. Hyde Park Central School District*, 1994).

In a special education case, an appellate court in California denied tort damages under the IDEA for a claim that a student was denied a FAPE because the appropriate remedy was an award of compensatory educational services (*White v. State of California*, 1987). Later, the Sixth Circuit affirmed that the IDEA does allow plaintiffs to recover damages for loss of earning power attributed to the failure of a school board to provide a student with a proper education (*Hall v. Knott County Board of Education*, 1991).

Against this backdrop, the debates in this chapter examine both sides of the issue of whether school officials should be liable for educational malpractice if students fail to make academic progress. In the point essay, Ralph D. Mawdsley, Cleveland State University, takes the position that if educators are to be treated as professionals, then they must be subjected to the same malpractice standards as doctors, lawyers, and other professionals. He essentially maintains that if students (and their parents) are to ensure that educators are performing their duties faithfully, then educational malpractice litigation must be permitted to proceed. Conversely, in the counterpoint essay, James L. Mawdsley, Stark State College, asserts that recognizing a tort for educational malpractice would be harmful because it would deter good people from pursuing careers in education for fear of the risk of liability. The counterpoint essay also argues that educational malpractice claims are likely to drive up costs for school systems while having little or no appreciable impact on student learning in addition to raising concerns about how hard it is to determine what is the teacher's fault as opposed to that of the students.

As you read these debates, ask yourself three interrelated questions. First, should school boards and individual teachers, regardless of whether children are in regular or special education, be liable for educational malpractice? Second, if so, what standards should apply? Third, if not, what remedies should be available to students and parents when children have not received education that allows them to progress academically?

Charles J. Russo
University of Dayton

POINT: Ralph D. Mawdsley
Cleveland State University

Litigation concerning educational malpractice has failed to gain a foothold in the United States despite a legal climate over the past four decades that has seen the expansion of student claims for damages against school officials and educational institutions for a wide range of common law, constitutional, and statutory charges. Malpractice is a negligence claim that is grounded in the essential elements of duty of care, breach of duty, causation, and injury, but with the added elements of professional standards of conduct and arms-length dealings, that is, nonconfidential relationships wherein parties are not related or on close terms and are considered to have about equal bargaining power. Although courts have found malpractice liability for those in the professions of law and medicine who have violated professional standards, federal and state courts have refused to recognize claims for damages grounded in the alleged failure of teachers, administrators, and educational institutions to provide effective instruction, assessment, or pedagogy for students.

The anomaly that exists in the U.S. educational system is that although educators are ethically and legally responsible for providing meaningful public education for students, teachers and administrators cannot be sued for damages if individual students fail to achieve their educational objectives. Without the recognition of educational malpractice liability for ineffective teaching, this point essay argues that students and their parents lack a meaningful legal measure for assessing whether school officials have faithfully performed their duties.

In light of emerging controversies over this issue, this point essay maintains that educational malpractice is a necessary remedy for students and parents. To this end, the arguments of the counterpoint essay notwithstanding, this essay argues for the proposition that the failure to furnish the same kind of remedy that is available in the legal and medical professions will result in having teachers and administrators not being subject to the same measure of accountability as those in other professions.

PUBLIC POLICY ARGUMENTS AGAINST MAKING EDUCATIONAL MALPRACTICE ACTIONABLE

At the heart of the controversy regarding educational malpractice in U.S. schools is the issue of remedies. The extent to which educational institutions, their teachers, and administrators should bear legal responsibility in damages for ineffective classroom teaching is the subject of this point essay. Federal and state legislatures and courts in the United States have addressed non-damages remedies where mandated by statutes. Yet, these same courts have resisted conferring damages where such awards would appear to sound in educational malpractice.

Perhaps the largest obstacles facing plaintiffs in educational malpractice litigation have been the three major public policy arguments that the courts have invoked in distancing educational malpractice from other claims of misrepresentation, breach of contract, or deceptive practices such as fraud. According to the first argument, although school officials are widely charged with outright failure in the achievement of their education objectives, they also are called on to bear responsibility for many of the social and moral problems of society at large. The public plight of educational officials in these respects is attested in the daily media, in bitter school board elections, and in seemingly countless surveys about the status and quality of public education, in particular. To hold educational leaders to an actionable "duty of care" in the discharge of their academic functions would expose them to the tort claims, real or imagined, of disaffected students and parents in countless numbers of school systems. Unfortunately, though, educators are already beset by social and financial problems that have gone to major litigation. The ultimate consequences, then, in public time and money, would burden them and society beyond calculation. Such reasoning, one can argue, is premised on the somewhat dubious assumption that because educational institutions have many functions to perform, no one expects school officials to perform any of them well. In other words, this position argues that school officials should escape culpability for negligence resulting from the (poor) quality of teaching because no one is willing to set standards that might serve as the measure for damages liability.

Second, with a variety of factors that can affect the educational performances of students, courts have refused to separate the wheat from the chaff regarding reasons how or why such ineffective work by a student who, for example, graduates as functionally illiterate, might be attributed to an unreasonably deficient provision of educational services. The reasons why students fail may be physical, neurological, emotional, cultural, or environmental; they may also be present but not perceived, recognized but not identified. Such subjective and amorphous determinants, courts have argued, neither lend themselves to judicial scrutiny nor are susceptible to certainty in determining damages. However, this reasoning has merit only if one assumes that multiple causes of poor student performance do not allow for multiple solutions in the same classrooms. In effect, this rationale presents an unflattering profile of teachers, who, unlike lawyers and medical doctors who must adjust their professional advice to the needs of their clients, need not be considered members of a profession and are expected to project only a one-size-fits-all approach to classroom instruction.

Third, courts fear the floodgate of litigation that can result from frivolous suits as plaintiffs seek to abuse the legal system. Whether this floodgate is more imagined than real is unlikely to be resolved in the United States because the courts have thus far simply foreclosed the possibility of exploring whether the explosion of new litigation is likely to materialize. Although a penchant for litigation in the United States is always a real concern for the time and expense associated with legal proceedings, the floodgate argument in education law may simply be an example of crying "wolf" once too often. As a practical matter, since U.S. education law already generates more than 2,000 reported law cases per year, not including disputes that are resolved via unreported decisions, administrative hearings, mediation, or other alternative dispute resolution methods, one can only wonder about the extent to which new case law involving educational malpractice would even be noticed to any significant degree.

DIFFERENCES IN THE NATURE OF PROFESSIONAL STANDARDS

The standard argument for judicial refusal to recognize the tort of educational malpractice—as compared, for example, with medical malpractice—is that pedagogy, unlike medicine, does not allow the kind of standards associated with medicine. This position posits that the arms-length physician–client relationship permits the application of professional standards of conduct appropriate to the profession. Yet, as to education, the judicial approach has been that it is not the job of the court system to engage in exhaustively policing the complex interactions between teachers and student to ensure that all children are educated in a manner consistent with the wishes of their parents.

Even if one were to argue that basic medical knowledge is more objective than pedagogy, one could still claim that something akin to a standard of good teaching, at least regarding certain core matters, does exist. Certainly, some would suggest certain kinds of cases do not involve second-guessing about pedagogical decisions. If a child is misdiagnosed as suffering from a readily identifiable learning disability, then justified reliance on such a diagnosis moves the student into the same position of relative helplessness as one who has been injured by an act of medical malpractice. Nonetheless, courts have refused to permit educational malpractice damages claims even in these more readily definable areas involving special education.

Congress, in enacting the Individuals with Disabilities Education Act (IDEA) in 1975, created statutory remedies where officials in public school systems failed to provide the appropriate evaluation, services, and placements mandated under its provisions. However, the IDEA, while having developed an impressive case law history involving the interpretation of rights and responsibilities under its provisions and despite a broad authorization that courts "shall grant such relief as the court determines is appropriate," has been consistently interpreted as not supporting a private cause of action for damages. At the same time, damage claims for students with disabilities are possible under the Rehabilitation Act of 1973 (section 504) and the Americans with Disabilities Act of 1990 (ADA). Even so, these are nondiscrimination statutes, and their focus is on prohibiting discrimination in teaching, not on imposing a duty to improve the quality of teaching. As such, the damages remedy under section 504 and the ADA is far more restricted than it would be under educational malpractice. One must also add, parenthetically, that the IDEA, section 504, and the ADA do not touch the overwhelming majority of students who do not receive services, placements, or accommodations and, thus, whose poor performance at present allows no justiciable causes of action, unless they sound in theories like misrepresentation or breach of contract.

In the most recent reauthorization of the Elementary and Secondary Education Act as the No Child Left Behind Act (NCLB), Congress has come much closer to addressing issues that touch the instructional functions of education. Congress has directed all states to adopt some form of student assessments and mandates that teachers who work with students with disabilities meet certain specified standards. In NCLB, Congress has set the requirement that all students must be able to achieve a passing score on their state's assessment test by 2014. This leaves open the kind of accountability standard that might invite negligence-type educational malpractice claims by those who are unable to pass these tests. For the time being, Congress has left the determination of assessment criteria to the states and has focused its attention on the quality of teachers.

Under NCLB, Congress has set highly qualified teacher (HQT) minimum professional requirements for teachers who work with all students, including those with disabilities. Congress, one can argue, has moved perceptibly in the direction of setting standards for education, something that to date has prevented viable claims in educational malpractice from proceeding. The NCLB's requirement that all students pass state assessments probably does not, in itself, create a cause of action for malpractice, but would seem to impose on school officials an obligation, at least, to explain their curricula and the pedagogies used to present the information that was assessed. The critical factor that has been absent in educational malpractice claims has been professional standards for teachers that are comparable with those set for medical doctors, attorneys, and other professionals.

LACK OF CLEAR PROFESSIONAL STANDARDS FOR EDUCATORS

To date, Congress has refused to set outcomes-based requirements for teachers. Still, to the extent that Congress has set, or requires states to establish, standards of effectiveness for teachers, it has taken, one can argue, a significant step toward creating measurable standards for evaluating what can be described as effective teaching. From the setting of such a measurable standard flows a cascade of potential liability areas relating to the duty owed by educators to students in the classrooms of ineffective teachers, the duty owed to ineffective teachers to remediate their deficiencies, the duty owed to parents of students in the classrooms of ineffective teachers, and the duty to third parties who allege harm from ineffective teaching.

The development of a cause of action for educational malpractice has stumbled largely because of a lack of professional standards for teachers and because of concerns about proving causation. The dominating presence of the IDEA in U.S. public schools augurs for a justiciable malpractice remedy for damages when students are denied effective evaluation and delivery of services. For the standards in IDEA to have meaning, Congress needs to amend its provisions and provide damages awards for statutory violations. Although the damages remedies for violations of the IDEA would be statutory rather than common law–grounded educational malpractice claims, the result would be the same in terms of having justifiable damages claims for violations of instructional requirements. At the same time, although opening up educational malpractice claims under the IDEA would help the 14% of students who receive special education, other children who are subjected to ineffective teaching for whom academic growth and development may be stunted would be deprived of a remedy.

CONCLUSION

Opening up potential liability for ineffective teaching would present causation problems and likely an indeterminate amount of new litigation. Even so, the arguments against educational malpractice have substance only because measurable standards have never been created to define effective teaching. In considering whether one is an ineffective teacher does not assume that students will have justiciable claims if they have not been successful in outcomes assessments. Yet, a determination of ineffectiveness would, at the very least, impose a duty on school boards to address and remediate ineffective teaching.

Congressional effort in the NCLB requiring school boards to hire HQTs and make annual yearly performance by students is the beginning of defining what may be described as effective teaching. This beginning represents only a small step toward teacher accountability for the practice of their profession. What has been missing from U.S. jurisprudence is outcomes-based accountability of the effectiveness of teacher instruction. However meritorious the NCLB's highly qualified teacher requirements may be, educational evaluation needs more than input assessments. No one is arguing that creating a viable educational malpractice claim will permit courts to march haphazardly through U.S. schools in assessing their liability for ineffective teaching. Thus, permitting claims in educational malpractice to proceed while setting both teacher standards and student yearly progress requirements pursuant to the NCLB is a viable first step to assigning teacher responsibility along with creating much-needed damages remedies against teachers and their boards when officials fail to address and remediate ineffective teaching.

COUNTERPOINT: James L. Mawdsley
Stark State College

Courts in the United States have so far refused to recognize educational malpractice as a cause of action. This is fortunate because there are no recognized standards of effective instruction that can be used to define the duty of care that teachers owe to their students. In addition, there is often no clear causal link between the actions of teachers in their classrooms and the failure of students to learn the prescribed material.

If educational malpractice were recognized, teachers would be placed in an unfair and untenable position. Absent a clearly defined duty of care, no teachers could be sure that they were teaching in ways that would meet their duty. Further, failing students would be able to claim that their teachers were responsible for their ignorance. Faced with the peril of litigation, and without the high salaries that other professions command, few people would choose to become or remain teachers. As such, this counterpoint essay stands for the proposition that parents and students should not be able to file suits for educational malpractice.

BACKGROUND

Peter W. v. San Francisco Unified School District (1976) is perhaps the most notable attempt to introduce the tort of educational malpractice into U.S. jurisprudence. After a student in California was allowed to graduate from high school despite the fact that he could only read at a fifth-grade level, an appellate court in California refused to recognize the novel cause of action. As numerous disgruntled students have discovered in the years since, every subsequent court addressing the issue has agreed with the appellate court in California that rejected the student's claim. *Peter W.* rested on the court's refusal to find that school board officials owed the student a duty to instruct him properly on the ground that such a duty would be impossible to articulate clearly. Indeed, even 35 years later, neither educators nor the courts are closer to articulating this duty.

As the point essay notes, there are generally no accepted standards for what constitutes an effective education. Some might argue that recent attempts to quantify what makes effective teachers, such as the highly qualified teacher's (HQT) minimum professional requirements under No Child Left Behind (NCLB), might be the first steps toward such standards. Yet, measuring teacher qualifications is a relatively simple task compared with measuring whether students have been educated competently. With the NCLB, Congress also required states to develop some kind of student assessment by which the progress (or lack thereof) of schools in improving student outcomes can be measured. The point essay believes that this is the first step toward creating standards that could be used in evaluating whether a teacher or school has committed educational malpractice. However, if this is the first step, it is clear that a very long journey still lies ahead.

The crucial question remains unanswered as to how badly students must perform on assessments to give rise to educational malpractice claims. Surely the point essay is not suggesting that any student who failed such a test could sue school officials. Permitting this to occur would be analogous to allowing unsuccessful litigants to sue their attorneys for malpractice, simply because they lost in court. Rather, before claims could proceed, there would have to be some minimal scores on assessments, lower than the ones necessary to pass. Moreover, this runs the risk of having courts treating any scores below that minimum as evidence of malpractice.

For the sake of brevity, this counterpoint essay leaves aside the myriad, well-known problems with high-stakes testing. The most that can be said for such tests is that they measure what students happen to know, not necessarily reflecting what they have been taught. Moreover, student successes or failures on test days are almost entirely in their own hands. Students may simply be so nervous that they forget what they have learned. Other students might get a poor night's sleep before tests. There are any number of reasons why students might do poorly that are outside of the control of their teachers. This author can think of no example in the field of malpractice where professionals can be liable for the failures of their clients. Engineers might be liable if they designed shoddy bridges that fell down, but are not liable if drivers who are inattentive accidentally drive off bridges. As a legal theory, educational malpractice fails because it is almost never the case that a single teacher's incompetence can be said to be the proximate cause of student failure.

NATURE OF MALPRACTICE

In fields in which malpractice is actionable, there are generally clearly defined, easily assessed outcomes. Patient in hospitals either recover or they do not, and if they do not, the failure of doctors to provide competent and timely care may be determined through expert testimony on the expected standard of care. If clients' cases are lost because attorneys fail to file suits within the time established by applicable statute of limitations, then malpractice is easily discerned by both attorneys and laypeople. In contrast, if an 18-year-old leaves high school lacking basic literacy and numeracy skills, there might be any number of reasons for this failure. The student might, for example, simply have refused to study or may have valued social life or athletics more than academics. A student might even have become involved in illegal drugs or gangs, neither of which was within the power of school officials to prevent.

By the same token, the fact that another student graduates with straight A's, having gained a thorough knowledge of the required subjects, may not have anything at all to do with the quality of school instruction. Perhaps that student simply has parents who are more educated and took the time to involve themselves in the child's studies. Perhaps the student is simply intellectually gifted. Or it could be that the student simply read a great deal outside of class. Factors such as parental involvement and students' enthusiasm for learning are entirely outside the control of teachers or school officials. Most school officials would probably be much more enthusiastic in claiming credit for the education their top graduates received than in accepting responsibility for their failing students. Still, the truth is that in both cases, school officials are at most only partially responsible for the achievements or failures of their pupils.

In general, clients are far more dependent on their attorneys, for example, than students are on individual teachers. There is no equivalent, in the day-to-day activities of classrooms, to situations in which attorneys fail to file suit until after statutes of limitations have passed. Students who fail to learn their multiplication tables today might learn them tomorrow or next year. They might learn them from their parents or from tutors rather than from licensed teachers. For persons to reach adulthood without learning basic mathematics at all, they would have to endure repeated failures over the course of many years. Although some of those failures could be attributed to instructors, many could be laid at the feet of the students themselves.

One might argue that the same is true in law and medicine. Criminal defendants might testify in court, contrary to the advice of their attorneys. Patients might refuse to take their medicine. Yet, this shows a crucial difference between teachers and other professionals. In the case of doctors or attorneys, there are clear and well-defined distinctions between those aspects of treatment or care that are the responsibility of professionals and those aspects that are the responsibility of the patients or clients. In contrast, considering how much of learning is attributable to teachers and how much to students is a much murkier business because the division of responsibility is different in every situation. Some students learn subjects only because they had classes with single, particularly effective teachers who took the time to explain the subjects in ways they could understand. Other students might learn the same material on their own, from parents, or from tutors.

MALPRACTICE IN EDUCATIONAL SETTINGS

That student outcomes are unique to individuals would lead to remarkable and shocking results if educational malpractice suits were allowed. A teacher might spend a year with a class of 25 students, giving them all the same lectures, assigning them all the same homework, and grading their work by the same standards. At the end of that year, when the students take their state-mandated assessment, the teacher would be liable for malpractice for some students but not others. Logically, the teacher should either be liable to all the students or to none of them because they all received the exact same instruction. If the instruction was inadequate for one student, it was inadequate for all, even for the students who managed to pass the test. And yet, the teacher could be sued by some of the students, but not others. This perfectly illustrates the difficulties in using student assessments as a measure of teacher effectiveness.

Although teachers may have a "duty," in some broad sense, to do a good job and to teach effectively, this is not susceptible to a legal definition. Still, there are other duties as well in the classroom. Students have a duty to make diligent efforts to learn. If courts were to recognize educational malpractice, they would also need to acknowledge the duty of students to mitigate the injuries they suffered from their incompetent teachers. This might not apply to elementary school students, who might be excused for not appreciating the extent of their own ignorance. However, if students like Peter W. reach their senior year of high school with only a fifth-grade reading ability, it is fair to expect that they and their parents must have noticed this problem and had a duty to do something to try to rectify the situation.

None of this is to argue that there are no bad teachers or that student achievement cannot be tied to the quality of instruction. Yet, students who leave school having failed to gain a full and complete education may have fallen short for any number of reasons. Even assuming, for the sake of argument, that students' failure results entirely from poor instruction, the problem is more likely to be systemic than the fault of a single incompetent teacher. A young person who graduates high school, as in the case of Peter W., with a middle school or elementary school grasp of reading or mathematics could not manage to fall so far behind in a single year, or under the instruction of a single teacher. Such failure is surely evidence of institutional neglect on the part of an entire school, or perhaps of an entire school system.

REMEDIES FOR EDUCATIONAL MALPRACTICE

One wonders what sort of remedy that plaintiffs could possibly seek if educational malpractice claims are permitted to proceed; not even the most activist court can mandate student knowledge of algebra. Perhaps courts could order boards to provide remedial instruction such as general equivalency diploma (GED) classes for students who have not learned all that they ought to have learned. And, surely boards would have to hire new instructors to conduct these classes or else the students would be stuck with the same incompetent teachers who caused the problems to begin with. If educational malpractice follows the model of medical and legal malpractice, then the remedy will be damages. This raises the question of how one could set the monetary value of having failed to learn specified material. Formulae would have to be devised; people who know algebra tend to make X dollars per year, while those who do not know algebra earn Y. Therefore, plaintiffs would be entitled to X minus Y dollars. In either of these cases, declaratory relief requiring remedial instruction, or awarding damages, the end result would be that school boards would be forced to spend a great deal of money that would otherwise have gone to the instruction of their current students.

Another, more frightening possibility is that plaintiffs might demand, and courts might order, school boards to make changes in their curricula, teaching methods, facilities, and so on, in attempts to prevent future students from suffering the same harms. Courts would have to oversee the changes, or appoint masters to oversee them. Further litigation over the sufficiency of the changes would be almost guaranteed. Those who can consider such a possibility with equanimity would do well to remember *Missouri v. Jenkins* (1995), a school desegregation suit lasting more than a decade. The history of litigation and court orders in this case serves as a dire warning of the perils of allowing courts to make decisions about what is necessary to improve the quality of schooling.

All of this is, of course, purely speculative because fortunately U.S. courts have thus far refused to recognize a cause of action for educational malpractice. The point essay seems quite sanguine about the prospect of the added expense to schools, the strain on school officials' time, and the increased burden on the courts from added litigation. Yet, suits need not be successful to prove burdensome. From the moment U.S. courts recognize a tort for educational malpractice, every school system in the country will have to worry about claims from their worst-performing students. All teachers would be faced with the possibility of having to explain and defend their instructional methodologies to juries. In such an atmosphere, it seems unlikely that many people would choose to become educators.

CONCLUSION

The true purpose of recognizing educational malpractice would be to give parents some leverage in dealing with failing school systems. Yet, the parents who bring suits (and their neighbors) will also be the taxpayers who have to pay for damages awards. Such suits would only drain scarce resources from already overburdened schools. Efforts at remediation would likely prove futile because, as noted earlier, students' failures are often largely their own fault. Students who prove unwilling or unable to learn to read properly in 12 years of primary and secondary education are unlikely all of a sudden to develop the necessary motivation and desire to learn when placed in remedial programs. All that would be accomplished would be a waste of time and money. The courts have been wise to reject the theory of educational malpractice, and this author hopes that they continue to do so in the future.

Further Readings and Resources

DeMitchell, T. A., & DeMitchell, T. A. (2003). Statutes and standards: Has the door to educational malpractice been opened? *Brigham Young University Education and Law Journal, 2003,* 485.

Flesch, R. (1955). *Why Johnny can't read.* New York: Wiley.

Henry, M. N. (2004). No Child Left Behind educational malpractice litigation for the 21st century. *California Law Review, 92*, 1117.

Mawdsley, R., & Cumming, J. (2008). Educational malpractice and setting damages for ineffective teaching: A comparison of legal principles in the U.S.A., England and Australia. *Education and the Law, 20*, 25.

Parker, J. C. (1991). Educational malpractice: A tort is born. *Cleveland State Law Review, 39*, 301.

Russo, C. J. (2008). Educational malpractice. In C. J. Russo (Ed.), *Encyclopedia of education law* (pp. 276–277). Thousand Oaks, CA: Sage.

Court Cases and Statutes

Americans with Disabilities Act, 42 U.S.C. §§ 12101 *et seq.*

Donohue v. Copiague Union Free School District, 418 N.Y.S.2d 375 (N.Y. 1979).

Elementary and Secondary Education Act of 1965, 20 U.S.C. §§ 6301 *et seq.*

Hall v. Knott County Board of Education, 941 F.2d 402 (6th Cir. 1991).

Individuals with Disabilities Education Act, 20 U.S.C. §§ 1400 *et seq.*

Missouri v. Jenkins, 515 U.S. 70 (1995).

No Child Left Behind Act of 2001, 20 U.S.C. §§ 6301 *et seq.*

Peter W. v. San Francisco Unified School District, 131 Cal. Rptr. 854 (Cal. Ct. App. 1976).

Rehabilitation Act of 1973, Section 504, 29 U.S.C. § 794.

Ross v. Creighton University, 740 F. Supp. 1319 (N.D. Ill. 1990), 957 F.2d 410 (7th Cir. 1992).

Suriano v. Hyde Park Central School District, 611 N.Y.S.2d 20 (N.Y. App. Div. 1994).

White v. State of California, 240 Cal. Rptr. 732 (Cal. Ct. App. 1987).

14

Do teachers have adequate rights when they are subject to the termination of their employment?

POINT: Michelle Gough McKeown, *Indiana Department of Education*

COUNTERPOINT: Allison S. Fetter-Harrott, *Franklin College*

OVERVIEW

Tenure, which originated in higher education, is a legal safeguard for the continued employment of teachers as long as they meet specified professional standards. In most states, statutes outline teacher tenure laws in the K–12 context. Typically, school boards grant probationary teachers tenure after they have provided satisfactory service for set periods ranging from 1 to 7 years. There are, of course, legitimate justifications for which boards may terminate the contracts of tenured teachers. State tenure laws indicate that boards may dismiss tenured faculty members on written notice of reasons "for cause," typically including justifications of incompetence, insubordination, neglect of duty, or immorality. Although the laws articulate justifications for protecting and dismissing teachers, legislators, educators, and other representatives of the public have long debated the value of tenure as well as its disadvantages. In fact, historical records indicate that these arguments about tenure can be traced back decades before the first set of state laws recognizing teacher tenure in the early 1900s, led by states including California and New Jersey.

State laws do not always use the term *tenure.* In 1938, the Supreme Court first addressed a case examining whether a dismissed teacher had an expectation of continued employment (*State of Indiana ex rel. Anderson v. Brand*, 1938). Although the statute was later repealed, the Court recognized that the prevailing law established a contractual arrangement between the school board and the teacher for continued employment absent a showing of incompetency, insubordination, neglect of study, immorality, or other just causes for dismissal. Thus, for all intents and purposes, the Court ruled that the teacher had tenure. Likewise, in *Perry v. Sindermann* (1972), the Court found that a public school's policies and procedures may manifest a de facto tenure policy. Here the Court acknowledged the right of a faculty member at a public college to continued employment. Today, only 19 states actually use the term *tenure* in their statutes. Others refer to continuing contracts, which by their nature form expectations of continued employment or job security absent actions falling in one of the enumerated grounds for teacher dismissal.

Teachers' expectation of continued employment is significant. As the Supreme Court articulated in both *Perry v. Sindermann* and *Board of Regents v. Roth* (1972), tenure at a public institution attaches a constitutionally recognized property interest in employment. Although the faculty member in *Roth* did not fulfill the statutory requirements to receive tenure, namely, 4 years of continuous appointment, the Court explained in some detail the significance of tenure, particularly in terms of the property interest that attaches. Specifically, the Court noted that if a public university as employer dismisses a tenured faculty member without cause and proper notice, the individual has a viable claim for the deprivation of one's due process rights under the Fourteenth Amendment.

As the Supreme Court of Arizona aptly stated in *School District No. 8 v. Superior Court* (1967), the purpose of teacher tenure is to protect

> worthy instructors from enforced yielding to political preferences and to guarantee to such teachers employment after a long period of satisfactory service regardless of the vicissitudes of politics or the likes or dislikes of those charged with the administration of school affairs. (p. 30)

Nonetheless, as critics of tenure have pointed out and the essays in this chapter debate, these constitutional rights may present substantial barriers when dismissing teachers whom administrators characterize as ineffective. These critics contend that the time and process involved discourages administrators from pursuing dismissal proceedings. Accordingly, these critics argue that these protections serve as roadblocks to school performance and accountability efforts. Yet, the Supreme Court's holding in *Cleveland Board of Education v. Loudermill* (1985) indicates that other public employees, here a school security guard, may have similar protections of continued employment absent just cause.

In the point essay, Michelle Gough McKeown, Indiana Department of Education, posits that the rights of teachers have been limited for some time, attributing these restrictions as largely functions of poorly crafted tenure laws that were actually intended to protect teachers' rights. According to Gough McKeown, these state tenure statutes have presented two unintended consequences. First, the laws have protected teachers with questionable records. Second, she believes that the laws have failed to protect teachers who have been subject to dismissal for cause beyond the legislation's original purpose. Gough McKeown adds that the protections for untenured faculty are equally lacking. She thus frames the problem not so much as an issue of whether teachers need more employment rights but whether they need more carefully crafted laws to actually protect their rights against the wrongful nonrenewal or termination of their contracts.

By contrast, in the counterpoint essay, Allison S. Fetter-Harrott, Franklin College (Indiana), contends that existing tenure statutes and employment arrangements as reflected in collective bargaining agreements sufficiently protect teachers from dismissal arising from discriminatory or arbitrary school board actions. She reasons that these laws and employment arrangements incorporate provisions to ensure fairness including detailed and at times cumbersome processes. Fetter-Harrott postulates that if anything, these extensive statutory procedural rights have created significant barriers to the dismissal of "ineffective or even harmful teachers," arguing that the school board costs along with the strains on administrators warrant reconsideration of teacher rights. In the end, she suggests that these protections actually harm the teaching profession when resources such as money are diverted to dismissal processes rather than salaries and when a disproportionate amount of attention is placed on poor teachers rather than students or qualified teachers.

As the preceding discussion highlights and both the point and counterpoint essays in this chapter illustrate in greater detail, the issue of teachers' rights remains controversial. When reading these essays, consider the following questions: What benefits and drawbacks are associated with the presence of teacher tenure? Should public school teachers maintain tenure as a form of job security given other laws and employment arrangements that afford them an array of employment rights? What employment rights should teachers have? Finally, what reasons should public school boards rely on in terminating the employment of teachers, and how much due process should they receive before dismissal?

Jeffrey C. Sun
University of North Dakota

POINT: Michelle Gough McKeown
Indiana Department of Education

With respect to their job security, teachers can be separated into two groups: those with and those without tenure. Tenure refers to the special protections afforded teachers after statutorily specified periods of time ranging from as short a period as 1 year in Hawaii, Mississippi, and Nevada, to as many as 7 in Ohio. Nontenured teachers are hired under term contracts that usually span the academic year. These two groups of teachers have significantly different levels of procedural due process protections with respect to whether their employment contracts can be terminated. More specifically, tenured teachers, who are considered to have a continuing contract and an expectation of annual reemployment, receive heightened procedural due process protections compared with their untenured colleagues, who work pursuant to annual contracts.

Teacher dismissal occupies a prickly role in the U.S. educational system. School boards and states want to provide good teachers with job security. Yet, boards also need flexibility so that they can terminate the employment of teachers who are not serving the best interests of their schools and students. As a result of the important role fulfilled by teachers, laws addressing dismissal, nonrenewal, and due process must straddle the two potentially conflicting goals of providing teachers with job security and providing administrators the needed flexibility to remove from the classroom teachers who are not serving students or, in the worst instances, even harming them. At the same time, the aims of such protections may be undermined when they are provided through broadly drafted laws and agreements that function to keep in place teachers who are not serving the interest of students. Unlike the counterpoint essay, which maintains that current protections are adequate, this point essay takes the position that the issue is not whether teachers need more rights when faced with dismissal but whether clearer statutes are needed to protect those rights.

EMPLOYMENT RIGHTS OF TENURED TEACHERS

The first tenure laws in the United States were developed to protect teachers from the whims of political processes. The aims of these laws were "to assure teachers of experience and ability a continuous service and rehiring based upon merit rather than failure to be rehired for reasons that are political, partisan or capricious" (*Hansen v. Board of Education of School District No. 65*, p. 471, 1986).

Once teachers have worked the requisite number of years and earned tenure, the grounds and processes for dismissal are statutorily governed, typically allowing firings for such specified causes as immorality or conduct unbecoming an educator; insubordination or a willful refusal to obey a lawful command; and incompetence. Of course, tenured teachers can also be dismissed through no fault of their own if their school systems experience financial exigencies or declines in student enrollment, or if their boards discontinue programs.

Providing the necessary job security for teachers is particularly important because history has shown that educators fill a critical and sensitive role. However, political whim may not be the biggest threat to their job security. The broad and nebulous language of many state teacher dismissal statutes has had the ironic effect of working against the aims of this legislation in two ways—by protecting teachers who fail to serve the interests of students and by providing mechanisms for dismissing teachers for impermissible reasons. Indeed, litigation reveals a long history of courts wrestling with the contours of these terms and whether the behaviors of teachers fell within these parameters.

Laws drafted in these broad and unclear terms have continued to facilitate the dismissal of teachers for violating the sensibilities of the community, or a particular segment of the community. A case from the Supreme Court of California illustrates how laws in the past have failed to protect the rights of teachers. In *Morrison v. State Board of Education* (1969), a teacher was dismissed for immorality as a result of engaging in a homosexual relationship. The court noted that the teacher worked for a number of years in the school district and that he had not received complaints of criticism for his job performance. Yet, after the board of education and superintendent learned that the teacher was involved in a 1-week, noncriminal homosexual affair, he was dismissed under the immorality provision of state law code.

The *Morrison* court described the challenge of interpreting the statutory terms:

> The problem of ascertaining the appropriate standard of "morality" in a secular society—America today—there may be a plurality of moralities. Whose morals shall be enforced? . . . There is a tendency to say that public morals should be enforced. But that just begs the question. Whose morals are the public morals? (*Morrison* at 227)

Although the teacher successfully challenged his dismissal, litigation indicates that misuse of the statutory terminology continues.

Rowland v. Mad River Local School District (1984) involved claims that a high school guidance counselor was suspended and her contract was not renewed after she mentioned that she was bisexual. After the Sixth Circuit upheld the counselor's dismissal, the Supreme Court denied certiorari, with Justice Brennan dissenting.

At the trial level, the jury in *Rowland* "made unchallenged findings that petitioner was suspended and not rehired solely because she was bisexual . . ." (*Rowland* at 1010). The jury also determined that the counselor's bisexuality did not affect her ability to perform her job and that she suffered damages as a result of not being rehired. Although the trial court entered a judgment in favor of the counselor on her First Amendment and equal protection claims, the Sixth Circuit reversed in favor of the board. As to the plaintiff's First Amendment claims, the court held that her statements about her bisexuality to coworkers did not have First Amendment protection because they were not a matter of public concern. As such, the court decided that it was permissible for the school board to dismiss the plaintiff on the basis of her statements to others. The Sixth Circuit further asserted the plaintiff's equal protection claims failed because she did not provide evidence that non-bisexuals were treated differently than she, despite the jury's finding that when the principal and superintendent suspended her and recommended that the board not rehire her, they "treated [petitioner] differently than similarly situated employees, because she was homosexual/bisexual" (*Rowland* at 1010 n.2).

Avery v. Homewood City Board of Education (1982) demonstrates this same type of rights violation under the broad statutory terminology in the context of pregnancy discrimination. The plaintiff taught in a public school system with a policy requiring teachers to give notice of their pregnancies no later than the fourth month of pregnancy. In November, the plaintiff, who was pregnant but not married, notified officials that she was due to give birth to a child in late December. When the teacher informed the principal, he commented that she violated the school's notice policy and directed her to speak with the superintendent.

In the ensuing litigation, the teacher alleged that the superintendent addressed her failure to adhere to the notice policy and encouraged her to resign because of the moral issue related to her being pregnant but unwed. In mid-December, the teacher received a letter from the superintendent stating that the school board was going to meet to consider canceling her contract for insubordination, neglect of duty, and immorality. The first two rationales for the cancellation of her contract related to the teacher's failure to give the board notice, and the third was based on the fact that she was pregnant and unmarried.

A federal trial court ruled that the teacher's dismissal was lawful because it was based in part on permissible grounds. The Fifth Circuit vacated in part because the trial court failed to apply the proper standard for mixed-motive discharge cases. Under the proper test, the court explained that the teacher bore the initial burden of proving that her having engaged in constitutionally protected conduct was a substantial or motivating factor in her dismissal. The court assumed that her out-of-wedlock pregnancy was constitutionally protected, observing that this test would have protected the teacher against the invasion of her constitutional rights.

The Fifth Circuit then held that the normal course of action in such a case where the trial court applied the wrong framework was a remand on that issue. However, on the record the court did not think that it was possible for the district court to find that the board would have discharged the teacher absent her out-of-wedlock pregnancy. The court then maintained that the board's action violated the teacher's rights under the Equal Protection Clause. In its analysis, the court cited *Andrews v. Drew Municipal Separate School District* (1975), in which it rejected three arguments put forth by a school board that its policy was rationally related to a government interest. The three arguments the court rejected in *Andrews* were "(1) that unwed parenthood is prima facie proof of immorality; (2) that unwed parents are unfit role models; (3) that employment of an unwed parent in a scholastic environment materially contributes to the problem of school-girl pregnancies" (*Andrews*, at 614). Here, the school again argued that unwed pregnancy was per se evidence of immorality and that an unwed teacher was a poor role model. The Fifth Circuit again rejected these arguments and remanded the case to a trial court for a determination of appropriate relief.

EMPLOYMENT RIGHTS OF NONTENURED TEACHERS

Boards have also misapplied the law in terminating the employment of teachers who were not tenured. Although school boards do not have to provide much in the way of due process when they do not renew the contracts of teachers lacking tenure, more due process must be afforded to teachers who are dismissed before their contracts expire. In the same way, nontenured teachers may be entitled to greater due process when they can make the case that they were dismissed for unconstitutional or discriminatory reasons. In *Cowan v. Strafford R-VI School District* (1998), for instance, a school board chose not to renew the contract of a nontenured second grade teacher as a result of her sending students home with a letter with a "magic rock" on the last day of school. The apparently well-intentioned letter, which stated that "the magic rock you have will always let you know that you can do anything you set your mind to" (p. 1156), commended students for working hard and suggested that they rub their magic rocks for support, but it raised concerns among parents who feared that she was promoting New Ageism. The teacher contended that the letter was simply intended to give the children something to serve as a confidence boost; it was not really about religious or magical beliefs.

After the principal received complaints from parents regarding the letter, he informed the teacher of the complaints and told her that two families moved their students to private Christian schools as a result of the letter and to avoid magical ideas. The principal also informed the superintendent who passed the information to the school board. The following August, the teacher received "job targets," which included that she needed to improve her interpersonal relationships with parents and her instructional process. The following spring, the principal recommended that the teacher resign because the board was not going to renew her contract. When the teacher refused to resign, the board chose not to renew her contract.

The teacher then filed suit alleging that the board refused to renew her contract "because she had offended the religious sensibilities of the Strafford community" (*Cowan* at 1157). The trial court applied the mixed-motive analysis, in which the teacher had to first make a prima facie case that religion was a motivating factor in the board's action. The board then had to show that it would have reached the same outcome without the illegal basis. The jury found that the decision not to renew her contract was motivated by religious concerns about the teaching of New Ageism. The Eighth Circuit affirmed; it hinted in its opinion that it questioned whether the teacher pled a prima facie case for religious discrimination, but did not address it because the school board did not challenge it. Although the Eighth Circuit refused to order the school board to reinstate the teacher to her former position, it did agree that 2 years was an appropriate length of time on which to grant her an award of damages in the form of front pay. It would have been even more helpful had the court addressed the appropriate standards for teacher dismissal in a case such as this that purportedly involved mistaken understanding of values.

CONCLUSION

Ultimately, the question of whether teachers need more rights when they are facing the termination of their employment is more complicated than a simple "yes or no" response. The litigation has demonstrated that school boards have most often violated the rights of teachers because of the lack of specificity in the laws that are designed to grant teachers employment protection. The failure of legislatures to draft statutes and state boards of education to promulgate regulations with sufficient specificity has undoubtedly led to the retention of teachers who have negatively affected the profession and their schools. At the same time, these laws have allowed boards to dismiss teachers for reasons unintended by the statutes and sometimes in violation of other laws.

More than 40 years ago, the *Morrison* court addressed the procedural concerns raised by teacher dismissal statutes, declaring,

> A sweeping provision purporting to penalize or sanction so large a group of people as to be incapable of effective enforcement against all or even most of them necessarily might offend due process. Such a statute, unless narrowed by clear and well-known standards, affords too great a potential for arbitrary and discriminatory application and administration. (at 226 n. 15)

However, as the litigation discussed in this point essay illustrates, when placed alongside current statutory schemes, the law has not made sufficient progress in this arena to protect the rights of teachers. Thus, it is not that teachers need more rights regarding the termination of their employment, but rather that their rights need greater protection through the enactment of better and clearer dismissal statutes.

COUNTERPOINT: Allison S. Fetter-Harrott
Franklin College

Public school teachers are essential to student learning. Although it is important to protect teachers from the arbitrary and unfair termination of their employment, a vast array of substantive and procedural protections exist to guard them from wrongful dismissal. Given the importance of providing educational leaders with the autonomy to govern efficiently and the many protections provided teachers, granting teachers greater protection when faced with the termination of their employment does not serve the public interest.

This counterpoint essay, then, disagrees with the point essay in contending that existing tenure laws and collective bargaining agreements provide sufficient protection for teachers facing the termination of their employment. If anything, this counterpoint essay maintains that the extensive procedural due process rights that are in place create significant barriers for school boards that want to dismiss ineffective teachers. To this end, this counterpoint essay posits that existing procedures harm the teaching profession both by often forcing school boards to divert scarce resources when teachers contest their dismissals and by placing a disproportionate amount of attention on poor teachers rather than on better qualified colleagues and on students.

TEACHER TENURE PROTECTIONS UNDER STATE STATUTES

Most jurisdictions in the United States have statutes in place that can grant public school teachers tenure. In the K–12 public school context, teacher tenure amounts to the right to procedural due process protections before public school boards may dismiss teachers. The range and nature of these many protections vary widely from state to state. Typically, teacher tenure statutory provisions provide that school boards cannot dismiss tenured teachers for cause unless they are engaged in one or more of the following grounds for dismissal: insubordination, conviction of a criminal offense, immorality, incompetence, other good and just cause. Tenured (and nontenured) teachers can also be dismissed as the result of bona fide reductions in the number of teaching positions resulting from declines in student enrollments, discontinuation of programs, and financial exigencies.

At the same time, many tenure statutes require school boards to afford teachers various procedural due process protections in determining whether dismissals are appropriate. These procedures often include timely notice of a school's intention to dismiss teachers, the alleged grounds for dismissals, and the right to fair and timely hearings such as arbitration procedures or appealable hearings before their local boards of education, administrative law judges, local judges, or others. Additionally, many statutes provide tenured teachers with additional rights in the hearing procedures themselves including the right to be represented by counsel or a union representative, the right to present and cross examine witnesses, the right to advance examination of the school's evidence, the right to request a transcript of the hearing (created at the school's cost), the right to multiple levels of appeal of the initial dismissal decision if adverse, and perhaps many other rights. In many locales, local unions use member dues to hire counsel or otherwise provide a teacher representation free of charge or at low cost for tenured teacher members facing dismissal.

In most states, teachers gain these extensive tenure rights simply by teaching for a relatively short specified period, often between 2 and 5 years. The attachment of such a wide array of procedural protections after only a handful of years in service distinguishes teachers from a host of other professional fields, including faculty in higher education, where individuals must often serve for 6 or more years before attaining tenure. In some states, teachers gain full tenure in one step, and in others individuals go through initial probationary periods during which they enjoy greater due process protection, and then advance to periods of full tenure.

Even when teachers have not yet gained tenure, they nonetheless ordinarily work under at least yearlong agreements with local school boards. These annual teaching contracts frequently are required by state statute and often provide even pre-tenure teachers with a host of procedural protections guarding them from dismissal, even for cause, during the time period covered by their contracts. For example, many pre-tenure teacher contracts provide for a range of procedural protections by their own terms. Sometimes, contracts simply refer to the teacher tenure statute. In other instances, contracts provide additional procedural protections in excess of those guaranteed by state statute. Additionally, many states add statutory rights to procedural protections from dismissal within the term of even a first-year teacher contract, several of which mirror the protections provided to tenured teachers, including notice, opportunity to refute charges, and a multilayered procedural process.

COLLECTIVE BARGAINING AGREEMENTS

In addition to their individual teacher contracts, most public school teachers across the country enjoy additional protections under collective bargaining agreements. These agreements, many of which are sanctioned by state statute, provide additional protections from dismissal. These protections might be related specifically to dismissal, such as by providing a range of specific and additional procedural advantages, or might be hidden protections from dismissal. For example, it is not uncommon for a collective bargaining agreement to limit the number of times and amount of time during which a school administrator might be able to observe a teacher's classroom performance. Others may prescribe specific methods of teacher evaluation that limit the manner in which administrators can give teachers feedback, including schemes that sometimes limit teacher evaluation to self- or peer-evaluation, that list the categories exclusively on which teachers may be evaluated, or that limit the number of times a teacher can be evaluated or the sources from which an administrator may draw to make an evaluation decision.

Many collective bargaining agreements may include grievance procedures that can embroil already busy administrators in time-intensive meetings and paperwork to challenge even oral counseling sessions on teaching methods or other aspects of performance. These various layers of rights and procedures provide many public school teachers extra layers of protection from the dangers of arbitrary dismissal.

CONSTITUTIONAL PROTECTIONS

In addition, the U.S. Constitution governs the actions of school leaders as government employers. Accordingly, as public employees, teachers have federal constitutional protection against discriminatory or arbitrary dismissal from their positions in many instances. Following the U.S. Supreme Court's decision in *Board of Regents v. Roth* (1972), where teacher tenure statutes or individual or collectively bargained contracts grant teachers of any level or experience some continued expectation of teaching employment, they have a right to protections guaranteed by the procedural Due Process Clause of the Fourteenth Amendment to the U.S. Constitution. Additionally, under the Equal Protection Clause of the Fourteenth Amendment to the U.S. Constitution, public schools may not dismiss teachers from employment based on discriminatory and arbitrary grounds such as race (*Wygant v. Jackson Board of Education*, 1986) and sex (*Southard v. Texas Board of Criminal Justice*, 1997). Similarly, as the Supreme Court found in *Pickering v. Board of Education* (1968) and a series of later cases, school boards may not dismiss teachers in retaliation for their exercise of free speech rights under the Free Speech Clause of the First Amendment to the Constitution.

HISTORICAL PERSPECTIVES ON TEACHER DISMISSAL PROTECTIONS

Many states began granting teacher tenure through statutory protections in the first quarter of the 20th century, especially around the time of World War I and the women's suffrage movement. Early teacher tenure and other dismissal protection movements were aimed at protecting the best teachers from arbitrary termination, such as termination for political reasons, firings carried out to make room for the close friends of new administrators, or for dismissals based on more invidious reasons such as pregnancy, gender, or race discrimination.

Few would dispute that each and every U.S. public school teacher is extremely important to the present development and future viability of U.S. children, and thus to our economy, our culture, and our communities. Accordingly, it is important that leaders in public schools have the capacity to make sure that each classroom is staffed with the most qualified and effective teacher. Cumbersome teacher dismissal protections pose a serious threat to this interest because they can make it exceedingly challenging to dismiss ineffective or even harmful teachers, often costing tens of thousands of dollars and untold amounts of administrator time to dismiss even one teacher who does not belong in the classroom. For example, perhaps because it is so difficult, sources reveal that in recent years, the school boards in New York City, Chicago, and Los Angeles have been able to dismiss only approximately one tenth of 1% of their teachers. Mere longevity alone leads to the granting of tenure under state statutes in many states, so exceedingly low rates of dismissal might be cause for concern.

Although state statutory protections may at one time have been necessary to protect teachers from arbitrary or discriminatory dismissals, educators across the country now enjoy a host of protections from such treatment. By way of illustration, the rights recognized earlier have largely evolved in the century since states began enacting teacher tenure protection statutes. Additionally, the past century brought with it as well a plethora of civil rights and funding legislation designed to reduce discriminatory and arbitrary dismissal. For example, Title VII of the Civil Rights Act of 1964 protects employees from discrimination based on race, color, sex, religion, and national origin. Additionally, an amendment to Title VII, the Pregnancy Discrimination Act, prohibits employers from discriminating against women because of pregnancy. Further, the Family and Medical Leave Act of 1993 provides full-time workers employed for more than a year with as much as 3 months of unpaid leave relating to individual or family medical needs, such as disabling pregnancy, the birth of a child, and other events. Finally, public school teachers enjoy the protections of Section 504 of the Rehabilitation Act of 1973, which prohibits discrimination against individuals with disabilities.

These federal statutory protections exist in addition to state antidiscrimination statutes and common law remedies for wrongful dismissal. Given the array of additional state and federal protections against arbitrary dismissal that have arisen in the last century, some argue that teacher tenure statutes and protections against dismissal provided in collective bargaining agreements are no longer necessary to safeguard public school teachers from wrongful dismissal from their positions. Rather, some worry that a troubling function of such provisions is to act as barriers to school leaders in managing teacher performance and in removing ineffective teachers from classroom positions.

Some more contemporary voices in favor of providing teachers additional procedural protections from dismissal argue that these protections and the ensuing job security that accompanies them are some of the few advantages of a profession that requires considerable skill but provides exceedingly little compensation. Given the elaborate web of increasing employment protections at the federal, state, and local levels, this incentive argument is perhaps the most compelling contemporary justification for teacher tenure statutes and other dismissal protections for teachers. Yet, many would argue that the prevalence of a costly array of protections is one cause of low teacher salaries overall because school boards spend money on administrative and procedural costs of teacher tenure that could otherwise have been allocated to recognize the many dedicated and effective teachers in U.S. classrooms.

Many doubt that the best and brightest current and future teachers are drawn to the profession by a belief that it will be more difficult to fire them, even if they are unsuccessful at their jobs. Additionally, many skilled and dedicated teachers would report that they resent a system that, because of the various layers of procedural protection against even dismissal for cause, might protect colleagues who are less committed, less professional, and less able to support or carry on their good work. This author alone has heard more than one qualified teaching professional bemoan that teaching alongside a poor teacher makes more work for the skilled peer, and any can imagine the distress caused by handing over well-prepared students to a subsequent teacher in whose care children will languish or regress. It is entirely possible that the dismissal protections afforded to poor teachers are demoralizing and contribute to a feeling of futility among their effective peers. Finally, others worry that the many teacher dismissal protections serve as shields more for teachers who are ineffective or unprofessional rather than for those who truly inspire and elevate children, the latter enjoying the greatest job security of all, bringing true expertise and value to schools and their students.

CONCLUSION

The importance of affording school leaders the authority to remove ineffective teachers from classrooms has increased. In many places, squeezed state budgets have translated to painful public school cuts where teacher salaries are the highest expense. Consequently, the importance of having the most effective teaching professionals has grown considerably, as boards have less and less to pay and fewer teachers to hire. However, most importantly, educational leaders must have the freedom to remove teachers who are simply not serving our nation's children effectively. Beyond the financial dimensions, the cost to children who languish for a year or more in classrooms of teachers who are ill equipped to advance their education is devastating. Our children cannot be repaid the formative years of their youth. Accordingly, we owe it to our children to maintain an educational system that protects the best teachers from discriminatory treatment while allowing school leaders to ensure that students will not bear the burden of a system that protects those who are unfit to teach.

Further Readings and Resources

Frels, K., & Horton, J. (2007). *A documentation system for teacher improvement or termination.* Dayton, OH: Education Law Association.

Greenblatt, A. (2010, April 29). *Is teacher tenure still necessary?* Retrieved March 15, 2011, from National Public Radio website: http://www.npr.org/templates/story/story.php?storyId=126349435&sc=emaf

Osborne, A. G., & Russo, C. J. (2011). *The legal rights and responsibilities of teachers.* Thousand Oaks, CA: Corwin.

Rossow, L. F., & Tate, J. O. (2003). *The law of teacher evaluation.* Dayton, OH: Education Law Association.

Russo, C. J., & Mawdsley, R. D. (2011). *Education law.* New York: Law Journal Press.

Court Cases and Statutes

Andrews v. Drew Municipal Separate School District, 507 F.2d 611 (5th Cir. 1975).

Avery v. Homewood City Board of Education, 674 F.2d 337 (5th Cir. 1982).

Board of Education of Hopkins County v. Wood, 717 S.W.2d 837 (Ky. 1986).

Board of Regents v. Roth, 408 U.S. 564 (1972).

Chicago Board of Education v. Payne, 430 N.E.2d 310 (Ill. App. Ct. 1981).

Cleveland Board of Education v. Loudermill, 470 U.S. 532 (1985).

Cowan v. Strafford R-VI School District, 140 F.3d 1153 (8th Cir. 1998).

Family and Medical Leave Act of 1993, 29 U.S.C. §§ 2601 *et seq.*

Hansen v. Board of Education of School District No. 65, 502 N.E.2d 467 (Ill. App. Ct. 1986).

Morrison v. State Board of Education, 461 P.2d 375 (Cal. 1969).

Perry v. Sindermann, 408 U.S. 593 (1972).

Pickering v. Board of Education of Township High School District 205, 391 U.S. 563 (1968).

Pregnancy Discrimination Act, 42 U.S.C. § 2000e(k).

Rehabilitation Act of 1973, Section 504, 29 U.S.C. § 794.

Rowland v. Mad River Local School District, 730 F.2d 444 (6th Cir. 1984), *cert. denied,* 470 U.S. 1009 (1985).

School District No. 8 v. Superior Court, 433 P.2d 28 (Ariz. 1967).

Section 504 of the Rehabilitation Act of 1973, 29 U.S.C. § 794.

Southard v. Texas Board of Criminal Justice, 114 F.3d 539 (5th Cir. 1997).

State of Indiana ex rel. Anderson v. Brand, 303 U.S. 95 (1938).

Title VII of the Civil Rights Act of 1964, 42 U.S.C. §§ 2000e *et seq.*

Wygant v. Jackson Board of Education, 476 U.S. 267 (1986).

Do teacher unions and collective bargaining improve the terms and conditions of teacher employment?

POINT: Bruce S. Cooper, *Fordham University*

COUNTERPOINT: Michael J. Jernigan, *Miami Valley Career Technology Center*

OVERVIEW

Ongoing controversy continues to rage over the status and continuing viability of teacher unions and the practice of collective bargaining concerning the terms and conditions of teacher employment in U.S. public education. With Wisconsin and Ohio serving as the epicenters of these conflicts, the resolution of the question whether unions and bargaining will continue as a major force has the potential to result in a fundamental reshaping of labor relations in U.S. public education.

The earliest steps toward public sector collective negotiations occurred in 1958 when New York City allowed city workers to engage in bargaining, and a year later Wisconsin became the first state to mandate the process for public employees. Further, President John F. Kennedy signed an executive order in 1962 recognizing the rights of federal workers to bargain collectively (Tyler, 1976). U.S. teacher unions became a force to be reckoned with in the early 1960s following a work stoppage in New York City (Kerchner & Mitchell, 1988). Together, these developments hastened the move toward using the process of collective bargaining nationally over the terms and conditions of the employment of school employees. As the process involving public teacher unions and school boards evolved in the states permitting collective bargaining, the parties adopted the largely adversarial model that emerged in the private industrial labor relations sector in the 1930s.

Putting aside a discussion of whether the industrial labor relations model of bargaining is appropriate in the world of education, teacher unions continue to function like their counterparts in the private industrial labor relations sector, wherein union memberships have plummeted to new lows. Regardless of whether they are in education, the automobile industry, or manufacturing, the primary purpose of unions is to save the jobs of members, particularly those with the greatest seniority, while increasing their pay and benefits. At the same time, teacher unions have garnered considerable political clout because they have been able to assert their influence by using mandatory membership and compulsory dues from members, not to mention so-called fair share or representation fees from teachers who choose not to join their ranks, to express their support for elected officials who are willing to do their bidding.

Conflict, if not resentment, has been steadily brewing in many places in recent years over the status of public school teacher unions and their use of bargaining. More specifically, taxpayers in many places have become frustrated with unions because at a time when the private sector is struggling to compete during the economic downturn, members of teacher unions continue to receive increases in salary and an array of benefits, whether in the form of tenure, medical coverage, or sick leave, often regardless of whether they have performed meritoriously.

In partial response to public frustration with the increase of compensation for public school teachers, a variety of elected officials and legislatures in states that allow for collective negotiations have sought to limit the reach of bargaining. Yet, attempts at reforming the scope of teacher unions and bargaining have been highly contentious. For example, a minority of legislators in Wisconsin, with strong support from public teacher unions whose members took to the streets and occupied the state capitol building, fled the state rather than vote on a proposal that ultimately restricted bargaining. After the statute was enacted into law, this disagreement went all the way to the Supreme Court of Wisconsin before it was upheld in a split vote (*State ex rel. Ozanne v. Fitzgerald*, 2011).

Against the preceding background, the two following essays debate the benefits of unions and collective bargaining in public education. The point essay by Bruce S. Cooper, Fordham University, maintains that teacher unions provide economic, political, social, and organizational benefits to their members and education as a whole. More specifically, he asserts that although unions provide significant benefits to their members, these gains enhance the process of education because they ultimately accrue to students who will gain from being taught by teachers who are well paid. Cooper believes that unions spur their members on to improve education and benefit all in the field of education by serving at the vanguard of educational reform.

Conversely, the counterpoint essay by Michael J. Jernigan, Miami Valley Career Technology Center, Clayton, Ohio, asserts that unions do not improve the status of their members. He argues that by focusing on salaries and benefits, unions do not necessarily advance teaching and learning or make for better teachers. If anything, he believes that unions are more concerned about sustaining their own existence than helping improve the quality of education. Jernigan posits that it is incumbent on teachers to recognize their ability to represent themselves in a professional manner when negotiating salaries and benefits rather than rely on their unions to act on their behalf.

As you read the point and counterpoint essays, ask yourself the following questions: First, have teacher unions outlived their usefulness? Put another way, do we need teacher unions? Second, if states were to eliminate unions and collective bargaining for public school teachers, what processes might you suggest to provide employment protections for these educators?

Charles J. Russo
University of Dayton

Ralph D. Mawdsley
Cleveland State University

POINT: Bruce S. Cooper
Fordham University

The case for the universal unionization of teachers and the application of the process known as collective bargaining in public, and some nonpublic, schools rests on four key arguments, each of which is grounded in a social science perspective. The first of these factors is that the economic conditions of the working classes are such that unions help reduce class strife and even class warfare because they afford teachers voices in their daily work lives. Second, given the politics of education, a major public service that is supported by all levels of government, unions are the key bargaining representative for teachers, particularly in the process of collective negotiations over terms and conditions of their employment. Third, the social role of teachers as contributors to the growth and development of children of virtually all ages and stages is such that individual educators benefit from belonging to unions. Fourth, the organizational development of unions as they operate major associations in local, state, and national arenas give voice to the interests and needs of teachers in a manner that is critical to supporting U.S. education in all of its many forms.

Viewed together, these four frames make a strong case for the proposition that teacher unions and collective bargaining do improve the terms and conditions of teacher employment. Further, in distinction to the counterpoint essay, this essay stands for the proposition that U.S. education would suffer economically, politically, socially, and organizationally if teachers were unable to either form unions or bargain collectively with their employers.

ECONOMIC ADVANTAGES OF UNIONIZATION

In 1867, Karl Marx, with Frederick Engels, wrote *Das Kapital*, extolling the importance of empowering workers who were exploited brutally and often alienated by "capitalists," the owners of the means of production. According to these authors, the workers had to labor long hours, in terrible working conditions, and be poorly paid with few needed benefits—all to enhance corporate profits at the economic expense of workers. Not surprisingly, Marx's prediction was that the workers would unite, hear "Power to the people!" and take over the industries and also the very nations themselves, tossing out the capitalists and establishing a "communist" or "worker state."

Although these class revolutions occurred in Russia and other European countries, the rest of the modern industrial world found another model. In this alternative model, democratically elected governments enacted national labor legislation that required owners/managers to recognize the rights of workers to form unions; that obligated them to bargain collectively with representatives of the union for wages, benefits, and conditions of work; and that called for the use of third-party arbitration if and when management and labor were unable to resolve their differences and to sign negotiated employment contracts.

Amazingly, what saved capitalism, and led to tremendous growth in the economy over the last century, were the democratic labor unions in many free nations. The United States, for example, enacted the National Labor Relations Act (NLRA), later the Wagner Act of 1935, signed into law by the newly elected Democrat President, Franklin D. Roosevelt. This law was one of the first major statutes enacted under Roosevelt's administration. The Wagner Act guaranteed the rights of workers, albeit in the private sector, to form unions, to bargain collectively, to strike, and to seek third-party assistance in settling differences with management.

After beginning in the early 1960s, most jurisdictions did not finally enact laws permitting unionization and collective bargaining for public employees until later in that decade and the early 1970s. Of course, these laws gave public school teachers the right to form unions and to bargain with local boards of education regarding the terms and conditions of their employment. These developments aside, unlike many other nations, the United States had no federal public sector bargaining laws. Rather, each state could, and many did, enact public employment relations acts that granted most public employees such as police, firefighters, state, county, and local government employees, and, of course, teachers the right to bargain and file grievances. However, in most cases, unlike the federal Wagner Act, teachers did not have a legal right to strike even though many have done so.

One could thus argue that what saved capitalism was much the same dynamic that saved and improved public education: giving U.S. teachers a collective, powerful voice regarding the nature and content of education and for their working conditions. This advances this essay's belief that unionization raised salaries, improved benefits, and made education a worthy profession with decent compensation. Without unions, Marx's predictions about the fall of capitalism might have occurred in more industrial nations. At the same time, unionization has allowed America's more than 3 million public school teachers to organize and act collectively to improve the status of education regarding the terms and conditions of their employment and how they can better serve children. Unionism was and is essential!

If teachers are to be recognized, given a voice, and rewarded economically, then their unions are crucial to the economic well-being of their members. What followed, too, was the adoption by state teacher associations and two major national teacher unions of collective bargaining. Through their unions, teachers were able to turn local strife into national and state power, giving power to teachers in a society that traditionally treated teachers at best as good men and women, but as "semi-professionals" (Lortie, 1980).

POLITICAL ARGUMENTS FOR TEACHER UNIONS

Public education is an enormous enterprise, involving federal, state, and local agencies of government—and thus widespread politics. These political actors include the legislatures that enact laws governing school, the governmental branches that implement the law via regulations, and governmental units at the state and local level that manage the schools, all of which are influenced by their local and national teacher associations.

Much of the funding and regulation of schools is government mandated and controlled. Unless teachers are unionized and active, they will fail to have a voice in politics from national to local levels, whether being active before the U.S. Congress, the state legislatures, or the 13,000 local public school boards as well as city councils in locales such as New York City and Los Angeles, for example, that have done away with elected school boards.

Linda Kaboolian and Paul Sutherland (2005) make just that point: "Public education has, by every measure, the highest density of membership and coverage by collective bargaining of any industry, public or private" (p. 15). As such, without teacher unions to represent both the institution of schooling and teachers, education could be publicly ignored and underfunded. The teacher unions, recognizing the importance of political power, have formed two large national associations, the National Education Association (NEA) with 3.9 million members, and the American Federation of Teachers (AFT), with 1.9 million members, and each has an association in the states, and local voice, depending on whether the teachers vote to affiliate with the AFT or the NEA. The AFT is also affiliated and chartered by the American Federation of Labor-Congress of Industrial Organizations (AFL-CIO).

Aware of the notion of strength in numbers, the two unions made strong moves to merge during the 1990s (Cooper, 1998), which would have created one of the largest public sector unions in the country. However, although the AFT, which is more urbanized and large-city, voted for the merger, the NEA, which is more rural and small community, voted no. Accordingly, the merger failed.

SOCIAL IMPORTANCE OF TEACHER UNIONS

Teacher unions are important devices for unifying and giving voice to teachers while providing a common social framework for advancing the quality of teaching. Teaching itself is a solo activity, where teachers close their doors and do their jobs alone or in groups of two (with an aide). Thus, teachers need to have, and benefit greatly from, the colleagues and collegiality that union membership provides.

As union members, teachers can meet, discuss common problems, share solutions, and have regional and national networks to press for ideas and resources. Teacher unions are becoming more committed to "organizing around teaching and learning quality," putting the NEA and AFT into the "quality of services" business. Both associations have endorsed "peer reviews, higher training standards for teachers, and teacher work schedules that treat professional development as part of a teacher's job, not as an add-on option" (Kerchner & Koppich, 2000, p. 283; see also Moe, 2011). Yet Charles Taylor Kerchner and Julia Koppich also assert that these unions' concerns for quality are actually a form of "accidental policymaking." As most will undoubtedly recognize, even though teacher unions were not created to be organizations of academic quality, they are now a strong social force that continues to press for school reform and improvement.

Members of all professions need mutual support, social networks, and chances to stay in touch with colleagues. Without teacher unions, these opportunities would be limited. The one room schoolhouse is gone. The United States is a highly interactive social community, connected by Internet, instant messaging, and shared ideas. The social activities of teacher unions give shape to the role of teachers while making their jobs workable, forceful, and effective.

ORGANIZATIONAL VALUE OF UNIONS

A final argument in favor of unions is their value as organizations that give form and structure to the needs and requirements of teachers in the United States. Of course, the Tenth Amendment reserves education to the power of states. Even so, public education is a complex enterprise with the federal government becoming ever more important in setting national standards, administering national tests, and funding areas of education, including services for children who are economically deprived and covered by the No Child Left Behind legislation (formerly the Elementary and Secondary Education Act), students with special needs who are covered by laws such as Section 504 of the

Rehabilitation Act of 1973 and the Individuals with Disabilities Education Act, and those who are protected be laws dealing with vocational education and other specialized programs.

As education increasingly becomes a national effort, teachers need organizations that can operate at all levels, giving form and structure to their needs and roles. Without unions, teachers would be lost in the nationalization rush and given little voice or notice. Education is organized and unions must follow.

Terrence Moe (2001) has found that teachers and their unions are key players in determining who gets elected to local school boards because turnout is often low and interest is diffuse. Moe observed that insofar as teachers and other school board employees are vitally interested in elections, they are 3 times more likely to cast their ballots in a local election than are the average, unconcerned citizens.

In furthering his position, Moe (2006, p. 255) noted that apathy should end in education. To this end, he noted that to ensure attention for education, teachers and other school employees, often through the work of their unions, have become deeply interested in funding, spending, allocation of resources, the hiring and firing of staff, rule-making, curriculum decisions, and whether schools are opened more or fewer days. He acknowledges that because these educators are invested in education, they have a greater stake in improving schools than many other interest groups have.

Teachers are well organized as their unions often sign up new members automatically (at hiring) and, as long as state laws allow them to do so, collect union dues right out of teachers' paychecks before they are distributed. Moreover, teachers often vote as a bloc, giving them a stronger voice in who is elected and how school boards vote on key issues. This form of organized, grassroots politics is effective and often essential to the relevance and authority of teacher unions.

CONCLUSION

The argument for teacher unions rests squarely on four legs. The first leg is that unions are critical to the economics of management-labor relations, giving a balance to their voices, and providing a platform for teachers to make decent livings and live quality lives. The second leg is that teacher unions have an important political role to play in policy making of education at all levels of government. Who else is there to represent the classroom, the instruction, and the teachers? The third leg is the reality that regardless of whether one agrees with them, teacher unions play a major role as social links for professionals.

The fourth leg is that teacher unions are a critical national organization, without which the nation's children would have no one to speak loudly and consistently for them in the halls of Congress, state legislatures, and local community school boards.

One supporter, Alan Singer (2010), wrote recently that one cannot imagine today the nation's teachers not being organized, with a strong voice for their work and their compensation. He pointed out that New York City (NYC) laid off 13,000 public school teachers in 1975 during a financial crisis. With fewer teachers, he maintained that the board of education and mayor had to work together to shorten the school day, eliminate elective courses, and enlarge high school classroom enrollment from around 32 to 60. Reportedly, he indicated that students were hanging out of windows because of the lack of supervision. Only the NYC teachers union, Singer posited, forced city officials to reduce class size, transforming schools from warehouses to learning environments.

Destroying teacher unions, as happened with the loss of mining as a viable industry when the miners' unions were destroyed, would mean that teachers would be ignored by the bureaucrats and budget cutters. Hence, just as with miners, the Race to the Top in education would become instead a "race to the bottom" and our students will get hurt.

Without a doubt, teacher unions have proven to be key levers in U.S. education, getting the candidates of their choice elected to high office while standing behind presidents and governors in their quest to fund and support schools, particularly when times are tight. Recently, one local union had a tough choice to make: whether to bargain for a 3% annual pay raise and witness the layoff of 85 new teachers for lack of funding, or to keep the teachers and forfeit the salary raise. Teachers voted in the majority for their newer colleagues and no pay raise, thus to keep more teachers employed and to hold class size down. What better argument for unions as colleagues and professionals, working together, to help their students, their families, and their community?

COUNTERPOINT: Michael J. Jernigan
Miami Valley Career Technology Center

Teachers have been described as semi- or pseudo-professionals by members of occupations that are considered professional, such as lawyers and doctors (Lortie, 1980). Perhaps this label results from the growth in teacher unionization over the better part of the past 50 years that created a group of college-educated workers who are represented by unions, organizations that are ordinarily associated with blue-collar workers. Unifying workers toward common goals including gaining recognition, improving the work environment, increasing wages and benefits, defining work hours, specifying work limits, and other related advancements has long been the calling card of unions (Renner, 2004).

The principle of unity for the common benefit that was applied initially to industrial settings has been extended to service industries and now includes teachers and other public employees (Kerchner & Mitchell, 1988). Even so, the application of the industrial labor relations model may not be appropriate for service industries such as education, even though it is used widely in the United States. The industrial model's focus was on salary, a day's pay for a day's labor. Initially, the emphasis for teacher organizations was recognition as professionals and earning the respect associated with professionalism (Renner, 2004). Against this background, the arguments of the point essay notwithstanding, this counterpoint essay raises questions about the viability of using this model to improve the terms and conditions of teacher employment. This counterpoint essay, which advances the case against continued unionization of public school teachers and some educators in nonpublic schools and against the growth of collective bargaining, rests on five major points: the blue-collar versus white-collar, or laborer versus professional status of teaching; the minimum entry requirements for teaching—bachelor's degree versus other union represented occupations requiring certification or licenses; union protection of workers and the focus on increasing salaries or benefits while ignoring the education of youth; safety in numbers or mob mentality (union vs. individual); and academic freedom versus contractual restrictions. When all of these factors are considered, this counterpoint essay believes that unions and collective bargaining simply do not improve the terms and conditions of teacher employment.

BLUE-COLLAR VERSUS WHITE-COLLAR, LABORER VERSUS PROFESSIONAL

Unions have represented workers in the United States since the 19th century. History reveals that the existence of sweatshops, poor pay, long hours, and unfair labor practices by employers caused workers to unite for better treatment and pay. These laborers were typically tradesmen or unskilled workers who were considered to be blue-collar workers. Blue-collar occupations are usually identified by the physical nature of the job requirements rather than purely intellectual occupations. Although unions certainly did have and may still have a place in protecting workers, those times seem to have passed. The federal and state governments have enacted laws and established organizations to protect workers and their rights. The U.S. Department of Labor, the Occupational Safety and Health Administration, the Equal Employment Opportunity Commission, and their state counterparts are all advocates for fair pay, reasonable working conditions, worker safety, and worker nondiscrimination.

A plethora of other city and local organizations also look out for the interests of workers. Insofar as the organizations identified in the previous paragraph are available for workers, the need for unionization seems to have diminished. The ongoing existence of unions may be more necessary to pay the salaries of national union representatives than to look after the best interests of education or teachers. To ensure their existence, unions must provide increased salaries that offset union dues while seeking to obtain better or improved benefits for members. This key item, membership dues, appears to be the sole item of interest for unions.

As long as their members receive higher salaries, unions can increase the cost of membership dues to ensure their continued existence. Although union membership initially appealed to less educated constituents, teachers have completed levels of education culminating in state certification or licensure, which should mitigate against their joining unions. The requisite level of education that one must complete before entering teaching is higher than that in the United Auto Workers, the American Federation of Labor and Congress of Industrial Organizations (AFL-CIO), and other similar unions where members typically have lower levels of formal education. Interestingly the American Federation of Teachers, the second largest teacher organization in the United States, derives its existence from the AFL-CIO. The largest national teacher union, the National Education Association, was designed primarily for education administrators but later excluded them to focus solely on teacher members.

MINIMUM OCCUPATIONAL ENTRY REQUIREMENTS

Union membership seems to be inconsistent with teachers' goal of being recognized as members of a profession. Moreover, as a collective group of public intellectuals, teachers should be able to negotiate on their own behalf. Other professions do so without undue difficulty. Most other union-represented occupations require at most a certificate of completion or a license. No other occupation requiring a college education as a minimum entry requirement is union represented. By completing a college education, prospective teachers have embarked on attaining status as professionals, but unionization seems to remove this status.

Teachers join unions and engage in bargaining to receive better salaries and benefits. These are goals that teachers should be able to achieve through self-representation. Other professions such as doctors, lawyers, and engineers negotiate their salary and benefits with the employer or client on their own behalf. Much like these other professionals, teachers are involved in an intellectual occupation. Teachers should thus be able to read and understand contract language and bargain for appropriate salaries and benefits without resorting to collective bargaining through union representation.

FOCUS ON SALARIES AND BENEFITS RATHER THAN ON STUDENT WELFARE

Unions must provide increases in salary and benefits to help satisfy their members and thus ensure their own continued existence. Unions also provide legal counsel and protection when union members are subject to discipline or dismissal, in addition to grievance procedures, appeals, and arbitration provisions. All of this contractual language establishes the level of representation required by the union in personnel matters and far exceeds the protection afforded taxpayers who fund teacher salaries and benefits. To remain viable, unions must "earn" their dues by providing membership higher salaries and better benefits. Unions must then convince their members that without the unions, these salaries and benefits would be unattainable. Interestingly, though, when negotiations falter, unions often discuss the possibility of strikes with their membership, sometimes without regard for what state laws may permit and without considering the detrimental impact of strikes on both teachers and students.

Teachers who are absent from work because of strikes do not contribute to the education of the nation's youth; they may also be fired if they engage in illegal strikes. Moreover, strikes are usually over the lack of salary increases and loss of or reduction in benefits, which do not affect the educational process per se or contribute to student learning. The reality is that changes in teacher salaries or benefits do not affect students in the classroom except when their teachers are not available. In these situations, striking teachers have a significant impact on the students that they left in their classrooms. Although teachers have historically been underpaid, recent information available through the U.S. Department of Labor reveals that their salaries are no longer lagging by substantial amounts and, in many places, have outpaced the rate of growth in the private sector. Fundamentally, unions try to obtain increased salaries for their members so that unions can receive the membership dues that ultimately sustain their existence at the local, state, and national levels. The upshot is that focusing on salary and benefits undermines the educational process.

When unions pursue increases in salaries and benefits for their members, they have relied on approaches such as meet-and-confer, good-faith bargaining, and the unexpected crisis (Kerchner & Mitchell, 1988), each of which has advantages and disadvantages. Yet, the current trend in collective bargaining is toward win-win, a process that is described as both sides sitting at the table with full disclosure of available resources, including fixed costs. This process seems to lend itself to negotiation by individual teachers rather than by their unions because it is an interpersonal interaction on the intellectual level that can be conducted individually rather than by a bargaining team as a group. However, some teachers may find safety in numbers even though it is unnecessary, as discussed in the following paragraphs.

SAFETY IN NUMBERS OR MOB MENTALITY

It is human nature not to want to be singled out. The general assumption is that if others are similarly situated, all will be treated the same. If not, those who are mistreated collectively can band together because they believe that their voices will be heard and that because of "safety in numbers," they will not be punished if they engage in actions such as illegal work stoppages. Unions appeal to this fundamental human feeling.

Unions use the fear of litigation, unethical disciplinary actions, and wrongful dismissals to lure teachers into joining. Unions "sell" the idea that as a collective group with a united front, their representatives have leverage that can be used to gain concessions from school boards that will lead to higher salaries and better benefits. Teachers may be unaware of the concessions earned by unions to receive salary increases and better benefits for their members. Although union members do ultimately vote on whether to approve negotiated contracts, they may not be aware of what they may lose in exchange for the salaries and benefits that they gain through unionization. More specifically, in exchange for salary and benefits, teachers may lose intangible, intellectual rights such as choosing one's own curricula or exercising academic freedom.

ACADEMIC FREEDOM VERSUS CONTRACTUAL RESTRICTIONS

If unions continue making inroads into areas considered to be management rights, such as determining class size, as terms and conditions of employment, then teachers may find themselves severely restricted in their classrooms because of language in their contracts. In other words, academic freedom, a right that is already constrained in K–12 education, may be the cost of continued collective bargaining as union representatives press for increases in salary and benefits. In the negotiating process, each side gives and takes until they reach a mutual agreement. This give and take may include academic freedoms currently enjoyed by classroom teachers.

Union representatives may agree to teaching restrictions, inflexible curricula, and prescribed delivery to achieve better salary and benefits for their members. Teachers must realize that their union representatives may have limited or no actual teaching experience. These representatives, who may be strictly union employees, may not understand the importance and relevance to teaching that academic freedom represents. Teachers may lose the autonomy to instruct and manage their classroom in the manner they think necessary to promote learning. Contracts may become more prescriptive in nature and restrictive with respect to classroom management techniques. In addition, differentiated instruction may not be an option for teachers to employ if contract language dictates method of instruction or delivery mechanisms.

The ability of teachers to assess their classes and select the best methods or combinations of methods to advance their students may not be allowed if union representatives concede to achieve salary and benefit concessions. The days of teachers closing their doors and preparing students in the best way possible based on their experience may no longer be an option, even though teachers are the best authority for classroom instructional methods and delivery. Teachers should not sacrifice this intellectual prerogative through unionization by allowing union representatives the authority to compromise the classroom-learning environment.

CONCLUSION

The argument against teacher unions is first and foremost an intellectual issue. Teachers have demonstrated their ability to accomplish intellectual endeavors through their completion of a college course of study, continued professional development as required for certification and licensure renewal, and completion of graduate degree(s) for increases in pay based on salary schedules. Earning a college degree is the beginning of professionalism. Continuation of this professionalism requires constant updating through professional development that is analogous to other professions using continuing education units to maintain currency. The assertions of the point essay notwithstanding, teachers possess the capacity to stand up on their own behalf, be heard, and complete contractual obligations without the need for intermediary third-party unions to act on their behalf.

Teachers should know what is best to help their students learn so that they may contribute positively to society. Unions do not necessarily advance teaching and learning in classrooms because they focus on salary and benefits, not education. Although an argument may be made that well-paid teachers are happy, better teachers, there are no data available to support this myth. Higher salary and better benefits do not necessarily make better teachers. The current economic reality dictates that all parties involved with taxpayer funds use these monies in the most efficient and frugal manner. U.S. society's entitlement attitude must not drive teacher salaries and benefits to the extent that school boards become financially strapped and unable to continue without state or federal fiscal intervention. In fact, as reflected in states such as Ohio and Wisconsin, recent events related to the economic climate have forced some legislatures to act to limit, reduce, or eliminate collective bargaining for public employees including teachers. As state legislators work to enact laws changing collective bargaining rights for public employees, their employee unions have staged demonstrations, sit-ins, and protests trying to garner public support against such restrictions.

Intellectually, teachers must recognize their ability to represent themselves in a professional manner when negotiating salary and benefits. Teachers do not need third-party representatives if they yearn to become or be considered professionals. Although this possibility has not been discussed earlier, continued entitlement expectations along with continued increases in salary and benefits may drive education toward technology that enables school boards to outsource educational needs to others, much as unions seemed to have driven many manufacturing occupations to other nations. Unfortunately, an economic recovery does not necessarily mean a return to the status quo previously achieved by teachers and their unions. Teachers need to be cognizant of the reality of this country's economic climate, the desire to be considered professionals, and their ability to evaluate, intellectually, the current employment atmosphere without the air of entitlement. Teachers must realize that the economy dictates resources available for school boards. One hopes the economy will recover and school boards will operate with fiscal responsibility allowing teachers to receive salary and benefits commensurate with the economic status of their communities. Teachers possess the individual ability to negotiate fair salaries and reasonable benefits that are affordable by school boards that are receiving fewer tax dollars because of the previously unforeseen and current economic downturn.

FURTHER READINGS AND RESOURCES

Cooper, B. S. (1998, March 11). Merging the teachers' unions: Opportunity amid complexity [Commentary]. *Education Week*, pp. 52, 34.

Cooper, B. S. (1998, May/June). Toward a more perfect union: An NEA-AFT merger would create the nation's largest labor group. That's good and bad. *Teacher Magazine*, pp. 55–58.

Herman, J., & Megiveron, G. (1993). *Collective bargaining in education.* Lancaster, PA: Technomic.

Kaboolian, L., & Sutherland, P. (2005). *Win-win labor-management collaboration in education: Breakthrough practices to benefit students, teachers, and administrators.* Washington, DC: Education Week Press.

Kerchner, C. T., & Cooper, B. S. (2003). "Ravening Tigers" under siege: Teacher unions, legitimacy, and institutional turmoil. In W. L. Boyd & M. Miretzky (Eds.), *American educational governance on trial: Change and challenges* (Yearbook of the National Society for the Study of Education, pp. 56–64). New York: Teachers College Press.

Kerchner, C. T., & Koppich, J. E. (2000). Organizing around quality: The frontiers of teacher unionism. In T. Loveless (Ed.), *Conflicting missions? Teachers unions and educational reform* (pp. 281–315). Washington, DC: Brookings Institution Press.

Kerchner, C. T., Koppich, J., & Weeres, J. (1997). *United mind workers: Unions and teaching in the knowledge society.* San Francisco: Jossey-Bass.

Kerchner, C. T., & Mitchell, D. E. (1988). *The changing idea of a teachers' union.* Philadelphia: Falmer Press.

Lieberman, M. (2000). *The teacher unions: How they sabotage educational reform and why.* San Francisco: Encounter Books.

Lortie, D. (1980). *Schoolteacher.* Chicago: University of Chicago Press.

Moe, T. M. (2001). Teachers unions and the public schools. In T. M. Moe (Ed.), *A primer on America's schools* (pp. 151–184). Stanford, CA: Hoover Institution Press.

Moe, T. M. (2006). Union power and the education of children. In J. Hannaway & A. Rotherham (Eds.), *Collective bargaining in education: Negotiating change in today's schools* (pp. 229–255). Cambridge, MA: Harvard University Press.

Moe, T. M. (2011). *Special interest: Teachers unions and America's public schools.* Washington, DC: Brookings Institution.

Renner, J. J. (2004). *The 1981 Mariemont teachers' strike: A lesson in leadership.* Unpublished doctoral dissertation, Miami University, Ohio.

Sharp, W. L. (2003). *Winning at collective bargaining strategies everyone can live with.* Lanham, MD: Scarecrow Press.

Singer, A. (2010, April 16). *Why I am pro-union and pro-teacher.* Retrieved from http://www.huffingtonpost.com/alan-singer

Tyler, G. (1976). Why they organize. In A. M. Cresswell & M. J. Murphy (Eds.), *Education and collective bargaining: Readings in policy and research* (pp. 12–21). Berkeley, CA: McCutchan.

U.S. Department of Labor. (2010). *Bureau of Labor Statistics, Career guide to industries* (2010–2011 ed.). Retrieved from http://stats.bls.gov/oco/cg/cgs034.htm#earnings

Walters, R. (2001). *Bargaining away teacher's rights.* Retrieved February 2, 2005, from The Buckeye Institute for Public Policy Solutions Perspective on Current Issues website: http://www.buckeyeinstitute.org/perspect/2001_8Persp.htm

COURT CASES AND STATUTES

Elementary and Secondary Education Act of 1965, 20 U.S.C. §§ 6301 *et seq.*

Individuals with Disabilities Education Act, 20 U.S.C. §§ 1400 *et seq.*

National Labor Relations Act (NLRA), 29 U.S.C. §§ 151 *et seq.*

No Child Left Behind Act of 2001, 20 U.S.C. §§ 6301 *et seq.*

Rehabilitation Act of 1973, Section 504, 29 U.S.C. § 794.

State ex rel. Ozanne v. Fitzgerald, 798 N.W.2d 436 (Wis. 2011).

Wagner Act of 1935, 29 U.S.C. §§ 151 *et seq.*

INDEX

Note: Bolded numbers refer to volume numbers in the Debating Issues in American Education series.

Budig, Gene A., **3:**259, **3:**264
Building Excellent Schools (BES),
    9:128–129
Bullough, R. V., Jr., **2:**48
Bully Police USA, **5:**63
Bullying
    antibullying policies, **5:**56
    awareness of issue, **5:**64
    in classrooms, **5:**59, **5:**60–61, **5:**65,
        5:66
    counselor interventions, **5:**61–62
    differences from cyberbullying,
        10:157–158
    educator responsibility for prevention,
        5:xxiii, **5:**55–69
    effects, **5:**59–60
    federal laws, **5:**63
    incidence, **5:**xxiii, **5:**55
    lawsuits, **5:**55–56, **5:**65–67, **5:**68
    locations, **5:**59
    prevention, **4:**263–264, **5:**56–57,
        5:60–63, **5:**64, **5:**65, **5:**66, **10:**156,
        10:170–171
    state laws, **5:**56, **5:**63, **5:**64, **5:**65, **10:**154,
        10:155, **10:**162–163, **10:**165–166
    suicides related to, **5:**xxiii, **5:**55, **5:**64,
        5:86, **10:**147, **10:**157
    targeted students, **5:**xxiii, **5:**55
    underlying causes, **5:**64–65, **5:**68–69
    See also Cyberbullying
Burch, Patricia, **3:**68, **7:**178
Bureau of Indian Affairs (BIA),
    1:257–258
Bureau of Indian Education (BIE), **1:**xxviii,
    1:254–255
    See also Native American schools
Bureau of Justice Statistics, **5:**24
Bureau of Labor Statistics (BLS),
    3:118, **3:**255
Bureaucracies, **6:**7–8
    See also Administration
Burn, Andrew, **2:**218
Burns, David, **1:**219
Burpee v. Burton, State ex rel., **5:**195
Bush, George H. W., **9:**xxvii, **9:**24
Bush, George W., **1:**49, **2:**130–131, **2:**205,
    5:190, **9:**60
Bush, George W., administration
    church-school partnerships, **3:**228
    community policing, **5:**168
    education policies, **6:**56
    Teacher Incentive Fund, **7:**36

teacher training programs, **3:**xxiii
Title IX amendments, **3:**210
See also No Child Left Behind Act
Bush v. Holmes, **1:**95, **1:**97–98
Business interests
    charter school operators, **1:**10, **1:**13,
        1:82–87, **6:**279, **6:**287, **6:**288, **7:**144,
        7:179–180, **9:**225
    cyberschool operators, **10:**81,
        10:84–85, **10:**87
    educational services, **7:**10, **7:**166–167,
        7:178, **7:**184
    effects on school governance,
        7:165–184
    efficiency, **9:**12–13, **9:**15–16
    engagement in education, **9:**236
    fund-raising services, **6:**294,
        6:296, **6:**304
    influence on public education, **7:**xxvi,
        7:6, **9:**15, **9:**32
    investment in education, **9:**233–260
    outsourcing to, **7:**166–167
    participative management, **2:**23–24
    performance pay, **6:**130, **6:**132–134
    profits, **9:**256, **9:**258
    school board elections and, **7:**10
    school improvement industry,
        7:170–171, **7:**173–174
    social obligations, **9:**258–259
    taxes, **6:**74, **6:**269, **9:**259
    technology funding, **10:**xvii
    technology skills needed by, **2:**237
    textbook publishers, **2:**29, **2:**32, **7:**166,
        9:18, **10:**21, **10:**22, **10:**93
    vocational education and, **1:**216–217,
        1:232
    See also Educational management
        organizations; Proprietary for-
        profit schools; Public-private
        partnerships
Business leaders, **7:**237, **7:**238–239, **7:**242
Business model
    in education reform, **7:**xxviii, **7:**47,
        7:247
    in private schools, **1:**72, **1:**78–79, **1:**81,
        1:82, **1:**88–89, **3:**68, **6:**266
    of Race to the Top, **7:**47, **7:**55, **7:**116
    See also Market competition
Business Roundtable (BR), **9:**247
Busing. See Transportation services
Butts, Calvin, **3:**138
Bybee, Deborah, **3:**24

CAEP. *See* Council for the Accreditation of
  Educator Preparation
Caldarella, Paul, **5:**243
Caldas, Stephen J., **3:**12
Calendars. *See* Holidays; School years
California
  Advanced Placement fees, **6:**230
  charter schools, **1:**15, **6:**xxiv, **6:**282,
    6:287
  constitution, **3:**179, **6:**202, **10:**108
  discipline policies, **10:**161–162
  diversity, **9:**58
  "English-only" curriculum, **3:**190
  extracurricular activity fees, **6:**218
  finance litigation, **3:**179, **6:**168–169
  for-profit schools, **1:**83, **1:**86, **1:**88
  property tax limits, **6:**27–28, **9:**202
  school district financial management,
    6:46
  school funding, **3:**177, **6:**27–28, **6:**64,
    6:99, **6:**200, **6:**202, **9:**191
  school shootings, **5:**24
  teacher compensation, **7:**210
  teacher licensing exams, **9:**85
  teacher training regulations, **9:**79
  year-round schools, **1:**237
California Charter Academy (CCA),
  6:287
California Supreme Court, **3:**179,
  6:168–169, **8:**2, **8:**233
Callahan, Raymond E., **9:**16–17, **9:**135
Cameras. *See* Video surveillance cameras
Camp Modin, **1:**139
*Campaign for Fiscal Equity (CFE) Inc. v.
  State*, **3:**182
Campbell, Amy L., **5:**237, **5:**242
*Campbell v. St. Tammany Parish School
  Board*, **4:**234, **4:**240
Camps, Jewish, **1:**126, **1:**132–133, **1:**136,
  1:139
Canada
  corporal punishment ban, **5:**110
  higher education, **6:**235
  Muslim students, **1:**59
Canada, Geoffrey, **9:**62, **9:**234
Canady v. Bossier Parish School Board, **5:**8,
  8:42–43, **8:**50
Cannan, John, **10:**180–181
Cannon v. University of Chicago,
  8:144–145
Cantwell v. Connecticut, **4:**xvii, **4:**44–45,
  4:98

Capper, Colleen A., **3:**249, **3:**251, **7:**106
CAPTA. *See* Child Abuse Prevention and
  Treatment Act
Care
  duty of, **5:**66
  ethic of, **5:**76
  meaning, **5:**100–101
  shown by teachers, **5:**150
  warm demanders, **5:**150–151
Career and technical education (CTE).
  See Vocational education
Carl D. Perkins Vocational and Applied
  Technology Education Act of 1990,
  3:127
Carlin, George, **2:**207
Carmichael, Sheila Byrd, **9:**26
Carnegie, Andrew, **9:**64, **9:**65–66,
  9:67–68, **9:**70
Carnegie Corporation of New York
  (CCNY), **9:**67–69
Carnegie Foundation for the Advancement
  of Teaching, **7:**174, **9:**65–67,
  9:177–178, **9:**183–184, **9:**185
Carnegie Units
  advantages, **9:**176, **9:**184–185
  alternatives to, **9:**176, **9:**181–182
  Common Core standards and, **9:**186,
    9:187–188
  creation, **9:**66–67, **9:**175, **9:**177–178,
    9:183–184
  criticism of, **9:**177, **9:**178–181, **9:**185,
    9:187
  definition, **9:**178
  potential elimination of, **9:**175–188
  proposed changes, **9:**181, **9:**185–188
  states abolishing, **9:**181–182
Carnoy, Martin, **1:**42, **3:**68
Carolina Abecedarian Project,
  1:202–203, **1:**205–206, **1:**213
*Carparts Distribution Center, Inc. v.
  Automotive Wholesaler's Association*,
  10:201
Carpenter, Linda Jean, **3:**209
Carrell, Scott, **7:**194
Carroll, Lewis, **7:**155
Carroll, Thomas, **9:**113, **9:**114
Carter, Deborah R., **5:**242
Carter, Jimmy, **7:**41, **7:**77, **9:**55
Carter, Stephen L., **10:**164
Catholic Church. *See* Roman Catholics
Cavalluzzo, Linda, **10:**90
Cavanaugh, Cathy, **10:**55

Colcy, Richard J., **3:**85, **3:**104–105
Collaboration
 among teachers, **7:**81, **7:**83
 with community agencies, **9:**201
 with parents, **9:**269, **9:**271–272
 in science, **2:**91
 use of technology, **10:**198–199
Collaborative learning environments
 engaging students, **5:**141–142
 establishing, **7:**152
 importance, **5:**xxiv
 technology used, **10:**40, **10:**214, **10:**217,
  10:223
Collective bargaining
 criticism of, **7:**26, **7:**34
 legislation, **7:**23, **7:**33, **7:**34
 by public employees, **8:**244, **8:**245, **8:**248,
  8:258
 resistance to reforms, **7:**27–32
 topics, **7:**33
 See also Unions
Collective bargaining agreements
  (CBAs)
 academic freedom and, **8:**256–257
 charter schools and, **6:**xxiv, **6:**281, **7:**132,
  7:140–141, **9:**168–169
 criticism of, **8:**xxiv, **8:**255–257
 effects, **9:**167, **9:**168
 effects on reform process, **7:**27–32
 employment protections, **8:**239–240
 financial provisions, **7:**29, **7:**36–37,
  8:255–256, **9:**169, **9:**171–172
 grievance procedures, **8:**239–240
 limits on administrative flexibility, **7:**23,
  7:25–26, **7:**28–32, **7:**35–36
 negotiations, **1:**77, **8:**245, **8:**255, **8:**256,
  8:257
 performance-based pay and, **6:**137
 public views of, **8:**245
 seniority provisions, **9:**168–170
 work rules, **7:**30–31, **7:**35, **8:**256–257
College Board, **3:**162, **3:**259, **3:**260, **6:**221,
  6:234, **6:**235, **6:**237–238, **9:**29, **9:**32,
  9:253
 See also Advanced Placement courses
Colleges and universities. *See* Higher
  education
Collegiate Learning Assessment (CLA),
  9:68–69
Colonial governments
 control of schools, **7:**xvii
 religion and, **4:**88–89

school systems, **1:**xvi–xvii, **7:**6,
  7:115–116
 See also Massachusetts Bay Colony
Colorado
 charter schools, **6:**xxiv, **6:**277, **7:**131,
  10:88
 debt limits, **6:**35
 finance litigation, **3:**180
 Pledge of Allegiance law, **4:**147
 virtual schools, **10:**88, **10:**89
Colorado Education Association, **7:**36
Colorado Supreme Court, **8:**58, **8:**69
Columbine shootings, **4:**277, **4:**278, **5:**xxii,
  5:16, **5:**24, **5:**28, **5:**64, **5:**190
Columbus City Schools, **9:**164, **9:**248
*Colvin ex rel. Colvin v. Lowndes County,
  Mississippi, School District*, **5:**20
Colwell, Brad, **1:**118
Committee for Educational Rights v. Edgar,
  6:158
*Committee for Public Education and
  Religion Liberty v. Regan*, **4:**6
Committee for Public Education v. Nyquist,
  4:11–12
Committee of Ten, **3:**153
Common Core State Standards Initiative
  (CCSSI), **9:**20–35
 adoption, **2:**62, **6:**14, **6:**82, **9:**39, **9:**40,
  9:62
 assessments, **2:**57, **2:**62, **9:**xxi, **9:**40,
  9:59–60, **9:**187–188, **9:**224
 assumptions, **9:**40
 Carnegie Units and, **9:**186,
  9:187–188
 criticism of, **9:**30, **9:**60
 development of, **2:**31, **6:**82, **9:**5, **9:**11,
  9:31–32, **9:**33–34, **9:**59
 failure predicted, **9:**35
 federal support, **3:**63, **6:**82, **9:**59, **9:**62
 funding tied to, **6:**82
 goals, **2:**31–32, **3:**63, **9:**xxi, **9:**20,
  9:34–35, **9:**230–231
 literacy standards, **2:**105
 need for, **2:**62, **9:**29–30, **9:**224
 technology standards, **10:**217–218
Common school movement, **4:**270
Communication
 with alumni, **10:**197
 cultural differences and, **2:**128–130,
  2:132–134
 between schools and parents, **3:**xxiv,
  9:268, **9:**269–270, **10:**195–197

curricula focused on, **2:**xxi–xxii, **2:**152
impact of digital technology, **10:**25,
   10:26–29
Hussar, William J., **9:**110
Husserl, Edmund, **2:**241
Hutton, Thomas, **10:**188
Hyland, Tim, **5:**178–179

Iacocca, Lee, **7:**237
Iannaccone, Lawrence, **7:**256, **7:**257, **7:**258
IASA. *See* Illinois Association of School
   Administrators
IB. *See* International Baccalaureate
IBM, **10:**144, **10:**210
ICS. *See* Integrated Comprehensive
   Services
Idaho
   charter schools, **1:**50–51
   finance litigation, **3:**180
   homeschooling laws, **1:**113
   prayer at graduation ceremonies,
      4:40
   suicide prevention programs, **5:**72
   virtual school funding, **10:**86
Idaho Digital Learning Academy (IDLA),
   10:86
*Idaho Schools for Equal Educational
   Opportunity v. Evans*, **3:**180
IDEA. *See* Individuals with Disabilities
   Education Act
Identity construction, **1:**64, **1:**65–70,
   2:218–219, **2:**222, **2:**225
   See also Ethnic identities; Religious
      identities
IDLA. *See* Idaho Digital Learning Academy
IEPs. *See* Individualized education
   programs
Illback, Robert J., **7:**255
Illinois
   moments of silence in schools, **4:**49–50,
      4:68, **4:**72–73, **4:**75, **4:**79
   school transportation funding, **4:**13
   See also Chicago
Illinois Association of School
   Administrators (IASA), **10:**199
Illinois Supreme Court, **1:**121, **6:**158
Illinois Virtual High School (IVHS), **10:**72
Imagine Schools, **1:**89
Imazeki, Jennifer, **6:**117–118
Imber, Mickey, **2:**122
Immigrants
   cultural capital, **2:**108–109

English language instruction, **2:**119,
   2:120, **2:**122, **3:**186–187, **3:**192,
   3:193–194
in Europe, **2:**131–132
families, **7:**194, **7:**204
frustrations, **2:**212
illegal, **7:**194, **7:**204
Muslim, **1:**57–58, **1:**59, **1:**60–61,
   1:63–64, **1:**69
nationalism, **2:**130
in public schools, **2:**132, **2:**134, **2:**138,
   3:152–153, **3:**161, **3:**186
See also Cultural differences; English
   Language Learners
Immigration laws, state, **2:**134–135, **2:**139,
   3:193
Immunity, governmental, **5:**82, **5:**189
iNACOL. *See* International Association for
   K-12 Online Learning
Incentive pay. *See* Performance pay
Inclusion classrooms
   accommodations, **8:**113–114
   co-teaching, **2:**178, **7:**46
   as default placement, **8:**113, **8:**121, **8:**124
   disadvantages, **3:**215–216, **3:**244–245
   discipline problems, **8:**101–102
   gifted students in, **2:**163
   instruction, **2:**179, **2:**185, **2:**191–193
   special education compared to,
      2:177–193, **8:**108–125
   student achievement, **8:**123–124
   students with disabilities in, **2:**178,
      2:179, **2:**185, **2:**187–193,
      3:215–216, **3:**218, **3:**244–245,
      3:253, **8:**110, **8:**112
   supporters, **8:**112, **8:**119–125
Inclusive learning communities, **7:**79–80
Income inequality, **9:**229
   See also Inequities
Income taxes
   corporate, **6:**74, **6:**269, **9:**259
   deductions, **1:**92, **6:**259, **6:**261–262
   equity, **6:**66
   federal, **6:**64, **6:**65
   local, **6:**65, **6:**71
   state, **6:**64, **6:**65, **6:**67, **6:**68, **6:**74
   See also Tax credits, educational; Taxes
Incomes. *See* Economic success; Teacher
   salaries and benefits
Incubation Model of Teaching, **2:**173
Indebtedness limits, **6:**21–38
Independent schools. *See* Private schools

Malpractice, **8:**216, **8:**223
 See also Educational malpractice
Managerial governance, **7:**180–182
Manhattan Institute, **6:**106–107
Mann, Horace, **4:**177, **4:**270, **6:**221, **6:**223,
 6:282–283
Marbury v. Madison, **6:**148, **6:**156–157,
 7:69
Marcus v. Rowley, **8:**22
Marina, Brenda, **7:**53
Market competition
 advocates, **6:**32, **7:**209–210, **7:**218–219
 benefits of, **7:**137, **7:**212, **7:**214–215
 effects on educational performance,
 7:208–23
 factors in increase in, **7:**218
 financing issues, **6:**34–35
 inequality and, **7:**219, **7:**220
 private schools and, **6:**262–264, **6:**266,
 6:269–270
 in public sector, **6:**29–30
 research on, **7:**220–221
 See also Choice
Marks, Helen M., **1:**192
Marshall, Catherine, **3:**212, **7:**103, **7:**104,
 7:105
Marshall, John, **6:**164
Marshall, Thurgood, **3:**5, **3:**10
Martindale, Colin, **2:**170, **2:**171
Martino, Gabrielle, **9:**26
Marx, Karl, **8:**247, **8:**248
Maryland
 AP Access and Success plan, **6:**237
 takeover of Baltimore schools, **7:**18
 teacher training regulations, **9:**77–79
 year-round schools, **1:**242
Marzano, R., **5:**142
Massachusetts
 antibullying law, **10:**162–163, **10:**164
 charter schools, **1:**16
 compulsory education law, **1:**xvii, **6:**221,
 7:149
 education department, **7:**xviii
 finance litigation, **3:**182
 full-service community schools, **3:**226,
 3:232–233
 property tax limits, **9:**202
 school funding, **3:**182
 school governance, **7:**12
 school laws, **1:**113, **6:**182, **9:**215
 special education, **6:**94, **6:**105,
 6:107–108

standards, **9:**23, **9:**27
 See also Boston
Massachusetts Bay Colony, **1:**xvi–xvii,
 4:176–177, **6:**62, **6:**182, **7:**xvii
Mastropieri, Margo, **2:**179
Matczynski, Thomas J., **9:**271
Mathematica Policy Research, **6:**140
Mathematics
 curricula, **2:**32, **3:**154–155, **7:**45, **7:**50
 as gatekeeper subject, **9:**11
 gifted students, **2:**164–166
 instructional approaches, **2:**96
 science and, **2:**104, **2:**105
 single-sex classes, **1:**183, **1:**185, **1:**186,
 1:188
 standardized test scores, **2:**104–105,
 9:8–9, **9:**237, **9:**238, **9:**239, **9:**241,
 9:242, **9:**253, **9:**255
 standards, **6:**82, **9:**5, **9:**25, **9:**59
 teacher education programs, **9:**77, **9:**78
 teachers, **3:**269–270
 tracking, **3:**154–155
 Trends in International Math and
 Science Study, **7:**213, **7:**259, **9:**23,
 9:30, **9:**255
 in vocational education, **1:**222
 See also Science, Technology,
 Engineering, and Mathematics
Mathis, William, **9:**29–30, **9:**32
May v. Cooperman, **4:**67
*Mayer v. Monroe County Community School
 Corporation*, **8:**194, **8:**208–209
Mayors
 control of schools, **7:**5–6, **7:**10,
 7:14–18, **7:**19, **7:**126, **7:**226, **7:**257,
 7:258
 school takeovers, **7:**7, **7:**14–15, **7:**19
 See also Elected political leaders; Local
 governments
McArdle, Nancy, **3:**84
McCain, Ted D., **1:**229
McCluskey, Neal, **9:**29–30, **9:**31
*McCollum v. Board of Education of School
 District No. 71*, **4:**93
McConnell-Ginet, Sally, **2:**133
McCormick, Alexander, **3:**51
*McCreary County, Kentucky v. American
 Civil Liberties Union of Kentucky*,
 4:23, **4:**120, **4:**133
McDuffy v. Secretary, **3:**182
McGrath v. Dominican College, **5:**86
McIntosh, Kent, **5:**242

Shen, Francis X., **7:**5, **7:**7, **7:**17, **7:**258
Sherman v. Community Consolidated School District 21 of Wheeling Township, **4:**138
Sherman v. Koch, **4:**49–50, **4:**68, **4:**75, **4:**79
Shift age, **9:**195–196
Shmurak, Carole, **1:**192
Shreve, David, **9:**25
Shulman, L., **3:**44
Siddiqui, Shahid, **1:**56
Siegel-Hawley, Genevieve, **7:**52
Sielke, Catherine C., **6:**37
Sikhs, **4:**267–268, **4:**276, **4:**277, **4:**288
Singer, Alan, **8:**252
Single-sex schools and classes
   benefits of, **1:**180, **1:**184–188
   history, **1:**184
   interest in, **1:**xxvi
   learning styles and, **1:**180, **1:**185
   legal issues, **1:**181, **1:**183–184, **1:**190–191
   number of, **1:**181
   opposition, **1:**xxvi, **1:**189–195
   private schools, **1:**181
   public schools, **1:**180–195
   research on, **1:**184–188, **1:**191–193
   school climates, **1:**192–193
   teacher preparation, **1:**188
SIS. *See* Student information systems
Skiba, R. J., **5:**206
Skills
   arts education and, **2:**145–149, **2:**150
   creative thinking, **2:**169–170, **2:**172–173
   critical thinking, **9:**18–19
   needed for future, **1:**xxvii, **1:**229, **7:**54
   technology-related, **2:**237, **10:**40, **10:**64, **10:**216, **10:**217–218, **10:**220, **10:**221–222
Skinner v. Labor Railway Executives' Association, **8:**63, **8:**77, **8:**78, **8:**83, **8:**84
Skoros v. City of New York, **1:**26, **1:**31
Skype, **10:**199
SLA. *See* Second language acquisition
Slaughterhouse Cases, **7:**66
Slavin, Robert E., **2:**112, **3:**155–156, **3:**163–164
SLD. *See* Specific learning disabled students
Sloan Consortium, **10:**xviii
Smartphones. *See* Mobile technologies
Smith, Adam, **6:**29–30, **6:**32, **6:**34, **6:**268

Smith, Marshall S., **7:**172
Smith, Thomas M., **9:**136
Smith-Hughes Act, **1:**216, **1:**219, **3:**127
SMPY. *See* Study of Mathematically Precocious Youth
Smuts, Gary, **9:**164–165
Snell, Julia, **2:**220
Snyder, Rick, **10:**61
Social capital, **7:**202–204
Social cohesion, **6:**18–19
Social Darwinism, **3:**153
Social justice, **7:**106–107
Social media. *See* Social networking sites
Social mobility, **6:**xxvi, **6:**226, **6:**263–264, **7:**222–223
Social networking sites
   ADA compliance, **10:**201–202
   cyberbullying, **5:**63–64, **10:**xxv, **10:**147, **10:**203, **10:**205
   definition, **10:**135, **10:**175, **10:**192
   disciplining students for activity on, **8:**180, **8:**183, **8:**184–185, **10:**174–190, **10:**204–205
   educating students on use of, **10:**176–177, **10:**184, **10:**190
   educational benefits, **10:**xxiii–xxiv, **10:**40
   free speech rights on, **8:**182–183, **10:**178, **10:**180–182, **10:**187, **10:**204–206
   legal issues, **10:**203–206
   misuse of, **10:**142–143, **10:**147–149, **10:**159, **10:**201, **10:**202, **10:**203
   parody profiles, **8:**182–183, **8:**184, **10:**159, **10:**169, **10:**180–181, **10:**183, **10:**187, **10:**190, **10:**204
   permanence of information, **10:**176, **10:**182–183
   policies on teachers' use, **10:**137, **10:**138, **10:**140–146, **10:**150–151, **10:**202–203, **10:**205
   political impact, **2:**233, **10:**145
   restrictions on use in schools, **10:**xxiii, **10:**174–175
   safety concerns, **10:**xxiii, **10:**xxiv, **10:**xxv, **10:**174, **10:**202–203
   school promotion on, **10:**192–206
   sexting, **2:**208, **8:**157, **10:**xxiii, **10:**147–148
   sexual harassment, **8:**157
   student use of, **2:**219, **10:**62, **10:**159, **10:**169, **10:**174–190, **10:**192, **10:**197, **10:**204–206